T0265922

100

YEARS

SIMON &
SCHUSTER

Playing *from* *the* Rough

A Personal Journey Through
America's 100 Greatest Golf Courses

Jimmie James

SIMON & SCHUSTER
New York London Toronto Sydney New Delhi

100 YEARS
SIMON &
SCHUSTER

1230 Avenue of the Americas
New York, NY 10020

First Simon & Schuster hardcover edition June 2024

SIMON & SCHUSTER and colophon are registered trademarks of Simon & Schuster, LLC.

Simon & Schuster: Celebrating 100 Years of Publishing in 2024

For information about special discounts for bulk purchases, please contact Simon & Schuster Special Sales at 1-866-506-1949 or business@simonandschuster.com.

The Simon & Schuster Speakers Bureau can bring authors to your live event. For more information or to book an event, contact the Simon & Schuster Speakers Bureau at 1-866-248-3049 or visit our website at www.simonspeakers.com.

Interior design by Wendy Blum

Manufactured in the United States of America

1   3   5   7   9   10   8   6   4   2

Library of Congress Cataloging-in-Publication Data has been applied for.

ISBN 978-1-6680-0597-2
ISBN 978-1-6680-0599-6 (ebook)

In honor of my mother, Thelma James, with love and appreciation to my wife, Erika James, and with hope for the brightest futures for our children, Jordan and Alexandra James.

CONTENTS

CONTENTS

INTRODUCTION

I dream my painting and I paint my dream.

—Vincent van Gogh

Standing over a ball on the first tee at Augusta National Golf Club, the most exclusive golf club in America, I flashed back to my six-year-old self.

In my mind's eye, I saw a skinny black kid in pinstripe overalls running barefoot down a dirt road that cut through the piney woods of deepest East Texas. I was playing baseball with a half-dozen other kids just like me—all barefoot, all raggedy, all poor. Our bat, a long, thin piece of discarded wood, had made its way down to us from the sawmill up the hill. Our bases were shorter planks that had drifted down from the sawmill as well; we lived in shacks with no plumbing or electricity, but we were filthy rich in junked wood. Our ball was made of rubberized plastic: a torn-off doll's head—pink face cracked, button nose flattened, blue eyes popped permanently open—the remnant of a toy donated to one of us at Christmas by the Salvation Army.

Here's what else we shared on that sweltering summer afternoon in the early 1960s: the unmistakable stench of poverty. We couldn't smell it—we were too used to the stink of accrued sweat and squalor and visits to our fly-infested outhouses. But everybody else sure could. It was a stink that the soap we made with lye and animal fat didn't even wash off during our weekly tin-tub baths.

But to those of us playing baseball on that hot, dusty day with a stick and a doll's head and the splintery bases we sprinted around as if gliding atop the wind, the stink we bore was simply the smell of . . . us.

Of everybody like us.

I wobbled for a moment at the memory. The disconnect was almost too vast to fathom: I'd come from a world that lacked almost everything to find myself standing in a world that lacked almost nothing.

A fresh white ball remained on the tee. I lifted my head: a small gallery had gathered around us. Some staff and the next group with their caddies were paying their respects to my host, Danny Yates, a legendary amateur golfer who played in the Masters twice and is considered, along with his family, to be Augusta National royalty. We'd flown there that morning from Atlanta on a private jet that belonged to another member of our foursome.

I rebalanced my stance in my neatly polished FootJoys and waggled a custom graphite driver, trying to ease my first-tee jitters.

I took a final peek down the fairway. A pristine green carpet unfurled slightly uphill, pines and tea olives lining both sides. Birds chirped, and a warm breeze whistled through the tall trees. Both rang in my ears like gongs.

I dropped my head and swung. The ball sailed long and true, a dimpled white dot that floated high into the clear blue sky.

On that late-spring morning in Augusta, with all of Georgia in full bloom, I followed my drive's trajectory from tee box to touchdown, no problem. It finally rolled to a stop a little short of Danny's drive. My butt cheeks relaxed a bit. The ball had traveled maybe 230 yards, modest by Augusta National standards, but the sight and the feeling of outsized, almost effortless power is something that has always thrilled me about golf. It's part of what lured me to the game in the first place and what keeps me coming back, no matter how disastrous my round.

I handed my club to a caddie in a spotless white jumpsuit—I couldn't help registering the contrast with the dingy, pinstripe hand-me-downs my friends and I had worn in my memory—and strode toward my ball.

For the rest of that day, I couldn't shake how surreal it all seemed. I don't think most minds can comprehend the gulf between the world I grew up in and the one whose freshly mowed grass I traipsed across at Augusta. I often felt as if I belonged to neither.

That sensation would stalk me through the ninety-nine courses that followed.

———

DURING MY YEARLONG ODYSSEY THROUGH America's most privileged golf venues, my life often unreeled before me like some serialized, uninvited movie. Just as my inaugural round at Augusta unleashed fraught memories from my childhood, the world I found myself in during the ensuing stops often triggered other recollections from my past that, as Faulkner famously wrote and I came to understand firsthand, is not dead; it's not even past.

Playing the country's one hundred best and often most exclusive courses is a lifetime goal for many avid golfers. It's a quest akin to mountain climbers scaling the world's Seven Summits. It has been done most often by "raters" sanctioned to evaluate courses for *Golf Digest*, the sport's consensus rating bible. As far as I knew, however, it had never been accomplished within a twelve-month period—and certainly not by a duffer like me.

But somehow I pulled it off. Beginning that day in Augusta, I played every one of America's greatest hundred courses, as determined by *Golf Digest*. My quest took me from coast to coast with dozens of stops in between: from Bethpage Black in New York to Pebble Beach in California; from Congressional Country Club just outside Washington, DC, to Gozzer Ranch in Idaho; from corn as high as an elephant's eye to a spectacularly isolated course built by a power equipment multimillionaire in the middle of his family's farm in southern Illinois.

I also played courses that casual fans, even nonfans, can appreciate as much for their beauty and design as for the sporting challenges they present.

There were Pine Valley Golf Club, which rolls through southern New Jersey's sandy Pine Barrens; Pikewood National Golf Club in West Virginia, which unspools atop a limestone deposit in the middle of a coal-country forest, and dares golfers to play around bluffs, rapids, gulches, and a natural waterfall right behind the par-three fifth hole; and Cypress Point Club, nestled along northern California's craggy coastline as if it had rolled in one night with the tide.

On and on I went. My odyssey felt equal parts travelogue, personal challenge, and dream come true.

And yet . . .

Amid all the beauty and history and privilege, there was something else. The barefoot six-year-old playing with that torn-off doll's head and the things he experienced on the long, unlikely road to the man he would become rarely felt more than a random flashback away.

I never knew when or where one would hit me: once as I rotated through my irons on a dew-covered practice range in Kentucky; another time as I strolled down a bucolic cart path between hidden tee boxes in western Oregon, the landscape so lush that the raging Pacific could be heard but not seen; and then again as I was pulled over by a police officer for speeding on a remote two-lane in the middle of Kansas.

I wasn't speeding.

It was during such moments that I'd find myself transported to another time and place—to other worlds filled with both light and dark.

I'd hear the hoots and honks of the drunken college kids who sped through the Sawmill Quarters on Friday and Saturday nights, shouting slurs and obscenities while I curled up with my brothers and sisters in the pitch black of our tiny shack.

I'd feel the hard, bad-man heft of my stepfather's fist, wrapped in the rage of his own inadequacies, as he pounded my face again and again from the front seat of a car, determined to beat the dreamer out of me before we set off on yet another family move.

Or I'd flinch at the terror of being trapped inside an abandoned refrigerator in the back of the house we moved to after my stepfather had pummeled me.

I'd also hear my own young-buck whoops and hollers as I taunted the cows that lazed in my grandparents' field out in the country. They offered endless entertainment along my route to the nearby pond where I collected bathwater, which later would almost always include the ticklish wriggles of tadpoles.

More than anything else, no matter where I was or what I was doing along my journey, I always, *always* sensed my late mother, Thelma James.

I'd envision her cooking over a wood-burning stove, scrambling eggs that I'd literally just squeezed out of our dirt-yard hens.

Or I'd see her proudly hand washing a worn-out suit coat, covered in mud and trash and rotting food, that she'd plucked from the city dump like a lost treasure for me to wear in church on Sundays.

When she appeared to me at those moments, vividly beautiful in my mind's eye, I'd be left to unravel the loving but incalculably complex woman that she was: a sixth-grade dropout who as a teenager was raped by a brother-in-law; a woman who would go on to bear eight children out of wedlock and raise all eight of us to be bright, empathetic, independent adults. We loved her fiercely, honestly, gratefully—right up until the day she died.

Amid all the darkness in our lives, Thelma James was our sliver of light.

Throughout my dream year, it seemed impossible to occupy one world without acknowledging the other. I circulated constantly through both. No matter how rarefied the tee box or fairway or green, that six-year-old in overalls and nothing else stood beside me, making sure I understood both the distance I'd traveled and how little separated us still.

THAT WASN'T MY EXPECTATION WHEN I set out.

Augusta was supposed to be a one-off present from my wife. We'd just moved our family from Virginia to Atlanta to facilitate Erika's new job as dean of the business school at Emory University. The move meant I'd have to travel back and forth to my job in Fairfax. From the early days of our marriage, as our budding careers sometimes took us in different directions, one or the other of us ended up making a long-distance commute.

To show her appreciation this time, Erika was determined to get me onto Augusta National. Not much gets in her way. So during one of her first meetings with the Emory business school's advisory board, Erika asked if anyone knew an Augusta National member who could invite her husband to play. Lin Rogers, an Atlanta businessman, was friends with Danny Yates and said he'd ask him about an invite. It was Lin's jet that carried our foursome to Augusta in a flight so short the descent seemed to begin before the ascent was complete.

Erika's gift planted a seed. By the time the invite came, I had already decided to retire after more than thirty-three years at ExxonMobil. I started there as an engineer, a recent graduate of Prairie View A&M, and ended up as an executive, overseeing logistics for fuel operations. My team was responsible for making sure that towns up and down the Americas, from just below the Arctic Circle to an hour's plane ride south of Buenos Aires, got the fuel they needed and that workers were kept safe, with the least impact possible on the environment.

The job was a grind—a challenging, rewarding grind. It involved sixty- to eighty-hour workweeks and kept me on the road at least two weeks every month.

I loved it. But as is true at many high-pressure corporations, I'd seen too many colleagues stay too long and leave bitter and disillusioned. They were worn down by the hours and pressure and jockeying for position that's all part of corporate America's life cycle—what makes it both dynamic and wearying.

So like an aging athlete, I decided to leave before I was past my prime. I'd accomplished everything I wanted as a globe-trotting businessman, far exceeding my wildest dreams. Now it was time to move aside and let others do the same.

I was fifty-eight.

I wanted to be home more while our kids were still in high school. It was my last chance to be with Jordan and Alexandra during those critical teenage moments before they sailed off to college. But I also had to be honest, both with myself and with them: I knew I couldn't go from working at a hundred-miles-an-hour pace straight into an idle retirement. I needed a project—I'd been a projects guy my whole career—to ease me into the transition. I'd been relevant in the corporate world. I'd sat at the head of tables; people had listened to me and often done what I asked.

For my own sanity, I needed to create a new sense of relevance, but not just at something I'd already been doing well—being a husband, a father, a contributing member of society. I didn't want to become some old guy who *used to be*. I needed to do something challenging that had rarely, if ever, been done.

My original plan was to reconnect with the country by visiting all fifty states and playing golf on two courses in each, taking my kids along to the most intriguing spots. I love interacting with people, and golf is a great vehicle for that. I didn't pick up the game until I was in my forties, when a vice president at work suggested I take it up to help me transition to a new position. It was something I had long wanted to do, but it just seemed so hard and expensive.

But once I started, I dove into it with the zealotry of a convert.

After Erika told me about her gift of Augusta, she followed up at Christmas with another present: a book by the renowned golf writer John Sabino that detailed how, during his lifetime, he had played the top courses in the world. Erika inserted a dozen or so pink sticky tabs in chapters about private courses in the United States that she thought she could help me get on—again, not much gets in her way—as an aid to my original plan of playing in all fifty states.

Running my finger down the courses in Sabino's list, I did what I've done since I vowed, as a skinny five-year-old, to be the first person I knew to graduate from high school: I set a new challenge for myself. I already had an invite to what is perhaps the most difficult course in the country to get onto, so I thought: Why not try to play the other ninety-nine? Why not do it in a year?

A month or so later, I opened an issue of *Golf Digest* that included its America's 100 Greatest Golf Courses list. My engineer brain kicked in. I viewed the journey as a logistics problem—that was my wheelhouse—knowing I'd have to juggle the schedules of whatever hosts I found and match them up with my own, all while making allowances for family obligations, in-house tournaments, bad weather, missed connections—anything that could throw me off schedule. There would always have to be a plan B and many times plans C and D. I created an elaborate spreadsheet to keep track of it all.

By the time I started, I felt sure I could get access to twenty-five of the courses. That sounds like a healthy number until you consider that it still left seventy-five private courses to breach. The twenty-five I felt assured of included one public course (Long Island's Bethpage Black) and twelve resort courses, which required only that one pony up enough money to play. In addition to luck, I figured I had three of the preconditions necessary to knock it all out: time, resources, and a supportive spouse.

Yet even with all of that going for me, I realized that to get invites to the other seventy-five clubs, I'd need to lean on something less quantifiable, something that wouldn't fit into a tab on my spreadsheet: an ability to sell myself and my vision to nearly everyone I met. Daunting as that might seem, I didn't view it as a new problem: it's the kind of thing I've done my whole life.

I did set parameters. The first involved a slight fudge of the calendar: though I played Augusta in mid-May, two weeks before I retired, because the course closes for the summer for repairs and improvements, I began my calendar year a few weeks after that—in early June, when I was scheduled to play my next round, at Kinloch Golf Club outside Richmond, Virginia. That became my start and end date, and I set it in stone.

I also determined that I would never directly ask anyone to get me onto a private course. I wanted the invitations to develop as organically as possible. When I was paired with others as a single, in the course of our normal, idling-on-the-tee-box conversation, I'd simply tell them what I was up to, the odyssey I was on, and hope that the audaciousness of my quest would compel them to voluntarily be sucked into my dream. If they weren't moved enough by what I was doing, that was okay, too. I'd simply enjoy our time together.

Another parameter: because some folks I played with at the top clubs could easily get me on almost anywhere else, I decided I'd accept help for no more than three courses from any given person. The goal was not just to play all of the courses but to see if strangers would voluntarily help me. I wanted to see if America could still be a place that was generous enough, enthused enough, and willing enough to help a stranger achieve his dream. With our public differences as a country seeming to swell with every news cycle, I feared that those traits were dissolving.

And then there was the elephant in the room: golf's relationship with race.

For the lion's share of its existence in America, golf had been a proud standard-bearer for segregation. Many of its clubs excluded Blacks, Jews, and women—until they were either sued, strong-armed, or shamed into acquiescing. I encountered people during my trek—white and Black, nonmembers and club presidents—who wondered if somebody like me would be welcome on all one hundred courses. As far as it had come, it seemed, golf still hadn't shaken its past. Would I run up against enough twenty-first-century resistance to short-circuit my quest?

It was a lingering concern. But the legacy of what I'd been through in life drove me to push past those doubts.

In the end, I completed the ninety-nine courses that followed Augusta—without a single day to spare. I flew 73,284 miles, drove another 17,472, and spent eighty-two nights in hotels or other people's homes.

I didn't calculate the distance I walked or rode on the courses themselves, but it did take me 8,796 strokes to traverse them.

I played across thirty-three states and needed six separate trips just to play the twelve courses in California—necessitated by my hosts' schedules and some biblically nasty weather. It's likely I would have failed to finesse the entire trip in time if, over the course of my working life, I had not accrued an almost unimaginable number of hotel, airline, and car-rental rewards points—and the status that allowed me to make changes at the last possible moment without incurring penalties.

That status came in handy whenever the golf gods chose, as is their habit both on and off the course, to challenge me.

———

WHILE TRAVELING ALL THOSE MILES and playing all those rounds— shaping all those drives and lipping out all those putts; befriending all those playing partners and heeding all those caddies; jostling through all those airports and eating in all those roadside diners—I reconnected with a country I found at once beautiful and flawed, bighearted and wrongheaded, proud and ashamed.

I found a country, in other words, much like my mother, a woman not only central to my biography but integral to my American experience. When I look back at what my mother taught me and my siblings, she emerges as a true wonder—despite her flaws. When I look at the sum total of the country where I was raised in the segregated South, with its racism and economic inequality and violent spasms of intolerance, I remain hopeful, even grateful.

More than anything else during that journey, I found myself, over and over. I found how the kid I was intersects with the man I've become. My frivolous odyssey trudging across some of the country's best-kept, hardest-to-get-on lawns, toting fourteen sticks and chasing a little white ball, stirred memories of a life filled with the types of stories that are rarely told by those of us who've endured them. Few of us ever move far enough beyond the prison of our abject poverty to gain a platform to tell those stories in our own voice.

History has often been written as if people like me were voiceless extras in a movie we were never intended to see.

While I was growing up, I not only knew we were poor; I knew we were poorer than all the other poor families we lived around. I cannot remember a time when we weren't the poorest kids wherever we lived. I can't remember ever being able to point to someone and say to myself, "There! There's someone whose circumstances are worse off than ours!"

As I began talking with friends and colleagues about writing this book, someone suggested I read the opening page of Frank McCourt's *Angela's Ashes*. Right away, he offers up a kind of dare to any memoirist who follows:

> People everywhere brag and whimper about the woes of their early years, but nothing can compare with the Irish version: the poverty; the shiftless loquacious alcoholic father; the pious defeated mother moaning by the fire; pompous priests; bullying schoolmasters; the English and the terrible things they did to us for eight hundred long years.

I won't brag or whimper in this book. But I can confidently compare McCourt's Irish woes to the Black, southern, sawmill-town version: the violent alcoholic stepfather; the flawed, illiterate, but protective and uncomplaining mother; the plantation-minded sawmill operators, whose company-store business model kept so many workers indentured; the racist and identity-erasing crimes visited on us for four hundred years. Yet here I am, writing about it all, from a perch beyond anything that up-bringing was supposed to prepare me for. I had no special talents.

My only true gift is one forged from a life where even the simplest of things were hard.

Perseverance.

There were many times in my life when I got so tired of the roaches, the shacks, the stink, the tattered clothing, the scorn, the ridicule, that I just wanted to quit. But I couldn't because of the one advantage I had from birth: a mother who never did.

She never played golf, of course, but if she had, no matter how deep or thick the rough, she never would've asked for relief or a mulligan. She would have played the ball as it. She never saw herself as a victim. Neither do I. The challenges and obstacles I faced did not deter me from trying to do things that were hard. Whether those things were overcoming poverty and racism or gaining access to America's one hundred greatest golf courses in a single year.

Who we become, what we achieve, and what we contribute are determined by whether we quit when our biggest challenges threaten to derail our biggest dreams or find a way to forge on. I chose to never quit.

CHAPTER ONE

AUGUSTA NATIONAL

Don't be pushed around by the fears in your mind.
Be led by the dreams in your heart.

—Roy T. Bennett

I was born invisible.

My birth certificate, yellowing in the Walker County Courthouse in downtown Huntsville, Texas, contains two details considered most vital about me in 1959:

COLORED and ILLEGITIMATE.

I never knew my father, Austin Riles, and he apparently didn't want to know me. He was an alcoholic who had a wife and another family, even as he kept growing ours. The arrangement didn't always go smoothly: his name was scratched out in pencil on my older sister's birth certificate after Riles's wife, the story goes, went to the courthouse in person and made a stink about her husband's name being attached to other children. By the time my brother Jerry and I came along, his name was officially, and permanently, replaced by ILLEGITIMATE.

I'm told Riles did visit me once, along with my siblings. The encounter lasted maybe fifteen minutes. I was about two years old, hanging around the porch of the house we were crowded into at the time with my mother's sister and her five kids. It sat in an unincorporated community on the edge of Huntsville that could have been named for our family's perpetual condition: Needmore.

My sister Jen, four years older than me, remembers Riles from that visit as being tall, like my grandfather, and picking her up and tossing her around playfully. She doesn't remember him doing anything with me; I just hung around the porch, curious but not that curious. When his time was up—my mother wasn't home, and my sister guesses that my aunt had arranged the visit—he gave each of us a dollar, or maybe it was just a quarter. Then he left. We never saw him again.

I don't recall any of it. The lone thing I do remember about Austin Riles is my grandmother telling me, four or five years later, that he was dead.

That's not the sort of origin story you just roll out over lunch inside the clubhouse dining room at Augusta. The simplest questions people ask when they're getting to know each other have always been the hardest for me to answer: Where are you from? What'd your dad do? Where'd your folks go to school? My early life didn't prepare me for the types of conversations I'd have in settings like that. From birth, I was marked as someone who shouldn't be seen, who didn't legitimately exist.

I was Needmore.

But at Augusta, I felt anything but invisible, with all eyes on the Danny Yates foursome and the tall Black guy playing with them. I felt exposed. I hid my unease, deflecting it with easy patter and small talk.

For all but the 1 percent of the 1 percent, Augusta National is more fantasy than aspiration. Golfers who know better don't try to figure out ways to play there. They just dream about it, like one might dream about playing center field for the Yankees or giving an acceptance speech at the Oscars. It happens—the club's closely held membership numbers about three hundred, including the likes of Bill Gates, Warren Buffett, Condoleezza Rice, and Roger Goodell—but it probably won't ever happen to you.

It certainly wasn't supposed to happen to me. It was in the same category as the fantasies my siblings and I had engaged in as kids, scrunched together on our slanting porch in the Sawmill Quarters, our eyes practically bugging out as we paged through a Sears catalogue that had made its way to us from our grandparents' house.

It was thick as a church-pulpit Bible. We'd take turns flipping through it, sometimes with our eyes shut tight in anticipation, then look on wide-eyed again at whatever glossy page we randomly opened it to. The item displayed on that page belonged to whoever turned to it, instantly becoming part of the dream life we imagined we lived.

"Oooh, look what I got!" my sister would exclaim, staring open-mouthed at the slim models displaying red leather pumps, patent plastic handbags, or silk-lined, elbow-length black gloves ("with dressy details").

"Whoa, look what I got!" I'd call out, ogling photos of chuckling, clean-shaven men in trim, stylish blazers ("Blazers belong in every man's wardrobe"), or an easy-to-assemble purple martin birdhouse ("An adult purple martin often eats its own weight in mosquitoes every day"), or a ten-by-seven-foot backyard toolshed complete with a lawn chair, garden hose, and gleaming red-and-white riding lawn mower.

We never expected to get any of those things, and for the entirety of our childhoods, we didn't. Yet we fantasized like that for hours, luxuriating in the pleasure of our daydreams.

Then we'd move on. I'd build miniature cities from stray wood. Jen would fashion a doll from a Coke bottle, using unraveled rope strands for hair. We'd all play baseball in the road; scratch hopscotch squares in the dirt; erect stilts from long two-by-fours, cutting off the bottoms with a rusty saw and making them into platforms to fit our feet so we could lope around the Quarters like giants or circus clowns or dinosaurs. The silliest beliefs held us rapt at the most random moments: if you stuck a needle in a telephone pole and put your ear to it when the sun came out while it was still raining, you could hear the Devil beating his wife. We shouted the whole time, to be heard above the hogs and chickens kept penned behind our shacks.

That was our world. That little patch at the bottom of the hill in the Sawmill Quarters had everything we needed—save security and first-class citizenship, things we didn't worry about as kids. I get nostalgic for the simplicity it offered. We all do. To us, at that age, that world was full of more light than dark. The constant grind that is poverty didn't feel like such a grind to us. Everything we did we created. It was empowering. We fashioned childhoods out of nothing.

Then, after the sun dropped and the stilts were put up and the doll stashed away and the hopscotch squares wiped clean by our bare feet, we'd repurpose the Sears catalogue inside our outhouse for toilet paper.

———

SEVENTEEN HOURS BEFORE MY TEE time at Augusta, I was trapped in another country. For all my meticulous planning, it looked as though I wouldn't make it.

I stood inside an ExxonMobil fuel facility in Sarnia, Ontario, where I'd just finished inspecting operations, a final run-through before my impending retirement. I was in a tiny conference room, explaining to a couple of work colleagues what the chance to play Augusta meant to me when a text from United Airlines alerted me that my puddle jumper to Toronto had been canceled.

A stunned silence fell over the room. There was no rental car service in Sarnia, and even if there had been, Toronto was a three-hour drive east. I wouldn't get there in time to make my connection. But missing out on Augusta was not an option for me. Even my colleagues understood that. So the three of us stood there, lost in thought, trying to devise a solution. Suddenly one of the men, a studious-looking Canadian named Rob, remembered a local who had a van for hire.

"If he can drive you to Detroit, you might get on another flight there," he said, noting that Detroit was only sixty-five miles south.

I called United immediately and asked if they could get me to Atlanta from Detroit that night. They couldn't. But Delta had a flight at 8:15 p.m. It was my only shot. I checked my watch: 4:30. I was an hour and forty minutes away. "I'll take it."

Thirty minutes later I was sitting in the front seat of a seven-passenger van, debating the decline of American politics with a burly Canadian as he skillfully steered us through the rush-hour traffic that crawled toward the border on I-94. He asked what I thought about the state of politics in America, and before I could answer he offered up his country as a new place of residence for me and my family. I smiled: politics was the last thing on my mind.

"I'll be just fine in the US," I assured him, then thought to myself, "If I make it to Augusta on time."

It was nearly midnight when I finally stepped into my house, slipped into bed, and kissed my wife awake.

"I was worried," Erika said.

"I wish you could caddie for me tomorrow," I told her.

"You couldn't afford me," she replied, smiling. "Get some sleep."

I glanced at a picture of us on the nightstand. Nearly twenty years had passed since I'd dropped to one knee on Mount Denali during a trip through Alaska and asked the most beautiful woman I'd ever met if she'd walk with me through my dreams. I'd chosen that vacation for the express purpose of proposing to her at the top of the world, and despite my over-the-top corniness, she said yes.

I turned to take a last peek at her, then drifted off to sleep.

I ARRIVED AT PEACHTREE DEKALB Airport just in time for the copilot to toss my clubs into the plane.

Lin Rogers introduced me to Danny, still lean and fit in his late six-ties, and as enthusiastic as ever about playing his favorite course, and an-other businessman, Bill Teberg, an affable midwesterner who had recently moved from Chicago to Atlanta. We all buckled in as the small jet taxied onto the runway. I finally breathed a sigh of relief.

We landed an hour later, and soon we were driving the four-lane that passes by the gates of Augusta National through what is perhaps the most disappointing tract of land in America. Three miles from downtown, it's a forlorn landscape of strip malls and neon signs. Nothing could prepare one less for what's at 2604 Washington Road.

When those front gates swung open, I was overcome with fear and awe. I was at Augusta National.

The club is built on what was originally the Fruitland Nursery. Between 1858 and 1859, a hundred years before my birth, the nursery's owners planted sixty-six magnolias on each side of the narrow, 330-yard-long driveway. Little did they know that Magnolia Lane would one day become the most prestigious driveway in golf.

Up ahead of us was the antebellum clubhouse, dubbed Fruitland Manor by the original owners, with its wraparound porch and square white columns. Attendants whisked our clubs away as soon as we got out of the van, and Danny led us to living quarters on the second floor, where we got ready. Framed photos of past Masters champions adorned the walls; I could almost hear Ben Crenshaw, Jack Burke, and Sam Snead snickering as I fumbled with my shoelaces.

As we stepped through the locker room, I took in the green carpet and mahogany lockers bearing members' names etched on brass plates. The Black attendants there nodded at me in the way that Black men do to each other to say, "I see you," silently acknowledging that, no matter our status, we're in the struggle together. I wanted them to know that they were not invisible to me and that—*hey! look!*—I was not invisible to myself, at least at that moment.

Our caddies were waiting with our clubs in the practice area. A man in his sixties, with bright blue eyes and slightly stooped shoulders, walked up to me and introduced himself. "Mr. James," he said, his jumpsuit gleaming, "I'm Eddie."

Eddie was white, as are most caddies at Augusta now. Fifty years ago—post–Civil Rights Act, post–Voting Rights Act, post–MLK assassination, post–March on Washington—the idea that a Black man would know someone who would be able to host him at Augusta, and that Augusta would be fine with that member escorting him onto the course, was unheard of. It would've been just as unheard of for a Black player to have a white caddie.

Until about forty years ago, almost all the caddies at Augusta were Black; Clifford Roberts, who cofounded the club with Bobby Jones in 1932, allegedly stipulated that all the caddies were to be Black and all the players white.

That began to change fifty years later, when, after years of arguing for a rule change, the pros were finally allowed to bring their regular caddies to work the 1982 Masters Tournament. From then on, white caddies outnumbered Black caddies. Today, a professional caddie company manages the club's caddie fleet, and there are 35 to 40 Black caddies out of a staff of 120.

Eddie and I shook hands.

"Where you from, Eddie?" I asked.

"Washington, Georgia," he replied. "What about you, sir?"

I told him I commuted for work between Atlanta and Houston.

"Where do you play golf in Atlanta?" he asked.

When I told him I was a member of the Cherokee Town and Country Club, he said he had played in a tournament there while he was in high school. That was all it took for us to make a connection.

I hit some balls while he sized up my swing; the practice range offers caddies an opportunity to get an idea of what they might be in for for the rest of the day—and how they should place their bets with one another. I fought to slow my tempo and keep my nerves in check. I worked my way methodically through my irons, then hit a few drives, feeling no better or worse than I normally do before a round.

After about twenty minutes, we all walked under the tall pines to the first hole of the club's intimate Par 3 Course, a short nine-hole warm-up before the main event. The place had already cast a spell over me, and rather than loosening up, my muscles tightened as the round progressed.

My scores increased as we skirted the larger of the Par 3's two stocked ponds—the same one Sam Snead had once pulled a six-pound fish out of before the 1972 Masters. (He later cooked and ate it in the clubhouse.)

I finished the nine holes at five over par.

Before heading over to the main course, we stopped in the clubhouse dining room for a quick lunch. My mind wandered as we all sat around the table talking. I kept trying to fit into the conversation, but all I could hear was the sound of myself chewing a pimento cheese sandwich, each bite echoing between my ears.

I don't even remember how we got to the first tee.

I WAS SO LIGHT-HEADED AFTER my opening drive I could hardly feel my feet on the ground. I couldn't help my nervousness. We were striding in the footsteps of those old champions framed on the clubhouse walls, the same ones I had felt chuckling at me earlier. I figured that maybe talking to Eddie would settle me down, bring me back to earth.

"How far to the pin?" I heard myself ask him before my second shot.

"One seventy-five, sir," he said.

"You don't have to call me sir, Eddie. I'll need my five-iron, please."

I put a good swing on it, but the ball struck the green and—true to Augusta's reputation—rolled off the right edge. Negotiating the putting surface's hollows and mounds proved too much for me. A poor chip and three putts later, I finished with a double bogey. Not the start I'd dreamed about.

Eddie must have sensed that I felt I didn't fit in. He offered support as I struggled through the next couple holes. "You'll get there," he assured me. "Putting on these greens is tough."

I've never accepted "tough" as an excuse. I needed to clear my head and concentrate.

The hole names at Augusta National recall the club's nursery roots and have become part of every avid golfer's vocabulary—Flowering Peach, Carolina Cherry, Yellow Jasmine, Nandina, Redbud. It was on Flowering Crab Apple, the 170-yard par-three fourth hole, that my fears began to dissipate. I reminded myself that I was there to play the game, one well-executed shot at a time. That was all that mattered. I needed to get past admiring the beauty and history of the place and just play golf.

I hit a high 6-iron that dropped onto the front of the green, just over a huge bunker. Eddie nodded his approval and handed me the putter. I walked to the green wondering if I could wash away the memories of all those previous missed putts with a single stroke. Eddie pointed to the line. I hit it delicately but squarely. The ball headed for the center of the cup but slowed before reaching the edge. It stopped two inches short.

"Pick it up," I heard Danny say.

I did, gratefully.

The high of that gimme didn't last long. Four tap-in bogeys and another insufferable double were all I could muster on the rest of the front nine.

———

FROM JUST ABOUT THE FIRST time I swung a golf club—atrociously, I might add—I dreamed of playing Augusta's eleventh, twelfth, and thirteenth holes: Amen Corner. It is considered the most hallowed, and bedeviling, section of golf geography in the world. Nestled back in the course's farthest reaches, it consists of a medium-length par four, a short par three, and a short par five. The triumvirate was christened in 1958 by *Sports Illustrated* writer Herbert Warren Wind, who used the term "Amen Corner" to describe how miraculously Arnold Palmer had played it to win his first major.

To kick-start the eleventh, I hit a low, stinging drive along the trees that hemmed the left side of the fairway. The ball disappeared beyond the hill. Eddie and I smiled at each other when we reached the crest and spotted it resting in the fairway. I feathered a fade with my 6-iron that rolled off the green, then clipped the pristine Augusta turf with my chip, leaving my ball six feet from the cup. It felt like twenty. Two strokes later, I tapped in another bogey.

We made our way up to the twelfth tee and looked down at the iconic par three. It's the hole everyone knows from watching the Masters on TV, with the stone bridge arching over Rae's Creek and the azaleas framing the green from the hill behind it. From the tee box, the green looked way too small, like a thumbprint, with bunkers at the front and back that seemed to take up an unreasonable amount of real estate. In a momentary lapse of concentration, I glanced at the men tending the azalea bushes to the right of the green.

I returned to the work at hand. At a little more than 150 yards, with a swirling, unpredictable wind, it's a tough hole to club. Eddie handed me a 6-iron, as he'd done for shots from that distance all day. This time, I questioned the man I'd trusted for eleven holes—who made his living surveying this course. The massive, slanting bunkers behind a green just 10 yards deep were intimidating; get stuck in one of those, and you have to chip onto a slick green that slopes toward the creek—and disaster.

Golden Bell, as the hole is officially called, has broken men far better than me. In 1959, a year after his miraculous play on Amen Corner, Arnold Palmer lost a two-stroke lead and any chance at a Masters repeat when he shot a triple-bogey six at the twelfth. At the 1980 Masters, Tom Weiskopf stubbed five balls into the creek and recorded the hole's worst score ever: 13. More recently, in 2016, Jordan Spieth, looking to win back-to-back Masters, held the final-round lead until he left the twelfth with a quadruple-bogey seven. As Rick Reilly wisecracked in 1990, alluding to the coat that's awarded to each Masters winner, "More green jackets have been lost at the twelfth than at the Augusta City Dry Cleaners."

Like every golfer who stands on that tee box, I was well aware of all of that.

"I think my seven might be better," I told Eddie.

He demurred silently. After looking away, he gave me his best counsel: "You need the six. There's a breeze." He was worried that I'd leave the ball in Rae's Creek.

I took the 6-iron and hit it flush. Eddie seemed to rise on his toes as the ball soared high above the green. When it splashed into the back bunker, he bowed his head. I told him it was fine.

"You were playing the odds," I said. "I was playing my ego."

Eddie snapped a picture of Danny, Lin, Bill, and me on the Ben Hogan Bridge before I made my way to the trap. I hit what I thought was a perfect sand shot that still rolled off the green. It stopped short of Rae's Creek, however. I chipped to within three feet, then rimmed out the putt before leaving with a double bogey.

As we approached the maintenance crew I'd spotted briefly from the tee box, I paused for a second. They were Hispanic, and I thanked them in my limited Spanish for the work they did to keep the place so beautiful. It was my way of again saying "I see you." They nodded back.

I had exchanged cordial nods with Mexican laborers and their families virtually every day as a kid, walking through their patch of territory on my way to and from the company store in the Sawmill Quarters. Though immigrants from south of the border were a rare sight at the time in small-town East Texas, Mexicans had been part of Boettcher's Mill for half a century. Mill founder Baldwin Boettcher, a German immigrant, hired many of them at his first mill in Westfield, just north of Houston, which supplied that city's early boom. When he closed the mill there, he brought along the Mexican immigrants to his new mill in Huntsville in 1929.

The mill's pecking order was on stark, undisguised display. Black workers and their families lived in the unplumbed and unelectrified shacks at the bottom of the hill, below the mill—what everyone referred to as "the bottoms." The Mexican immigrants were settled right above us, in shacks that also lacked running water and lights but were equipped with natural gas for cooking and heating. It was a literal and figurative step up. At the top of the hill, white families lived in the plumbed and electrified homes nearest the sawmill, where they also held the prime jobs. The living arrangements were a kind of handy Jim Crow–era racial pyramid, just so nobody got confused. It was reinforced when Miss Johnnie Mae and Old Man Cole, an elderly Black couple, got into a fight. She chased him with a cast-iron skillet before packing up her clothes and getting us to help her move them and her furniture up the hill into a vacant house in the Mexican section of the Quarters. It took just one day for the Sawmill overseers to show up and dump her possessions onto the dirt road that ran in front of the shack.

We didn't mix. Sometimes white kids shot at us with slingshots—what they called "nigger shooters"—when we walked past their houses. They called us niggers and we called them white patties. Our refrain, "White patties, white patties, you don't shine, call me a nigger and I'll kick your behind," was no match for the deep, painful history of their slur.

There were never antagonistic interactions like that with the Mexicans. We had no issues with them, and they had no issues with us. When we passed by, it was just cordial nods and smiles, with the language barrier often putting a stop to even elementary conversation.

———

AFTER MY BRIEF PAUSE ON the way over to the thirteenth hole, Azalea, I crossed another bridge, stepped up to the tee, and hammered a great drive. The 455-yard par five has a sweeping dogleg left, and my drive set up perfectly to get onto the green in two and give me a real shot at birdie—or better.

I stood next to Eddie before my approach, examining the creek that snaked deeply and ominously along the front of the green. Two hundred thirty yards remained to the pin.

"You want to leave eighty yards for your approach?" Eddie asked rhetorically; considering the round I was having, laying up would normally be a given.

I stared hard at the green. Without turning to him, I asked, "How much to carry the creek?"

Eddie, of course, was offering sound advice when he suggested laying up. But all I could think was that I'd probably never get back to this privileged place, and that if I reached the green with this shot, I would have a putt for . . . eagle! I glanced at the pine straw beneath the trees to my right, where, during the 2010 Masters, Phil Mickelson had hit an immaculate second shot from behind a tree that stopped five feet right of the flag.

This was my moment.

To Eddie's disappointment, I asked for my 3-wood. It felt great in my hands—right up until I sent the ball careening off to the right. It came to rest on the tight grass at the confluence of the thirteenth and fourteenth fairways—a bad shot with a decent outcome, and a rare gift from the golf gods. My pitch over the creek to the flag sixty yards away rolled twelve feet past the hole.

As he cleaned my ball on the green, Eddie said, "Let's take our time and get you a birdie."

That would be nice, I thought. As he pointed to the line, all I could see was the image of Tiger Woods's first-round putt there during the 2005 Masters that had picked up speed and eventually trickled into Rae's Creek; Augusta's history competed with my own on every hole, it seemed. So with the gentlest of nudges, my ball rolled end over end along a perfect line to the cup. I anticipated my impending triumph. When it stopped dead a foot from the hole, I closed my eyes and sank to my knees.

"It's a par," Eddie offered. "All pars are good."

Under a still-warm afternoon sun, I struck a pair of lovely drives on fourteen and fifteen that flew high above the trees and dropped softly into the fairway. I squandered them both with haphazard approaches; as one saying goes, the hardest shot to recover from is a great drive. By then my mind was focused on scoring rather than just making a good swing. That led to two bogeys and then two more on sixteen and seventeen.

Any chance I had at recovering my rhythm was gone, especially as I looked at the narrow uphill chute that greets players at eighteen. I pulled my tee shot into the trees, where Eddie and I hunted for it, waists bent and heads bowed, like a forensics unit canvassing a crime scene. "Right here," Eddie finally called out. I used my driver to punch it under some branches but back toward the tee box and, thankfully, into the fairway.

Albert Einstein taught us that the passage of time is an illusion of our consciousness. My day at Augusta proved it. The hours evaporated in an instant.

A two-putt double bogey ended my round with a suddenness that caught me off guard. My playing partners removed their caps and started shaking hands. It was over. I stood completely still for a moment, the world around me silent, until Eddie took my hand and thanked me.

"You were great," I told him. "Without you I would've shot a hundred and five instead of ninety-five."

Eddie had to know I'd never forget the four hours we'd just shared at a place I might never get the chance to return to. He'd be back tomorrow.

I stopped by the modest pro shop and bought Erika a shirt with the Augusta logo, along with a hat and a ball marker for myself to commemorate the day. The other guys were staying in Augusta, but I had two weeks of travel and meetings ahead of me and needed to go home.

Danny walked me to the waiting van, which would escort me to the same private jet I had flown in on. I told him I didn't know how I could ever properly thank him. He grinned and placed his hand on my shoulder. "My pleasure," he said.

I sat alone in the shuttle van as it rolled back down Magnolia Lane, toward the front gate and the commercial hodgepodge on Washington Road just beyond it. I turned for a moment to glance back at the clubhouse, then looked toward the heavens, gripped by the thought of how proud that day would've made my mother—a sixth-grade dropout who didn't learn to read or write until she was in her forties but raised her invisible kids to be seen.

Thelma "None" James—so called because she never had a middle name—had her first child at seventeen and was in a field picking cotton two days before giving birth to me. An outcast to many, she was a rock to us. She maintained a moral compass set without regard to what or how anyone else thought. The principles that guided that compass weren't complicated, but they were firm: don't lie, don't steal, don't talk badly about others.

Simple.

She was aware of how others looked at her, including her sisters and at times her evangelical preacher father. She was the one who kept having babies without getting married.

One Sunday, I was seated with her and some of my siblings in the middle pew of the little whitewashed Fellowship Baptist Church in La Marque. The pastor, Reverend Price, delivered a sermon to the modest gathering that Sunday about women having babies out of wedlock. He went on and on in his thunderous voice about how awful it was, about how sinful those women were. It was clear to me that he was preaching directly to my mother. She just sat there, my three-month-old brother cooing in her arms, listening but not reacting.

I finally had enough. I shot up from the pew—I was twelve, tall and gangly for my age, sporting that ill-fitting suit my mother had rescued from the town dump—and laid into him. I asked him who he thought he was, passing judgment like that when there were plenty of other vices and transgressions, many of them his own, that he'd stayed quiet about—like his own drinking and smoking, and his welcoming Aunt Willie Mae's paramour into the church as a deacon for no other reason than he was one of the few adult men who actually showed up on Sunday. Aunt Willie Mae and her lover's extracurricular liaisons were a secret to nobody, including me and Reverend Price.

I threw all of that at him. Yet there he was daring to condemn my mother. I don't recall everything I said, but whatever it was, I knew Reverend Price had it coming. When I finally finished, my ears ringing with rage, I plopped back down beside my mother. I don't remember a reaction to my outburst beyond the congregation's stunned silence. My mother just continued to stare ahead, patting Alfred to keep him from fussing.

In the days, weeks, and years that followed, I never heard my mother say a single disparaging word about Reverend Price. Fact is, I never heard my mother utter a disparaging word about anybody. Ever.

I did, of course, and very publicly, but unlike Reverend Price, I knew who my mother really was. A couple of years earlier, she'd sent me to the store to buy food. I'd walked what felt like a mile or two to get there and picked up everything I was told to get, but when the woman at the checkout line gave me change, she made a mistake. She gave me more money than I'd started with.

When I got home and told my mother, a woman who rummaged through landfills for clothing and dishes and toys, all she said was "You know we don't steal."

I explained, "But Momma, I didn't steal it. The woman at the register gave it to me by mistake."

"You knew she made a mistake," my mother responded, "so that means you stole it."

She made me walk back to the store and not just give the money back, but apologize.

I did as I was told.

Back at Augusta National, the late-afternoon sun flashed through the arbor of sweet-smelling magnolias, dappling the van's back seat as we rolled out and toward the front gate. As I rearranged my legs, I felt something in my pants pocket. I reached in and pulled out one of the matchboxes I'd taken earlier from the bar counter. I've never smoked in my life, but with the club's logo stamped on them, I thought they'd make great souvenirs to hand out at work.

Then a smile broke across my face. I knew exactly what my mother would say if she were seated there beside me.

"Who said you could take those matches?"

CHAPTER TWO

EAST POTOMAC

When someone tells me "no," it doesn't mean I can't do it,
it simply means I can't do it with them.

—Karen E. Quinones Miller

Before continuing on my panoply of privilege, I thought it only fitting I head to the mottled, unremarkable, yet solemn and historically rich municipal course that stretches across an island made from reclaimed land in the middle of the Potomac River.

East Potomac Golf Links unrolls within shouting distance of the Lincoln Memorial, occasionally framed by cherry blossoms. It would have been within listening distance of Dr. Martin Luther King, Jr.'s, amplified voice in 1963 when he delivered his "I Have a Dream" speech.

When we lived across the river in Virginia, I sometimes drove into DC to escape the undulating fairways of the suburbs in favor of the flat terrain along the tidal basin. You won't find the Blue Course at East Potomac on any Top 100 lists. As one golf writer described it, "The land is flat, the holes are ordinary, the traps are shallow, the greens are slow and the conditioning is only adequate. But the price is right ($35, walking)." The park's Red and White courses, both nine-hole layouts, can be played for less. The Blue draws every shape, size, color, and level of golfer, accommodating about forty thousand rounds every year, a little more than are played at Bethpage Black, the lone municipal course among *Golf Digest*'s Top 100. I was happy to return.

A few years earlier, Erika and I had taken our kids to see the newly opened Martin Luther King, Jr., Memorial. Our son, Jordan, who was nine, read the inscription chiseled into the monument's base, a line from Dr. King's "I Have a Dream" speech: "Out of a mountain of despair, a stone of hope." Jordan looked beyond the statue of Dr. King to the two stones behind it, separated by the narrowest of spaces.

"They didn't have a lot of hope," he observed.

"Just enough to change the world," I told him.

That same sliver of hope was all I needed to hold on to the belief that I could draw others into my dream and complete the remaining ninety-nine courses.

DESIGNED BY AMATEUR CHAMP WALTER J. Travis in 1917, East Potomac became an epicenter of Black golf when the rest of the sport was still almost entirely white—though, as one of the three Black retirees told me when I eventually joined them on the front nine as a single, "You know, when this course first opened, Blacks couldn't play on it, either."

The Professional Golfers' Association of America inserted a Caucasian-only clause into its bylaws in 1934 that wasn't lifted until 1961, almost a decade and a half after Jackie Robinson integrated baseball. The Masters didn't extend an invitation to a Black competitor until 1975. Augusta National didn't admit its first Black member until 1990; its first female member was admitted in 2012.

East Potomac, part of the National Park Service, was integrated in 1941—way ahead of the curve—but it didn't happen without a fight. On June 29, 1941, three Black golfers—a postal employee, a schoolteacher, and one of the city's top amateurs—arrived with their clubs to play there in protest of the horrendous conditions at the Langston Golf Course, where all three were regulars, and their lack of access to the city's best, whites-only muni courses. Built just a couple years earlier and then one of only twenty courses in the United States open to Blacks, Langston's greens lacked grass, and an open sewer ran alongside two fairways. It was also part of the National Park Service.

Told that they couldn't play at Potomac, the three men left, only to return a short while later. This time they strode onto the course and teed off, each man nailing his first drive down the fairway. Tailed throughout by six US marshals, they played all eighteen holes, despite catcalls and threats from hecklers.

All three men broke 80.

Their round was the first attack on unlawful segregation in the District of Columbia. It created such a stir that Harold Ickes, the secretary of the interior, issued an order the next day to end discrimination not only at East Potomac but at all federally owned golf courses around the country.

In the years that followed, East Potomac hosted several championships of the United Golfers Association, the all-Black tour that birthed the careers of Charlie Sifford, Lee Elder, Ted Rhodes, and many others.

But its reputation among Black golfers goes well beyond that: it became fertile, if still mottled, ground for making extra cash. According to Jim Thorpe, one of the course's most prolific gamesters (not to be confused with the Native American Olympian and football player), there was nothing subtle about it: "Guys came to the golf course with paper bags of money and wads of cash in rubber bands." Players could walk off the course with more folding money than they won at tournaments.

Thorpe, the son of a North Carolina groundskeeper, eventually became one of the PGA Tour's most successful Black pros. He lived across the river, in Falls Church, and often played East Potomac with his older brother Chuck, a hard-living legend in his own right and the unquestioned star of the National Golf Tour, better known back then as the Black tour, which existed into the early 1990s. They'd play fifty-four or seventy-two holes a day, arriving at 8:00 a.m. and not finishing until dark.

They came in search of money games and were rarely disappointed, playing against guys with names such as Possum and Potato Pie—and anyone else with a lucrative side hustle and a set of clubs. One guy named Waldo wore pants three sizes too big with at least twenty thousand dollars stuffed in each pocket.

The Thorpes' favored game was the Wheel; variations of it—such as Rabbit and Squirrel, in Atlanta—exist around the country. In the Wheel, Jim and Chuck were the hub and every other twosome on the course was a spoke that emanated from them. That meant that every twosome was betting not only on themselves against Jim and Chuck, but on everyone else beating them, too. Tens of thousands of dollars were often riding on a single day of golf—with Jim and Chuck sometimes not carrying enough cash to cover a loss.

"There are no 'life and death' putts on [the PGA] Tour," Jim once said. "It's life and death when you play against those guys at East Potomac. If you don't have money in your pocket, you better win."

Thorpe never had a formal golf lesson in his life but developed a swing that was pure, self-taught serendipity, beginning outside the line and then finishing, on his follow-through, with a kind of helicopter twirl over his head; Johnny Miller once said it "had more moves than kung fu." Thorpe won three times on the PGA Tour and thirteen times on the Champions Tour. He also had two top-ten finishes at the U.S. Open. Still, despite his indisputable success as a professional golfer, he said he had never felt comfortable playing anyplace with a chandelier in the clubhouse.

I understood. Growing up, I saw the world divided between two groups: Those People and Us. Golf was definitely a Those People thing. I felt the same way when I began at Exxon. The idea that one day I'd rise to the executive level, outranking the people I had once worked under, never crossed my mind—not after a refinery inspector pulled out his grandfather's KKK hood as we crawled through a narrow, dark tower, thinking I might find it historically interesting; and certainly not when a box of rocks was placed in the middle of the table we sat around for a daily meeting for several weeks of my first year. The rocks were supposed to represent how smart the other people around the table thought I was.

They were Those People. And more often than not, it seemed, Those People played golf.

I didn't take up the game until I was in my forties, while living in Beaumont. The course I learned on was what golfers call a dog track: a cheap, barely maintained, town-run muni—several steps below East Potomac. On weekends I would return to Virginia and play at a country club where every time I swung and took a divot, I feared that I was destroying somebody's front lawn and worried that I was unwittingly doing something inappropriate.

I went on to play at great courses all over the country, even before my quest to play the Top 100, and Erika and I eventually bought a house on Kiawah Island, South Carolina, a golfer's paradise. But the feeling that I'm somehow trespassing—that I'm still the kid whose first suit was pulled from a town dump and that I shouldn't be let through the front gate—has never completely left me.

———

THAT FEELING VANISHED, HOWEVER, WHEN I pulled into East Potomac Park. The low-slung Greek Revival clubhouse had an air of faded glory, with community tables on the veranda where people can sit and eat burgers and hot dogs from the snack bar inside. A public pool and putt-putt course are just part of the milieu.

Once I teed off, striding in the footsteps of Thorpe and all the lost-to-history legends who had had to hustle for everything they got, I felt . . . at home. The only thing that mattered there was how I played golf.

As a businessman, I traveled a lot. After meetings in unfamiliar cities, I'd go out for something to eat or sit at a bar, even though I don't drink. Invariably, I'd be surrounded by white businessmen. I would see white strangers meeting with other white strangers—talking, joking, laughing—and I always felt like an outsider. It wasn't that they were hostile to me, but there seemed to be something about being white that allowed them to simply meet and strike up conversation. That feeling was reinforced constantly: it was their world, and I was merely an extra in it.

The corporate world's solution to that predicament is "inclusion." It never felt satisfactory to me. The word automatically establishes a hierarchy and becomes part of the power dynamic. Instead of saying "This is our world, and we're all a part of it," to me, "inclusion" says "This is *my* world, and I've decided to let *you* into it."

All of that was irrelevant at East Potomac. I teed off by myself on the first couple holes that sweltering weekday afternoon before calling out to the older Black guys a couple hundred yards ahead. "Can I join you?" I asked, with the ease of a white businessman approaching white strangers at a bar. Their carts were parked nearby as they searched the rough for an errant ball on the 565-yard par-five third hole on the Blue Course.

The tallest of the three turned to look at me, saw I was walking the course with a pull cart, and yelled back, "Only if you can keep up."

I was sure my long strides and fast play would quickly ease their concerns. They watched as my drive soared down the fairway: 265 yards.

I hurried down the fairway with my pull cart in tow. As I approached my ball, the trio walked over to introduce themselves: Mike, the tall fellow with a clean-shaven head who had called back to me; Richard, a light-skinned guy with a gray mustache; and James, whom they affectionately called "Pops" and who, even if he stood on his tiptoes, would struggle to reach my shoulders.

They glanced at one another curiously as I pulled the driver from my bag. A steady head and smooth swing sent a low-flying scorcher toward the green. They looked stunned, then offered approving nods as the ball came to rest fifty yards short of the flag. My near birdie on the hole seemed to ease their concern about whether I could keep up.

The piercing 7-iron I hit to within six feet of the flag on the par-three fourth hole sealed the deal. After I rolled in my putt for an easy bird,

Mike winked before admitting that his true concern had been whether I could play.

I laughed and said, "Don't be fooled. The wayward shots will come."

He looked skeptical. But my double bogey on the next hole probably helped convince him.

I kept the wild shots at bay as I parred the next three holes. On the tee box between shots, Mike, Richard, and Pops told me they were long-time friends, veterans, and retirees from second careers. Smiles spread across their faces when the conversation turned to their kids. There seems to be something about a common passion for golf that can produce instant camaraderie among strangers. It was that magic I was counting on to get invites to the country's most exclusive clubs.

"I've just retired myself so I can spend more time with my teenagers before they head off to college," I told them. "But I'm taking some time first to transition by traveling across the country to see if I can play golf at places where guys like us were once unwelcome."

All three men nodded.

They were good golfers. I don't know if their swings were self-taught like Thorpe's or whether they learned golf from a club pro as I did. But they sure knew how to get the ball in the hole for par or close to it.

When you learn from a pro, you learn the mechanics of a perfect swing. When you teach yourself, all you're worried about is perfecting a swing that will connect with the ball and make it go straight. You don't worry about how much of a turn you make or shifting your weight; you don't worry about any of that technical stuff. You worry about getting the clubface squarely onto the ball. That's how you learn when you develop on hardpan fairways, ball-eating roughs, and lumpy greens.

To my eye, those guys were unconcerned about form and technique. But they knew how to play golf. They were just having fun on a hot June day.

Our dynamic remained relaxed. That made it easy to swing the club. How well you play golf is directly proportional to the amount of tension in your body; tension is the enemy of a smooth swing. When you're relaxed and comfortable with your playing partners, you stop thinking about golf. You're just talking and swinging.

I completed the front nine with a 38.

As we made the turn, however, the temperature rose to well above ninety, without so much as a breeze off the river; it's my firm belief that a steamier ninety doesn't exist outside the DC Tidal Basin. The wisdom of the older men's choice to ride in carts came into clear focus. My sweat-soaked red shirt clung to my body as I hit my 5-hybrid down the left side of the fairway. The ball drew slightly, with a gauzy blue sky as backdrop, and landed in the rough a hundred yards from the pin and just a few yards behind a wide tree.

Golf is counterintuitive, but the laws of physics still apply. I placed my sand wedge on the ground, stepped on its face, and confirmed that the angle of the shaft would produce a shot that would clear the tree. I steadied my head and swung: the ball rose instantly, arced over the tree, and landed ten feet left of the pin. The laws of physics held as I pushed my birdie putt to the right of the cup.

Several bottles of water and two large bottles of Powerade had not been enough to keep me hydrated under the searing sun. As we approached the thirteenth hole, a pain rippled through my head and I quivered from a sudden chill. I tried to push through it but struggled visibly. Pops had seen enough. "Hop on the cart with me before you pass out," he said.

That act of kindness probably saved me from a serious medical condition I was too stubborn to acknowledge. I regained my strength and composure and rattled off three straight pars. One more and I'd break 80, a feat I rarely accomplished and a goal I'd set to achieve at least once on my remaining Top 100 course list. At East Potomac, it would put me into company with the first three Black men who had played there.

As a boy, my mother tried to teach me to never get ahead of myself. "One thing at a time," she'd say. I should've heeded her advice on eighteen. Preoccupied with my score, I popped my drive straight up, leaving me with two hundred yards to the flag. My approach sailed left and landed on the other side of a tall row of hedges. A high wedge over the hedges and a three-putt for double bogey brought my round to a bitter end with a score of 80. But I'd treasure the company I played with that day forever.

"Cherish the time with your kids," Mike called out to me after we all shook hands and parted. "They grow up fast."

———

THE CONTRAST TO MY NEXT stop could not have been starker.

The following morning, I drove two hours, finally winding through a posh neighborhood that deposited me at the gate of Kinloch Golf Club, a dozen miles northwest of Richmond. I'd gotten a tee time there through a connection with a head pro at one of my former clubs, but I still felt apprehensive as I approached. Several people had warned me that there would be places where I would not be welcomed, and for no good reason, other than perhaps the profound ghosts lingering with me from the day before, I feared that that meticulously groomed course in the shadow of the former capital of the Confederacy might be one of them.

All of that was going through my mind as I entered the access code on the keypad at the gate. When a voice echoed from the other end, I ID'd myself, said I had a morning tee time, and was instantly buzzed in.

As I made my way up the drive, the neighborhood's pillared mansions gave way to an expansive, almost paint-by-numbers property of tall trees, perfect fairways, pristine greens, raked bunkers, and glistening ponds. There can't be many more well-conditioned acreages; there wasn't a mottled blade of grass in sight.

It was New South golf heaven. When it opened in 2001, Kinloch was instantly declared *Golf Digest*'s "Best New Course." A calm came over me, akin to the serenity I had felt during solitary walks through the woods as a kid, soothing my anxiety. It had been less than two weeks since my retirement dinner, during which I'd thanked many people who had believed in me and supported my dreams. Now I was here, living a new one.

A young guy greeted me as I pulled up to the front of the Tudor-style clubhouse, then grabbed my clubs, directed me to the gentlemen's locker room, and told me, "Your caddie will be waiting for you with your clubs on the practice range."

With its dark wood bar, the locker room was as expansive as the grounds. Another man approached me and asked if I'd care for an early-morning cocktail. I declined but asked him if I could get the dust from East Potomac wiped off my golf shoes before I went out.

His reply: "Absolutely."

When he returned with my sparkling FootJoys, I found my way to the pro shop and asked the assistant behind the counter if there might be a member interested in a round with a guy on a mission to play the hundred greatest courses in the country. I didn't think I'd have to say much more than that to rouse a playing partner in a golf paradise like this.

The slender, dark-haired assistant pro seemed amused. His stunning reply: "Members here don't even play with each other."

Fears of being unwelcome pricked at me again as I walked to the driving range. My caddie, a college kid named Brian, was waiting with my clubs, and after a brief warm-up and a couple of putts on the flawless practice greens, we were off to the first hole, a wide-open, midlength par four with a blind landing zone.

As I waited behind the first tee box for my turn, my anxiety over being marginalized dissipated. Member after member teed off, one at a time, alone. I felt guilty for having thought that the assistant pro's response was anything other than the truth. I settled in and lined up my first drive. Brian advised me to hit left to avoid running down the slope and into the rough.

A full turn and follow-through sent the ball left of center, but it still rolled down the slope and into the right rough. Golf gods! I muscled my approach shot to just left of the green but failed to get up and down for a par. My round on the second of one hundred courses was under way.

It was just Brian and me out there, of course. He was an affable kid: grew up in Richmond, rising senior at Virginia Tech, spent summers as a youngster on Kiawah, where his parents had a house. It turned out that his childhood memories there were much like my own kids'. We talked the whole way. By the time I stood over my three-foot birdie putt on the short par-three fourteenth along the edge of the property's lake, I was feeling good about my swing and enjoying my time with Brian. I lost focus momentarily, hitting my putt through the break as I marveled at how easily the differences between a fifty-eight-year-old Black man and a twenty-one-year-old white college kid could vanish during a round of golf.

The final three holes, with trees bordering one side of curving fairways and water bordering the other, were three of the most magnificent closing holes I'd ever seen. Though this was only the second course on my list, I couldn't imagine how the fifty-two higher-rated courses could be much better.

After a round-ending bogey, Brian said what caddies say: "An eighty-five isn't bad for your first time playing here." It never gets old and never goes unappreciated.

But Kinloch has an epilogue. The nineteenth hole here is an actual hole, not the bar. It's a 150-yard par three over a pond with a green guarded by a large bunker that gives golfers a chance to break ties and settle their bets.

Jim Thorpe would have approved. I would've lost the tie.

I returned to the locker room hoping to finally talk with a couple of members, but none was lingering around. I turned down a beer from the locker room attendant and headed to my car. The valet had ensured that the interior was cool, providing a refuge from the blistering heat. As I wound my way back to the gate, I wondered if my strategy for getting onto the more exclusive courses—playing with, or at least meeting, members who'd make connections for me elsewhere—was still viable.

The problem didn't appear to be what I'd feared: racism. I know it exists, believe me. I'm still stopped for driving while Black, and white women still clutch their purses a little more tightly when they spot me on a train or sidewalk.

I also know, having lived with it for sixty-plus years, that racism affects some of us less, despite being talked about more, than it did just a couple decades ago. Though particular slights are still rooted in hatred and prejudice, not every slight is. For every person who doesn't like me for an immutable trait such as race, many more don't like me for something else altogether—including the fact that they just might not like themselves.

That was the lesson I drove away with from Kinloch Golf Club, whose members were more indifferent to me than anywhere else on my journey. Yes, I was invisible. But on that day, at least, I was merely as invisible as everyone else.

CHAPTER THREE

VALHALLA

What difference do it make if the thing you scared of is real or not?

—Toni Morrison

Once again there were golfers everywhere but no members looking for a stranger to join them. Standing alone inside the Flint Hills National Golf Club clubhouse, an exquisitely crafted two-story log cabin, I fretted about my strategy of finding contacts to gain access to the more exclusive clubs through players I would be randomly paired with as a single.

I'd made the nine-hour drive from Houston to Kansas to play three courses in two states over the next five days. The country's poverty and prosperity were both on full display just outside my car window, flashing by like a time-lapse reproduction of my personal journey. I'd passed the Oz-like buildings towering toward the sky in downtown Dallas before crossing the Red River, where wood-framed shacks, just a notch above the shacks I'd lived in during my youth, dotted Oklahoma's flat, desolate terrain. A wavy sea of ranchland finally rose up to greet me as I rolled into the Sunflower State.

Except for the native grasses that make its secondary rough so treacherous, the topography of Flint Hills is a more prettified version of the state's actual Flint Hills, a geologic formation of tallgrass prairie plateaus. Almost six thousand transplanted trees—cedars, maples, pin oaks, pines, sixty-foot-high cottonwoods—add texture and perspective to Tom Fazio's soft-rolling design. Tending to them all: the club's staff arborist.

I had forty minutes until my 8:00 a.m. tee time, so I made my way past the other golfers to the practice area, which included carefully groomed fairways, complete with bunkers and receptive greens.

My caddie arrived just as I was completing my warm-up. Easygoing and sixtysomething, Ken introduced himself as "Nebraska by birth but Kansas by heart." His experience as a caddie and his comfort with strangers were undeniable. He didn't hesitate to offer his guidance as we made our way around the course, where each hole, separated from the others by a partition of trees, offered its own solitary stroll through the wilderness. With no one else in sight, it felt as though we were toddling through our own private sanctuary. I had a bounce in my step after Ken gave an approving nod following my successful navigation of the par-five fifth hole for my third par of the round. But the air quickly went out of my inflated sense of pride as I made more double bogeys than pars on the next four holes. Golf has a way of reminding you not to let your pride exceed your skill level.

On the way to the tenth hole, I told Ken I'd grown up in Texas. When I listed the towns I'd lived in along the Gulf Coast—Texas City, La Marque, Hitchcock—he laughed and said he'd coached track during the seventies in nearby Lake Jackson. It turned out we'd been at some of the same meets during my junior and senior years in high school. We talked about several of the more memorable superstars I'd competed against from other small towns in Texas, including Donnie Little, a multisport athlete from Dickerson who became the first Black quarterback at the University of Texas, and Mike Mosley, another multisport phenom who played quarterback at rival Texas A&M. They were athletes whose talents had taken them well beyond their original stations in life.

I wasn't a good enough athlete for sports to be my route out. But sports taught me confidence and allowed me to believe that one day, somehow, I could be seen. I had more self-assurance on the track than on the gridiron. Running came naturally to me; it was what I had done while growing up, flying around those wooden bases in the Sawmill Quarters; leaping over the ditches that lined our streets in La Marque; racing down a road that ran beside the seawall in Texas City. I even beat Donnie Little and Mike Mosley in one semifinal heat: when I shot out of the blocks first, I expected to hear the starting gun go off again to signal a false start. When it didn't, I was shocked that there was nobody in front of me for the rest of the race.

Ken shook his head and smiled. It had taken nine holes, but that great-grandfather from Nebraska and I had found our nexus. Our walk together on the back nine became even more relaxed, with every ounce of outsider tension now gone from my swing.

Listening to Ken, I was struck by how much the former coach reminded me of those I'd played for in high school. A favorite was my varsity football coach, Phil Bennett. He died way too young, in his late thirties or early forties, not many years after I graduated from high school, but he left a big mark on my own young life.

At a glance, Coach Bennett looked as though he'd fallen straight off the Texas Football Coach assembly line: a balding good ol' boy with a comb-over and a country twang who dipped tobacco and drove a pickup truck. He was the Bum Phillips of high school football, except that his teams weren't very successful. Hitchcock High rarely won, but he maintained an ability to judge players at face value—he started the school's first Black quarterback—and he engendered a loyalty among his players that far exceeded his record. When our team heard rumors that he was going to be fired, the captain asked me to write a speech for him to give from the press box during halftime of our next game. I don't remember why the speech was never delivered, but I suspect that Coach Bennett got wind of what we were up to and stopped it in its tracks. I'm sure he figured a stunt like that wouldn't do him any favors in Texas.

Like a lot of other teachers at my school, Coach Bennett viewed me as a quiet leader, and there were times he treated me almost as a peer. It wasn't a leap. I was a poor but precocious kid—not the kind of kid all the girls wanted to date, but the kind of kid a white football captain would ask to write him a speech.

Even so, I lived such a simplified life; I was almost always preoccupied with making sure I had enough to eat, clothes on my back, and some type of shelter. I didn't have time to worry about being popular, who liked me and who didn't, or any of the other normal things high school kids obsess over. (Though when I ran for student council, every one of my classmates voted for me—the first unanimous election in our school's history.) For me, it was the basics, period. Getting free lunch in the cafeteria was a victory. It left me with one less meal to worry about. Being teased or bullied about it barely registered on my emotional radar. I had no real role model for surviving high school, so I simply learned what I could and applied it as I went. It was like building a bridge, beam by beam, and walking across it at the same time.

What I lacked in money and support I made up for with curiosity and intelligence. I'd take tentative steps outside my poverty-limited world to see, and often gawk at, what was out there; I was the only kid in the high school who regularly attended school board meetings, eager to know how and why things ran the way they did, the way a kid in the electronics club back then might have been fascinated by transistors.

It was after one of those school board meetings that Coach Bennett approached me (mistakenly) as an equal. The basketball coach had just resigned, and Coach Bennett, who also served as athletic director, was under a lot of pressure to hire a stellar replacement. Basketball was the one sport the school was known for. The expectation was that he'd promote the fresh-out-of-college junior varsity coach, Coach Wilson, who was also Black.

We sat in Coach's old pickup truck for a few long minutes while he chewed tobacco and stewed over the decision.

"You know, Slim Jim," he said, his tired face lit by the lot's lone streetlamp, "I want to do the right thing. I just don't know what the right thing is. Everybody's expecting me to name Coach Wilson, but I don't think he's ready, and if he doesn't do a good job, his career is probably over before it has a chance to get started. But if I don't give it to him, people will accuse me of being racist."

Coach had confided in me before. He knew he could trust me to keep our conversations private. In Texas, high school coaches are the biggest stars in town, and the pressure often left men like Coach Bennett feeling isolated. I became his sounding board. I was the only football player in the honor society, and he'd often use me as an example to the rest of the team, telling them "You could be like Slim Jim" before letting me leave practice early to attend some academic function. Like other teachers and coaches, he respected me because I didn't quit; I was the kid who showed up at school wearing rubber flip-flops because they were the only shoes I owned. They perceived me as mature because I was responsible and driven. But the fact is that I was incredibly naive about most things.

Nonetheless, there I was in the passenger seat of an old pickup truck with a good ol' boy of a football coach who occasionally leaned over to spit into a paper cup, asking me what he should do. And all I could think to say to him was "You got to do what you think is right."

"You know, Coach, people know you're not a racist." I went on. "But you have to figure out what you think is right and then do it."

That was what my mother told us all the time. But there was another dimension that I hadn't learned yet: you have to do the right thing *in the right way*. I think that was what Coach was struggling with.

I don't remember now what he ended up deciding. He left town sometime after I graduated and got another coaching job in another small town, north of Houston. He lost more games than he won there, too, and when I visited him once while I was attending Prairie View, he looked a lot older than he was. Not long after that, I heard he died of a heart attack.

AFTER MY ROUND, THE CLUB pro introduced me to Jeff Johnson, the president of Flint Hills. He immediately invited me to lunch with some other members and staff, and within minutes I no longer felt like an intruder. They seemed impressed that I'd already checked Augusta off my list, although J.J. expressed concern that there still might be clubs that wouldn't accommodate me. His was not one of them; not only would he invite me to become a member, he eventually introduced me to members who also belonged to some of the most remote and exclusive Top 100 courses.

I had arrived at Flint Hills that morning concerned that my central strategy of winning over strangers to help me complete my quest might be wishful thinking. I left with renewed confidence that it was the right way to go.

That confidence carried over during the next couple days at Prairie Dunes Country Club outside Hutchinson, an hour away.

Designed in the 1930s by the legendary midwestern golf course architect Perry Maxwell, the original layout was considered the top nine-hole course in the country; Maxwell had died by the time the club expanded twenty years later, so the additional nine holes were designed with the same discerning nuance by his son, Press. The seaside links-style course is set in the heart of the country about as far as you can get from the actual seaside, adhering to Perry Maxwell's belief that "the golf course should be there, not brought there." It seamlessly incorporates the sand dunes, prairie grasses, and cottonwoods that surround it.

It's a challenge. The greens can be severe, and the rough, composed of the prickly native grasses referred to by locals as "gunch," is among the most difficult to play from in all of golf. My caddie would confide that "This course is only hard when the wind is blowing," then pause a beat and deadpan, "The wind is always blowing."

The small local club attracts a cultlike national membership, yet it remains as humble and unassuming as its heartland address. I drove right by it even though my GPS said I'd arrived, and I had to ask a jogger by the side of the road for directions. "It's right back there," she said, pointing not far behind me. The simple white clubhouse with an asphalt shingled roof caught me off guard. The pristine surroundings of Augusta National, Kinloch, and Flint Hills had conditioned me to expect more than the unassuming setting of Prairie Dunes, which *Golf Digest* has ranked as high as thirteen since it permanently joined the magazine's list in 1969.

So it seemed fitting that a serendipitous conversation with the golfer warming up next to me on the practice range wound its way through several degrees of separation and terminated with a connection to a member at one of the courses I'd had the most difficulty finding a contact for. That alone made the next two days of tottering through the gunch worth it.

―――

I FINISHED MY LAST ROUND at Prairie Dunes early in the afternoon and hit the road for the eleven-hour drive to my next stop: Valhalla Golf Club in Louisville, Kentucky.

But thirty minutes after leaving Hutchinson, rolling east down US Route 50, I looked in my rearview mirror and saw flashing lights atop a white truck with blue stripes. I slowed, expecting the truck to pass me on the rural two-lane highway, but it slowed, too, and the officer behind the wheel finally motioned for me to pull over.

Being stopped by the police while driving alone in the middle of nowhere is one of a Black man's worst nightmares. On one of my Sunday-afternoon walks with Jordan, I'd taught him how to handle himself if stopped by the police. It's a talk that all Black parents must have with their sons. I'm mindful that most officers make sacrifices to protect and serve us, but it takes only one having a bad day to end my life. I told Jordan to always keep his hands on top of the steering wheel, not make any sudden moves, follow the officer's instructions, and never get into an argument—pretty standard, almost left-unsaid stuff for most people but details that can't be emphasized enough for people of color. "The police don't radio in that they are pulling over a smart kid with dreams of a great future," I emphasized. "They simply say they are stopping a Black male."

I know this because I'd been pulled over three times for Driving While Black during my young adult years. The first time was in 1980, while I was still in college, driving from Prairie View to my brother's apartment in Houston. I'd stopped to return a movie I had rented the day before at a video store. As I pulled up to the store this time, I noticed a woman inside run to the front door and lock it. She seemed so out of sorts and moved at such a hurried pace that I thought she had diarrhea and was locking up to go to the bathroom. I waited in my car for a while, expecting that she'd come back to unlock the door after she finished her business. After about twenty minutes, I assumed she was in really bad shape, so I got out of the car and went to pass time in another store nearby.

Minutes later, a police officer walked in and asked me to come with him. It was not a request. He then asked if that was my car parked in front of the video store, and when I said yes, he told me to get in the back seat of his police cruiser. He took my license, got into the front, and called in my ID. After I heard whoever he was talking to say, "No history," the officer got out, opened the back door, and told me I was free to leave. When I asked what had just happened, he explained that there had been a robbery in town and the woman inside the video store had called when she saw me. He said I fit the suspect's description: Black male, five feet, six inches tall, blue shirt, gray pants.

Only one of those applied to me: Black male.

The next time came after I graduated. I was behind the wheel of a sporty red Miata with the top down on a Saturday night, driving home from a friend's house in a ritzy section of Houston. A police car pulled up behind me, lights swirling, and an officer with a bullhorn ordered me to pull over. I eased into a lighted parking lot, one hand on the steering wheel, the other on the stick shift. In a display of force and intimidation one officer walked up along each side of the car, hands on their guns, and ordered me to put both my hands where they could see them. As they towered over me in my small car, they yelled, *"Do it now!"* Then one of them glanced toward the front of the car and said, "Oh, your registration is on your windshield," and they left without another word.

They'd known my registration was there before they pulled me over. They were just messing with me.

The third time came a few years later. I was driving an SUV in another swanky neighborhood in Houston, with an inspection sticker that had expired the day before. After the officer pulled me over and asked for my license, he returned to his car and phoned it in. Seconds later, six police cruisers raced in and lined up behind me. I waited another thirty minutes before the cop came back to my window to tell me, "You need to take care of that."

I'm a numbers guy. I know around a thousand people are killed by police officers each year. I also know that about a quarter of them are Black and only a fraction of them are unarmed. But when you've been pulled over and harassed time and time again, numbers don't matter. Only lived experience matters. The fear and anxiety, whether logical or illogical, are real.

That was what was running through my mind when that police pickup truck—*pickup truck!*—pulled me over in small-town Kansas. I let my window down so that I could keep my hands visible once the officer approached. After he asked for my license and registration, I asked why he stopped me. He said I had been speeding.

I knew I hadn't been speeding; in fact, a half-dozen other cars had passed me not long before he pulled me over. A familiar feeling gripped me, despite having spent the past month playing golf at some of the most exclusive courses in the country: I felt small, as if my six-foot, four-inch frame had shrunk to half its size. I felt the shame of letting a blatant lie go unconfronted. But I was not about to challenge the officer. You fight false accusations in court, not along the side of the road. I hoped he'd simply give me a ticket and leave.

The officer returned from his truck with a traffic citation and told me, "Call the number I circled, and they'll discuss our deferment program with you." He said my ticket could be expunged simply by paying a $450 fine and fee.

It occurred to me that perhaps he hadn't pulled me over because I was Black, but because of my Texas tags. It was just an old-fashioned shakedown for the most time-honored small-town crime: Driving While Out of State.

I pulled back onto the highway and made it across the Mississippi River into Illinois before fatigue got the best of me, still five hours from Valhalla. I checked into a hotel to bed down for a short night.

———

VALHALLA IS TRUE TO ITS myth-inspired name: idyllic, immaculate, seemingly removed from the trials and tribulations of the earthly world. Nestled near the eastern edge of Louisville, where the redbrick river town gives way to stretches of bluegrass interrupted by deep woods of beech, bald cypress, and the random big-leaf magnolia, Valhalla is a tract of wild landscape that Jack Nicklaus tamed for the golf gods. His Jekyll-and-Hyde design—mostly open and linkslike on the front nine, untouched forest choking the fairways, and thick bluegrass collaring the greens on the back—transports and challenges anyone who plays it.

The gated entryway signals exclusivity: whitewashed fences run along the long drive to the clubhouse, giving visitors the impression of entering a well-maintained horse farm. Though the driveway is not quite Augusta National's Magnolia Lane, its splendor cast an almost equal spell on me. Opened in 1986, Valhalla is already inching toward iconic, having hosted a Ryder Cup and three PGA Championships, including Rory McIlroy's thrilling win in 2014.

As I soaked it all in, I was once again nagged by a feeling that I didn't belong. I had moved through the world with an acquired knowledge and grace that was unimaginable to me during my childhood. Yet no matter how educated, worldly, or wealthy I became, I remained that barefoot kid swinging a discarded stick at a crusty doll's head or rubbing the pages of Sears, Roebuck catalogues together to soften them before wiping my butt during trips to our maggot-infested outhouse. My stomach still clenches when I think about the overpowering stench of those visits.

On that late-summer afternoon a month into my quest, I struck up a conversation between swings on the practice range with an intern standing there to make sure everyone was taken care of. His name was Dylan Rowe, and I asked him where he was going to school. He proudly told me he was studying golf management at Sam Houston State University in Huntsville.

I practically froze midswing. Miles and years from the piney woods of East Texas, I'd encountered someone associated with the place where the demons that still stalked me had been created. So many unpleasant memories came rushing back, overpowering my thoughts as I stood beside that poised, polite kid who couldn't have been much older than my own teenage son.

Back then, the Sawmill Quarters' humdrum routines gave way to chaos on Friday and Saturday nights. My stepfather's sister, Aunt Essie Pearl, had converted her shack next to ours into an ad hoc juke joint on weekends, serving marked-up, bootlegged liquor and beer while a couple of musicians played something her patrons could dance to. She'd somehow jerry-rigged her place so that it had electricity, and a dozen or so neighbors from the bottom of the hill and beyond would show up as the sun went down.

I was too young to know all that went on there. But around midnight, after the liquor and electricity petered out and everyone wove their way home, another ritual commenced: college boys from the university that Dylan attended would arrive, roaring through the pitch black, seven or eight of them crammed into some two-tone Rambler or Bel Air the way a previous generation had stuffed themselves into telephone booths.

Their wild eyes and lopsided grins were lit through open windows by an inside dome light, the sole illumination on our unelectrified street, save for the moon and the stars. They whooped it up and shouted "Nigger! Nigger! Nigger!" at the top of their lungs, every syllable audible through the cracks between the boards separating the inside of our shacks from whatever went on out there. There was no real distinction between the dirt road the students drove on and our dirt yards.

Their howling of the N-word became so commonplace in our lives that we grew nearly immune to it. The reaction inside our shack was negligible, more like the annoyance of being awoken by the screech of an owl or the rustle of a rat. If any of us got up at all, it was merely to peek out a window to confirm what we already knew. "It's those college boys again," someone would mumble before turning over and dropping back to sleep.

I don't recall anyone ever confronting them, certainly not the one Black cop who was usually sent in to resolve conflicts between us Coloreds. There was no way a Black man was going to arrest white kids in the Jim Crow South. But it didn't matter. Young as I was, I don't remember ever being scared. Like those times years later, when the police pulled me over in my car for nothing, all I really felt was the powerlessness of being on the colored side of white. We were mere props for someone else's amusement. Huddled in a single bed, my siblings and I usually just fell back to sleep, understanding, if only subconsciously, that even the minimalistic world we lived in between these pines was not our own. My volatile stepfather, drunk-snoring beside my mother in the front room while the rest of the shack reeked of his boozy vomit, never budged.

Those soirees were loud and disruptive, but they were also brief: our road wasn't long, so the liquored-up kids simply drove past the dozen or so houses that lined it until they reached its dead end, punctuated by a little wooden, steepled church. Then they'd spin around and speed back out. They didn't even speed, really; the road's loose dirt was so unstable they couldn't drive all that fast, though I'm sure that hardly mattered in their raucous retellings. It was only in the morning, when we'd find empty or broken Lone Star or Pearl beer bottles littering our small grassless plots, that we'd remember they'd been by at all.

Until the next Friday and Saturday nights.

Incidents like those were a constant reminder that being Black conferred a greater sense of powerlessness than being poor. Though poverty was a constant presence in our lives, it just seemed like the natural order of things for people like us. But the racist acts we dealt with almost every day were a relentless reminder of our status as second-class citizens. There were still WHITES ONLY signs posted on doors and windows around downtown Huntsville to remind us. Black folks, including my stepfather, held the most menial jobs in the sawmill, and the women who worked outside the mill, like my mother, cleaned the houses or looked after the kids of the town whites.

Decades later, after I led a post–oil spill cleanup effort for Exxon in Montana, I had a long conversation with Rex Tillerson, then the company's CEO and later, briefly, secretary of state under Donald Trump. At one point, we veered from the business at hand and talked about the things we had in common: we were both civil engineers, our birthdays were only days apart, and we'd both lived in Huntsville, where he'd moved as a kid when his father worked for the Boy Scouts of America. What I was too ashamed to mention was that my mother or some other relative may have worked in his family's home or yard.

All of those circumstances made us feel less than—but at least we were less than together. They gave us a common community. We never felt less than one another; if no one else could see us for who we really were, at least we saw one another.

I assumed that Dylan, when he was back at school, didn't drive drunk through the Sawmill Quarters on weekends. In fact, nobody did anymore: my family's shack, along with all the others, had been razed or crumbled and rotted into pieces sometime after the lumber company had shut down in the late 1960s. The land, since purchased by the university, is mostly reclaimed by forest now, and student apartments are planned for where our shacks once stood.

Yet on the grounds of Valhalla, where I was reminded of the powerlessness of my youth, I chose not to mention to Dylan my experiences with those who had preceded him by half a century at Sam Houston State. There had been progress, and as the loop from those nights streamed through my head, Dylan's generosity and gentleness jarred me from my reverie.

He told me that his father was the head pro at Whispering Pines Golf Club, a Top 100 course. Located in Trinity, Texas, it's only about thirty miles from Huntsville.

He then said he'd be happy to ask his dad to get me on.

I was no longer less than.

———

BEN HOGAN ALLEGEDLY ONCE SAID, "I play golf with friends, but we don't play friendly games."

I played Valhalla with two former Exxon colleagues, Kevin Hobbs and Richard Byrne, along with Kevin's brother-in-law, James Hourigan. Kevin had gotten the director of golf at his home club in the Woodlands, Texas, to arrange our reunion—or what we dubbed the "Bout in the Bluegrass." Our trash-talking emails began the day our tee time was confirmed. I told Kevin that I was going to kick his butt in his own backyard; he'd grown up on a farm not far from Louisville and had attended the University of Kentucky. Richard, a former federal prosecutor, told me to be sure to bring enough money to pay off my bet.

We didn't actually put any money on the line. The game was about pride, about bragging rights, which is what golf bets are about anyway, at least among recreational golfers. Nobody cares about the dollar or two or ten that are grudgingly handed over on the final green. We only care about rubbing our victory in.

During our previous rounds together, I had given them three or four strokes. I did so again that day. I'd spent the bulk of the month since my retirement playing golf, so Kevin and Richard, five or six years younger than me and still toiling in the fields of Exxon, figured my game had only improved. Sandy haired and around six feet tall, Kevin was the better athlete, but I was the better golfer, and Richard, a gentle giant who can drive the ball a long way, generally hits enough wayward shots in between those drives to sabotage his score.

Their equalizer: mind games. Richard, especially, knows how to get me to start focusing on something other than my swing, a carryover from his years of dueling in the courtroom.

Kevin tossed a tee into the air to determine who'd go first, and it hit the ground pointing toward me. I immediately turned to my caddie, a spirited guy with football-sized calves named Ted. "How far to where it makes that dogleg left?" I asked him.

Ted informed me that it was about 240 yards, and I stroked a high-flying drive that sailed past the trees on the left before landing in the middle of the fairway. From there I had a clear line to the pin at the front of the green. I picked up my tee and stared down Kevin and Richard as if to say, "Take that!"

Their drives also landed in the fairway, but without a direct approach to the green. That forced them to lay up short on their next shots. My approach flew by the pin and settled near the back. "Don't worry too much about the line, just get your speed right," Ted advised. My seventy-two-foot birdie putt sped toward the front of the green before it halted three feet short of the cup. Kevin and Richard had already putted out for bogeys. With Kevin's brother-in-law just along for the ride, my par putt dropped in to win the hole.

Having laid down my marker that I'd come to play, I strode with a slight swagger to the par-five second tee. Kevin and Richard pretended to ignore me.

I thought about the friendship Kevin and I had forged over the years. He and I had met early in our careers as young engineers with strong personalities. We were competitive in the workplace and on the basketball court in the intracompany league. We habitually clashed in meetings and at times didn't get along. Neither of us was shy about expressing our views— Kevin dispassionately and me passionately. He often recoiled at my fervor. But later we were assigned to the leadership team at the Beaumont refinery, where we gained a mutual respect and genuine admiration for each other while working together to improve the refinery's performance.

Beaumont was also where we had both learned golf. After long days at work, we would escape to the Henry Homberg Municipal Golf Course in Tyrrell Park, the local muni, and unwind on its hardpan fairways. Under the warmth generated by our shared zeal for learning the game, our differences began to melt away. We soon bonded and formed a deep friendship. I worked directly for Kevin the last three years of my career, and although we solved a lot of business challenges at the office, we also worked through issues our teams were facing while we chased the little white ball.

More than that, we talked about things we would never have discussed during meetings or over business dinners. Kevin shared some of his own life story. He told me that his parents had worked hard to make sure that he and his siblings got an education. Because of their efforts he had been able to gain admission to the University of Kentucky and earn a chemical engineering degree.

Just as I had my demons, Kevin had his. And although our demons were different, they strengthened our bond. His background helped explain his strong work ethic, which sometimes made him seem stoic and stern. But when Kevin's young sons accompanied him on our Saturday golf trips, I saw a side of him few people at work got a glimpse of. I learned a lot about his compassion and empathy as I watched how tender and attentive he was with his kids. Our common passion for golf gave me an insight into Kevin that I would never have discovered otherwise.

My caddie pointed beyond the creek crossing the front of the second tee, toward the right side of the fairway, and said, "Kick a field goal with your drive directly between the two most prominent trees in that cluster."

A confident swing propelled the ball on a line that perfectly bisected the trees, and two swings later I was lining up for a thirty-foot birdie putt. The ball stopped a foot short. Richard then sank a ten-foot birdie putt to steal the par five.

"Take that," he said before retrieving his ball from the cup.

I walked off the green without congratulating him. All's fair in psychological warfare.

No blood was drawn on the third hole, a par three with a well-bunkered green guarded by a creek called Floyd's Fork, as we all played it poorly. But things got more interesting on the short par-four fourth. By now I'd established credibility with Ted on playing the game. A good caddie can size up his golfer within the first couple of holes, but my play had been unusually consistent, so he had no way of knowing that I was playing much better than normal. He had also established his standing with me as a solid looper. "Hit your ball over that bunker off the left side of the fairway," he told me now. "It's just two hundred fifteen yards to carry it." I didn't catch the ball cleanly, sending it into the rough on the upslope above the bunker.

That was where I was going to need Ted to earn his keep. At eighty-five yards from a back-pin position, I asked him if I should hit a three-quarter sand wedge to the middle of the green or try to get back to the pin with a slightly less lofty three-quarter pitching wedge.

His advice: "A sand wedge off that slope will fly straight up and land short of the green. So hit the pitching wedge back to the flag."

I did what he said and caught the ball cleanly with a three-quarter swing. It flew on a nice arc and hit a foot left of the flag, took one hop, then rolled over the back of the green. I was disappointed that the ball didn't stop next to the flag but asked Ted for my lob wedge, thinking I had a short chip and putt for par. When we reached the back of the green, however, I was surprised to see that it sloped steeply down to a creek, which was where we found my ball.

I was steamed. I gave Ted a look and asked, "Why'd you tell me to hit it back to the flag with that steep drop-off?" He seemed stunned by my reaction but didn't respond. I plucked the ball out of the water, took a penalty stroke, pitched back up to the green, and two-putted for a double bogey.

I rarely allow what happens on a golf course to get to me anymore. It's just a game; I know that no matter my results, my wife and kids will still get to eat. But this felt different—this was the Bout in the Bluegrass; this was Jimmie versus Kevin versus Richard. Pride was on the line. I let my ego cause me to lose my sorts. I overreacted and took it out on Ted. I didn't say another word to him for several holes. Thelma James would not have been proud. Ted continued to offer his advice. I refused to acknowledge it.

It wasn't my finest moment, and it showed in my score. I reeled off three triple bogeys and a double over the next five holes to finish the front nine over 50. I'd let the pressure of the match frustrate me and destroy my swing. I didn't just want to beat those guys, those former colleagues, those friends; I wanted to dominate them. I wanted them to know that I had gotten much better than they were at golf. But in the end, only I was responsible for my score. And even though I was in no mood to be sensible, I shouldn't have blamed Ted.

Yet as we moved to the more densely treed back nine, it seemed to me as though Ted started to intentionally offer bad advice. He suggested I hit a 3-wood out of the deep bluegrass rough. Then Richard picked up on my undeclared war with Ted and went in for the kill. "Your caddie is terrible," he whispered.

It was a sly attempt from that former prosecutor, who'd regularly gone head-to-head with drug dealers, murderers, and other hard-core criminals, to keep me off-balance. At Exxon, as one of our in-house attorneys, Richard had helped me handle several legal matters during the final years of my career. We'd grown close over long days and late nights spent pursuing the facts to make sure we got them right. So I was mildly amused to see that excellent but pedantic lawyer playing courtroom head games to gain an advantage on the golf course.

It took until the twelfth hole, the toughest on the course, for me to get my swing back. I parred it, then three-putted from fifteen feet for a bogey on the beautiful thirteenth hole, with its green just below a cascading waterfall. Suddenly, midway through the tougher of the two nines at Valhalla—narrow, tree-lined fairways bordered by deep rough—I was interested in the match again. But I'd lost track of who had scored the most points. I didn't dare ask; I didn't want Kevin and Richard to know I still cared who won. Kevin's brother-in-law, who wasn't participating in the blood match, was playing better than all of the rest of us. I decided I could declare him the real winner and deny Kevin or Richard the pleasure of gloating.

I don't think we men ever stop being boys.

When my ball hit the rocks along the side of the fifteenth green, then kicked into the creek on my approach shot, I was ready for my long nightmare of a day to end. When we finally reached the closing hole, a 470-yard par five, Ted pointed to a plaque noting that it had been Nicklaus's closing hole in his final major, the 2000 PGA Championship. By that point, it was clear that Jack would miss the cut, so he was probably as ready for his round to end back then as I was for mine. His playing partner that day, Tiger Woods, who would go on to win in a three-hole playoff at the peak of his career as he pursued Jack's record for total majors won, said to him, "Let's finish it in style." They both carded birdies.

Inspired by Tiger's quote, I looked at Kevin, Richard, and James and said, "I don't know who's ahead, but let's finish it in style."

I promptly hit a hundred-yard pop-up that dropped into the rough, between the tee box and fairway. Undeterred, I asked Ted for my new Epic driver and smashed a 270-yard shot out into the fairway, leaving me just 140 yards to the pin. Kevin and Richard accused me of propping the ball up in the rough for leverage. I just hit it as it lay.

Confidence restored, I proceeded to hit a soaring approach shot that landed eight feet from a finishing-in-style birdie to match Tiger and Jack. But as soon as the ball left my putter, I knew I hadn't struck it hard enough. I tapped in for par as Kevin gleefully informed me, "If you had made the birdie putt, you would've tied me for the match." I told him it wouldn't have mattered; James had beaten us all anyway. We laughed as we shook hands and headed to the pro shop so I could say goodbye to Dylan. None of us was proud enough of our play to taunt anyone else.

I didn't have time to hang around. In less than twenty-four hours, Erika and the kids and I would be boarding a flight to Ireland for a family vacation. I offered to give Richard a ride to the Louisville airport before starting my seven-hour drive back to Atlanta. On the way he said nothing about our match or about our banter leading up to it, but he had one last question: "Did you tip that terrible caddie you had?"

"Yes," I told him. "And I gave him a good tip, too."

He left the car without another word, satisfied that he'd set me up for next time.

CHAPTER FOUR

WHISTLING STRAITS

The world is merciless, and it's also very beautiful.

—Hajime Isayama

I was my mother's fourth live birth. Ultrasounds weren't available to forewarn her of the possible miscarriages she suffered between the births of me and my brothers and sisters. I don't think she even visited a doctor during any of her earliest pregnancies. All but the last two of us were delivered by a midwife.

My mother endured so much that I only learned about or appreciated in retrospect. She'd already had six kids when we drove from Huntsville back to La Marque in Frank's car, with four of us kids scrunched up together in the front seat to let my mother lie by herself, sick and moaning, in the back. The two-hour drive was extended by frequent stops whenever the radiator overheated. She was in agony.

It wasn't until we were almost home that Frank finally pulled up to a hospital emergency room. Only later in life did I understand that she had been having a miscarriage.

"It's incompatible with life."

Those were the words used by a doctor to tell me and Erika about the condition that could kill the baby growing inside her. I tried to process them but found it impossible.

Moments before, we had been sailing through the first ultrasound of Erika's early pregnancy. The technician was chatting away as she swabbed Erika's abdomen with gel and waved a wand over it, images of the fetus appearing in real time on a monitor. That was when the blood suddenly rushed from the tech's face. She went silent, then asked if we could excuse her for a moment. A few minutes later, she returned with a radiologist. He introduced himself but didn't say much more. He grabbed the sensor and again rubbed it across Erika's abdomen.

After studying the images, he explained that there were two choroid plexus cysts on our baby's brain and that the cysts were one of the markers of a chromosomal disorder called trisomy 18. "What does that mean?" we asked. That was when the radiologist, with a clinician's matter-of-factness, uttered the four words I'll never forget.

"It's incompatible with life."

Over the next two months, I researched everything I could about trisomy 18. I learned that choroid plexus cysts are just one of several markers for the disorder. Our baby had none of the others. My brain went into full math mode: I assured Erika that the probability of our baby having trisomy 18 wasn't zero but that it seemed as indistinguishable from zero as you could mathematically get. I told her that according to my research, the cysts would most likely disappear by the time she had her next ultrasound. I told her all of that mostly to comfort her, but I believed it, too, because that was what the data showed. Still, it was a long two and a half months before we returned to the doctor's office to see whether or not it was true.

The cysts were gone by that second ultrasound. Three months after that, inside a hospital delivery room, I asked the doctor during a brief pause why receiving a baby from the womb was often called a "catch."

He told me to scrub up and put on a pair of surgical gloves. Then, just before Erika's final push, he showed me where to stand and how to hold my hands. Seconds later, a slippery baby shot right into them.

"That's why they call it a catch," the beaming doctor said.

Tears ran down my face.

"We have a son," I shouted to Erika right after our firstborn went from his mother's womb straight to my heart.

———

FIFTEEN YEARS LATER, WITH HIS Afro soaring atop his six-foot frame, Jordan sat next to me as I drove him from our home in Atlanta to Durham, North Carolina, for a two-week writing camp at Duke University. Jordan loved writing. At camp, he had written poems, then turned them into lyrics for songs for which he composed music. Words and music were the stray pieces of wood he used to fill his own childhood.

Family travel had kept all of us away from home for much of the summer, so the drive gave me and Jordan a chance to get caught up on our talks about things that matter. That was what we called the conversations we had during walks through our Buckhead neighborhood on Sunday afternoons before I headed back to Houston or elsewhere for work.

The walks started after we moved from Charlottesville. Erika and I hadn't seen any Black teenagers in our almost exclusively white neighborhood. We thought it would be beneficial for our neighbors to become accustomed to seeing a Black teenager with an Afro walking by their homes with his father before he ventured out alone in a place where some might question whether he belonged. I also wanted to make sure that he fully understood the risks of being the only Black male kid in a white neighborhood.

As a teenager, I was once forewarned about the risk of white neighbors thinking I didn't belong. It happened during college one summer while I interned at a Department of Commerce bureau just outside

Washington, DC. A woman who lived in an upper-class Chevy Chase, Maryland, neighborhood, just across the line from the District, had invited me to board in her home. She worked at the bureau and had gotten my name from a list of summer interns looking for a place to stay. When I arrived at her house, she was taken aback when she opened the front door and saw I was Black.

It wasn't an issue for her; her house sat across the street from Lindy Boggs, the longtime Democratic congresswoman from Louisiana and mother of NPR's Cokie Roberts. She spoke admiringly of them—but she let me know that there were no Black residents in the neighborhood. Though Black domestic workers could be seen during the day, it would have been unusual to see one walking through the neighborhood at night. She was concerned that if I walked the tree-lined streets after dark and was confronted by neighbors or the police, it could become a problem, especially if it were to happen while she was away on one of her frequent business trips.

Fortunately, I never experienced any incidents. Perhaps the neighbors got used to seeing me leave the house for work in the mornings.

Once at Duke, Jordan quickly reunited with his friends. As I stood and watched him walk toward them, I noticed a swagger I'd never seen in him. I felt proud and sad at the same time: proud of his commanding presence but sad as I thought about how little time we had remaining before I'd drop him off at college for his first semester, not just camp.

As I drove away, I thought of Harry Chapin's perennial dad anthem, "Cat's in the Cradle," wherein a father too busy with work when his son was a boy discovers that his son has no time for him when he becomes a man. It's a song almost any father can relate to, no matter his age or musical taste. I worried that I would come to regret the moments I had missed during all those work trips to Paris, London, Tokyo, Bogotá, and beyond to fulfill my own dreams. And now here I was darting across the country again to play golf.

I wrestled with that conflict constantly. I could justify the frequent separations from my family when what I did provided for them. Of course I would have preferred to be home with them every evening, but my career didn't allow for it. It was the key to their well-being. But now I was doing something totally discretionary, and it was harder to justify. It was a conflict I'd never completely resolve.

The fact is, after having a career with so many responsibilities for so long, I needed something to help me fight off the thing I feared second-most in my life: boredom.

The thing I still feared most was poverty. That never leaves.

I feared poverty more than death.

I FLEW INTO CHICAGO THE next morning and made my way north to the American Club in Kohler, Wisconsin, a lake resort town about halfway between Milwaukee and Green Bay. Herb Kohler, who made his money in plumbing products, had hired Pete Dye to build two distinctly different public courses along the shore of Lake Michigan and the banks of the Sheboygan River. Both courses, Blackwolf Run and Whistling Straits, were on the *Golf Digest* Top 100 list.

I arrived at the River Course at Blackwolf Run an hour ahead of my tee time only to discover the single I'd been paired with had decided to tee off earlier in the morning when a slot had opened up. I accepted the assistant pro's offer to pair me with two Australian brothers who were teeing off an hour after my scheduled tee time. My caddie, Bill, a wisecracking carpenter who'd provide a running commentary throughout my round, said he didn't mind waiting. With two hours to kill, we headed to the practice range, where I worked on hitting fades and draws on command. I quickly felt in full control of my "A" game.

We met up with the two Aussies, Tom and Alastair, on the way to the first tee. Tom now lived in San Francisco, but Alastair had flown all the way from Down Under just to play golf in America with his brother. Oh, the miles we golfers travel just to strike a tiny white ball with a stick over the green contours of an open field.

Our round began on a par five with a fairway bordered by trees and fescue that separated it from the Sheboygan River flowing off to the left. The river, darting in and out over the entire course, is as much a feature to deal with as the bunkers and trees, by both its presence and its absence, with golfers challenged to play from the valley, the delta, and the land abutting both banks.

Bill's time with me on the practice range had given him a good sense of my ball flight and distances. After my drive landed in the deep rough, he stared it down. "You probably shouldn't hit more than an eight-iron," he advised.

I swung hard to cut through the rough and caught a flyer. My ball sailed 175 yards before plopping down onto the fairway. "Hit one less club on your approach shot than you normally would," Bill said, "so that you don't risk going over the green." I asked for a 6-iron, then made a relaxed swing as if I were still on the driving range. The ball landed on the right side of the green before chasing toward the back, stopping just eight feet from the pin. Bill handed me the putter, and I made the long walk in the short grass with high hopes of opening my round with a birdie. But my heart sank as I pushed my putt to the right.

As I waited on the fifth tee for one of my partners to hit, trying to forget the three double bogeys that had followed my first-hole par, I asked Bill if he went south to caddie during the off-season, which is a very long season up here.

He told me he'd bought a fixer-upper and spends the off-season working on his house. "I'm not married and I don't have kids," he said. "What I make caddying during the season is enough for me to live a decent life."

Funny and personable as he was, I sensed that Bill was a loner. Like me, he was at ease interacting with others but also comfortable with his own solitude. Maybe too comfortable. As much as I love people, I can go long stretches without interacting with anyone. I find comfort on lengthy road trips by myself, with nothing for company but my thoughts and the views on the other side of my windshield.

My mind drifted back to Jordan. Having grown up without a father, I had no personal experience with a father-child bond. My mother had nurtured me and cared for me, and I have no doubt that she gave me and my siblings the best she had. But I never had an opportunity to cultivate a relationship with my father—let alone a love for him.

I was sure that both Jordan and Alexandra would have special memories of moments we shared, such as the annual trips Alexandra and I took to purchase the doll of the year in whichever city had the newest American Girl doll store. She would also surely remember my cheering her on at her basketball games, dance recitals, and horseback-riding competitions. Jordan can't possibly forget the train rides across the country he and I took together each year. As a toddler, he loved Thomas the Tank Engine, but at three he told me he was ready for trains without eyes. He and I rode Amtrak from city to city, then explored the subway system in each one. He'll remember my applauding his performances in plays and piano and violin recitals and cheering him on at baseball games, soccer matches, and basketball games.

They would both remember the family vacations that took us all over the globe, such as the three-day safari at Singita's spectacular sanctuary near Kruger National Park in South Africa; they'd remember my teaching them to drive, helping them with school projects, drying their tears, and putting Band-Aids on their skinned knees and paper cuts—things big and small that I never experienced with a father. More important, neither of them will ever say the words "My father never said he loved me."

But will any of those memories make them feel as attached to me as I felt to my mother? Is that even possible? Will they see those experiences as being provided out of love and a commitment to their future or just the trappings of a privileged life?

Those thoughts evaporated as I slowly recovered my game with a hard-earned bogey on the fifth hole, its tee box carved between the trees high above a left-to-right fairway bending along the river. Alastair and Tom were also struggling, so I don't know why I had so much tension in my swing.

"I don't like this course. I've traveled too far to play this poorly," I told Bill and my playing partners, almost forgetting that Alastair had traveled all the way from Australia.

As we started the back nine, I asked Bill if he had siblings. He told me he had several. He didn't tell me exactly how many, nor did I ask him how big the house he had grown up in was, but I'm sure that the small, packed houses I shared with my siblings growing up influenced my own appreciation of solitude. Crowded, cramped, and dirt poor—a family environment like mine could either breed cooperation born of necessity and the fear of hunger or blow apart in the desperate heat of despair. For Art, Jen, Jerry, and me, it established the seeds of independence but also an interdependency that we would carry with us for the whole of our lives.

Art was born a month after my mother turned seventeen. Twelve years later, Frank moved in and Art moved out. For six years he was my mother's only child—her "little man," working in the cotton fields beside her. Frank was an abuser, and Art saw him as the monster he was. When we moved to the Sawmill Quarters, Art stayed with another family in a house across the street.

I idolized him. He was tall, handsome, and smart. He'd had to grow up fast, partly thanks to the years he had spent alone with our mother. He saw her refuse to be bitter and learned from her quiet strength and perseverance in the face of adversity. Then, after he left the house, he lived with people who didn't have it quite so bad; he experienced normality, at least what others considered normality, before the rest of us. Another brother might have left us behind. Not Art. He always looked out for us. He'd learned that strong sense of duty from our mother, too.

Art, as much as he could at thirteen, replaced our father. Though he didn't live with us, he was never far away. He was our protector. He'd stop Frank from hitting my mother and make sure he didn't come after us. Years later, after Frank disappeared, Art gave Momma money and brought groceries to the house. By then he had already dropped out of school and started working odd jobs. He gave me my first suit that didn't come from a landfill.

Jen was born six years after Art. For as long as I can remember, she's exuded strength and resilience. She was Momma when Momma wasn't around. She entertained us kids with stories she made up on the fly. Her bedtime tales frightened and enchanted us, and her imagination fueled ours. She taught us to create toys out of whatever we found: dolls from Coke bottles, bows and arrows from sticks and string and soda bottle caps. More than anyone else, she helped us build a childhood out of thin air.

In many ways, she had to grow up quicker than Art. She was a beautiful "light-skinned" young girl, and men always had their sights on her. She learned early how to elude and outsmart them. She was a survivor. After Frank abandoned us and the food ran out and the rent was due, it was Jen who took our mother to the welfare office, helping her fill out the forms so we could get a monthly check for rent; it was Jen who made sure we wouldn't go hungry by signing us up for handouts of hard cheese, powdered eggs, potted meat, and powdered mashed potatoes. She was fourteen, I was ten. She always had an outsized sense of responsibility.

Like Art, Jen was smart and beloved by all her teachers, yet she also dropped out of school when her first child was born. She married the father soon after, and they went on to have two more children together.

They were a family. They lived the type of life I dreamed of as a kid: they had a home, they took vacations, they had family portraits hanging on the wall—a common concept that nonetheless was foreign to me. There are no portraits of the family I grew up in.

For most of my childhood, Jerry and I were inseparable. He was my mother's third-born, two years older than me. If someone mentioned one of our names, the other's often followed. He was just ahead of me in school. He told me what to expect in first grade and taught me how to tie my shoes. Unlike Art and Jen, however, whose brilliance was clear to anyone who interacted with them, Jerry got caught in one of poverty's pitfalls. It took him slightly longer to read and sort through simple arithmetic, yet he always did. But that was enough to get him labeled a slow learner from the moment he walked into first grade, our introduction to formal education. There was no Head Start for kids like us; there wasn't even kindergarten. The label haunted him. He came to hate school, and in tenth grade, when he was cut from the basketball team, the one thing at school that held his interest, he dropped out.

From an early age, I lived my life with a certain intentionality. At ten, I hit a crossroads. Jerry started hanging out with boys who'd steal bicycles from yards in the nicer neighborhoods on the other side of Sixth Street in Texas City. Then they'd go to Big Chief's, the local supermarket, to swipe packs of Juicy Fruit and Wrigley's spearmint gum. It was mostly mischief born out of boredom; I don't even know that Jerry did those things, but he liked hanging around the kids who did.

I worried that if I went with them, even if I didn't do anything wrong, I'd get into trouble and that even the slightest misstep, such as getting caught stealing gum, would ruin my life. Poverty can be like quicksand. You get stuck. You get pulled down farther. Eventually you get to a point where nothing can pull you out. You suffocate. When you are born poor and Black in Jim Crow Texas, you have no margin for error. I understood that in my bones. Though Jerry was comfortable hanging out with boys who took so much risk with their futures, I wasn't.

It forced me to make one of the most consequential decisions of my young life: I chose to stop hanging out with my big brother. I lost my best friend and spent my time wandering the streets alone.

Our worlds became irreconcilable. It started with one degree of separation, then another. I went on to college; he worked odd jobs in construction. My first assignment with Exxon took me to Baytown, Texas. While employed there, I once saw Jerry working in the same plant as a laborer, cleaning up after the welders, machinists, pipe fitters, and other craftsmen. He worked as a contractor in several of the plants in the area, yet I was surprised to see him in the one where I was employed.

Jerry did all right for himself, and whenever we are together, we pick up right where we left off. But it isn't the same. There was never any conflict or animosity, but we lost the intimacy we'd once shared. The bonds of our childhood have been difficult to regrow.

———

AFTER RUMINATING ON MY RELATIONSHIPS with my siblings, I tried to refocus on my golf game. However, my dislike of the River Course at Blackwolf Run solidified when, on the thirteenth tee, Bill said, "You need to hit a two-hundred-ten-yard high draw over the trees to the left to avoid the risk of going in the river on the right."

Who puts a par three on a resort course that requires a shot very few recreational golfers can pull off? I watched as my ball clipped the top of the trees and dropped out of sight. Weirdly, I finally felt relaxed. My horrible play on that stupidly designed hole caused my anxiety to evaporate; there's something freeing about having nothing left to lose. Self-doubt accompanies me, and most golfers, on every round, especially when playing with strangers. It's just a matter of when it's going to show up. I usually start my rounds with a par or birdie; then one bad shot has me wondering "Do they think I'm that bad?" My body tenses, it becomes a self-fulfilling prophecy, and I play worse.

But with the tension gone, I striped a 3-wood over the lake to the fairway on the three-hundred-yard fourteenth hole, then put a good swing on my lob wedge to land my approach ten feet left of the flag. "You got this," Bill said. He pointed to the line, I pulled the putter back and pushed it toward the ball, like a perfect pendulum. My putt dropped into the cup for a life-affirming birdie.

By the time we finished the eighteenth hole, I was back to feeling stressed: exhaustion from the previous two days on the road was catching up to me. I had made no new contacts to help me moving forward. But Bill's lightheartedness and my reflections on my relationships with my kids and my siblings made for a remarkable day—despite my contempt for the course.

———

THE NEXT DAY I RETURNED to Kohler, with the mist off Lake Michigan blanketing Whistling Straits. The layout doesn't need any extra challenges. Carved along two miles of rugged, windswept shoreline, Whistling Straits is known as a course of a thousand bunkers. They're everywhere—so much so that Dustin Johnson, unsure if he was in one or not, lost the lead and his chance to capture the 2010 PGA Championship title after grounding his club. (He was in one of those bunkers after all.)

The bunkers didn't trip me up as much as my swing did. I started the round with a bogey, then a triple bogey. One of my playing partners put it into perspective: "On a beautiful course like this, who cares about the score?" We all agreed to enjoy our time along the shore of Lake Michigan and not get caught up in how poorly we played.

As the mist lifted on the back nine, my resolve to enjoy the day got stronger as my game continued to unravel. I learned that both my playing partners worked with a company that aligned with government agencies to improve education for students at every economic level. I wondered if their company could have helped Jerry escape his learning disabilities label. It was a label I'd barely escaped myself. My second-grade teacher had questioned my cognitive abilities after we moved from Huntsville to La Marque. It wasn't until fourth grade, when we moved to Texas City, that teachers realized that the quiet kid with the runny nose and tattered clothing had an uncommon aptitude for math. Even so, at fourteen, when we moved to the government projects in Hitchcock and I enrolled in a new school, I was automatically put back onto the slow learners' track. Fortunately, my English teacher at the time, Mrs. Porter, recognized that my understanding of grammar and verb conjugation was ahead of that of the rest of the class.

"When you registered for school, did your parents say you were behind in English?" she asked.

I didn't tell her I had just one parent; I just answered, "No."

She asked to see the rest of my schedule and said, "Come with me." She stopped class and marched me to the counselor's office, where she demanded that I be put onto the regular academic track. Hitchcock High School was not a haven of academic excellence at the time, but my life could have turned out much differently had it not been for the bold actions of Mrs. Porter. Things turned out differently for Jerry.

Those circumstances were brought home to me as we headed to the seventeenth tee on a splendid summer day along Lake Michigan, one of my playing partners looking around, taking it all in, and remarking, "Life just doesn't get any better than this."

———

IT WAS STILL DARK AS night on my final morning in Wisconsin. My car's wipers struggled to clear sheets of rain from the windshield as I made my way to Erin Hills. The three men I'd been paired with invited me to join them for breakfast as we waited for the storm that beat against the clubhouse roof to subside.

In the middle of breakfast, as if someone flipped a switch, the dark clouds turned white and the downpour stopped. I might have been better off getting rained out. The narrow fairways, brutal fescue, and scraggly bunkers at Erin Hills were a lot more menacing in person than they'd looked on TV during the U.S. Open weeks earlier.

My caddie spent the round trampling through the tall fescue that lined most of the fairway or over hill and dale searching for errant shots. To his credit, Mike found my ball every time, no matter how deeply it had burrowed into the grass, except for once. Even Mike couldn't find my ball in the high, wispy tall grass left of the fifteenth hole. It's a short, drivable par four, where Patrick Cantlay attempted to drive the green but instead hit into a small but harrowingly deep bunker that now, ignominiously, bears his name; he lost the hole and later his U.S. Amateur Championship match.

My fate: live to play another day.

The next morning, I awoke in Indiana for the final round of my trip to the upper Midwest. Doug Hicks, one of my wife's work colleagues, had gotten his brother to host me at Pete Dye's famed Crooked Stick Golf Club in suburban Indianapolis. The storm that had delayed my round at Erin Hills had swept over Crooked Stick the day before, taking out the iconic oak tree that marked the signature par-three sixth hole. My round was almost canceled, but the grounds crew worked all day to clear debris from the course and make it playable.

Crooked Stick is known for that tree and John Daly's debut in the 1991 PGA Championship, when he used his superior driving distance to dismantle the course hole by hole. One of his most impressive feats was reducing the fourteenth-hole approach shot to a short iron. Pete Dye, the master of using water and sand to make holes play longer than they should, had designed the hole as a hard dogleg left with a niggling creek running along the left side of the fairway. Clearing the creek on the most direct line to the green required a carry of more than three hundred yards. (That was before technology and better fitness made three-hundred-yard drives routine on the PGA tour.) The carry forced golfers to lay up to the right, then hit a long iron or fairway wood into the green. Daly said to hell with all of that. He hit his drives over the creek during each of the four rounds, leaving him a short iron to the green. Back then, no other golfer on tour could drive the ball far enough to match that.

We golfers spend most of our lives chasing that one pure shot we hit during some random round in our past. The pursuit for mine temporarily ended with a swing on the third hole at Crooked Stick. Mind and body became one. There was barely a sound. I felt no vibration in my hand. And the ball soared higher, longer, and straighter than any ball I'd ever struck before with a 5-iron. It floated atop a cushion of air before dropping into the bunker off the back side of the green. It was a beautiful stroke wasted, but I'd didn't care. In that fleeting moment, I'd found perfection in striking the ball and a reminder of one of the reasons I love this game so much.

My tee shot on the 180-yard par-three seventeenth hole flew over a narrow strip of land sandwiched between two ponds before landing twelve feet from the pin. Mike, who hosted me on the course along with Doug's brother, complimented me on the shot, then pointed behind us across a field at the stump from the lone tree where Pete Dye had found the crooked stick that inspired the name of the course. Atop the stump sat a golf club with a crooked shaft. Dye had imagined that golf originated with a guy finding a stray piece of wood and using it to hit a rock into a hole in the ground.

Maybe golf wasn't so different from playing baseball on a dirt road with a stick and a doll's head after all.

My final drive of the round sailed into Pete and Alice Dye's backyard. I thought about walking over and knocking on the door to see if I could retrieve it. Then I thought better of it. I took the drop and ended my trip with another double bogey.

CHAPTER FIVE

DALLAS NATIONAL

Our lives begin to end the day we become silent about things that matter.

—Dr. Martin Luther King, Jr.

"Why did you agree to have dinner with me?" I asked Darren Woods, the CEO of ExxonMobil, after we were seated inside an intimate Italian restaurant.

"Because," he answered evenly, as he always did, from across our small, square table, "you asked."

The night before my round at Dallas National Golf Club, I met Darren for dinner. I didn't plan on a drawn-out evening. I was staying with friends and wanted to be back at their house early enough to visit with them before turning in for the night, ahead of our golf round the next morning. And it's safe to say that Darren, recently elevated to ExxonMobil's top perch, had more pressing matters on his plate.

Yet three hours later, after an intense and at times heated conversation that centered primarily on diversity, we found ourselves closing the place down.

Years earlier, before he had moved to Dallas, Darren and I had often worked closely together. We had sat across from each other on the company jet during business flights across the country or to Canada and

South America. He'd also been management's liaison for the company's Black affinity group, one of several formalized associations of underrepresented employees, which I'd led for several years. Our relationship was both collegial and frank, with no question or answer off-limits. I trusted and respected him.

But what Darren knew about me—what everyone inside the company knew about me—is that I always spoke my mind. For many, that realization stemmed from a single question I asked at an employee meeting back in 2001.

It was February—Black History Month—and despite the snow falling outside, three or four hundred mostly Black employees were gathered inside a large auditorium on the corporation's Fairfax, Virginia, campus. A half-dozen or so presidents of companies under ExxonMobil's purview, along with their direct reports, were seated together in the front row. They were there to hear Eugene Renna, second in command of the newly merged Exxon and Mobil, talk about diversity.

At the end of his prepared remarks, Renna took questions from the audience. They were all softballs, including queries such as "What were the most significant moments in your career?" Despite his gruff, cigar-chomping demeanor, Renna often answered with a humor that filled the room with laughter.

Meanwhile, I'd sized up the long row of senior execs up front. All but one were men, and all of them were white. They listened attentively, and approvingly, as Renna spoke about diversity and how much ExxonMobil valued it. To me, they were the proverbial elephant in the room; as representatives of the company's leadership positions, there clearly wasn't any diversity at all. I decided somebody needed to point that out.

That somebody was me.

I had no intention of embarrassing Renna or putting him on the spot. He was too well respected for that. I also had an interest in his understanding the point I wanted to make. Still, I knew I could be putting my career on the line. I recalled a promise I'd made to my boss when I had been promoted to supervisor twelve years earlier: I'd told him I'd hold Exxon to its commitment to diversity. More than that, I told him that although it was the company's responsibility to implement the goals and objectives set in the C-suite, I wanted to be the company's conscience. I would hold myself responsible, too. All I asked for was his support.

I stood up. I tried to calm my nerves and lighten the moment by saying that I had enjoyed coming to work each day for the last seventeen years and that I hoped to enjoy the next seventeen as well. That was my heads-up to Renna and the rest of the room that something risky was on its way.

I dove in. I said that we do a lot of benchmarking at Exxon, comparing our outcomes with our competitors', as a way of gaining a sense of what's possible. I allowed that I'd like to do some benchmarking now. I then asked if all the presidents and their direct reports could please stand.

The packed auditorium turned deathly silent; I swear you could hear the snowflakes hitting the pavement outside. The prevailing thought bubble that seemed to appear over every Black head in the room: "Oh, no, he didn't." It was like the start of a car wreck unfolding in super-slow motion.

After what seemed like an interminable pause, the first executive stood up: the vice president of my division. I had worked on a diversity project with him years earlier, and afterward he had told me that he'd never forget how much I'd done, even though diversifying the company wasn't my job. I had never forgotten his words. Now, when he stood, the rest followed: several white men and one white woman.

I turned back to Renna. "As a young Black person in the company, if I were to benchmark this to see what was possible for me"—I gestured gently toward everyone standing—"what would I conclude from what I see?"

It was now quiet enough to hear the snow outside melting.

I don't know how many beats followed, but Renna eventually broke the silence. "We need," he began, "to have people in the company with enough courage to ask questions like that one."

My heart was pounding so hard that I didn't hear another word he said.

About a year later, at the company Christmas party, Renna spotted me and Erika and came right over.

"Oh no," I joked before shaking his hand. "You remember me."

"How could I forget?" he answered in his signature growl. He then added, "If anybody gives you a hard time about that day, lemme know."

A few years later, as diversity came into even greater focus, I became one of ExxonMobil's public faces. I appeared in TV commercials and newspaper ads and on the front of brochures handed out to shareholders at one of our annual meetings.

Despite the progress made during my career—some of it due to my efforts and trailblazers like Jesse Tyson and John Holmes—there was still a ways to go. I saw the dinner as a last-ditch effort to salvage what I considered my failure to inspire more progress on diversity within the company. I told Darren that right away.

He didn't understand why I took any perceived failure personally, that it was hardly my responsibility. I explained that although the company hadn't given me that responsibility, my life had. No matter the setting, I was always that kid running around the Sawmill Quarters in raggedy overalls. That remained true even as I sat across a table from the leader of one of the most powerful corporations in the world.

The conversation moved from my merely wanting to share what I thought the issues were to telling Darren what I thought he should do to improve the company he was now leading. That was the rub. That's almost always the rub when it comes to race in America. We both saw and understood the challenges. But we came to different conclusions on how to address them.

After Renna's talk in Virginia, two of the presidents I'd pointed out in the front row approached me. They told me that too little time had passed since we had started hiring African Americans for professional positions in the early 1980s for them to have risen through an organization as byzantine as Exxon. My reply: if you're depending on time to take care of it, it's not going to happen. As engineers, we know the equation: output is the result of effort over time. There's more than one variable. Time alone does not lead to progress. The work that's done over time—the *effort*—is what gets results. So when those presidents said to me, "Give us time," I told them that I thought enough time had passed. What wasn't happening was the right kind of effort.

I told Darren I thought that the company needed to be more aggressive in advancing individuals and less bound to its strict protocols. As executives, we spent a lot of time developing people for leadership positions, putting together extensive plans for their career paths. My solution: take the underrepresented employees on those lists and move them up as soon as possible. They've already been identified as being capable and competent, and as they proved themselves in positions of increasing accountability, more will follow. I told Darren what I'd told two of those presidents in Virginia: progress isn't made just by the passage of time; it comes from the efforts of great people over time. And I certainly thought Darren was that.

I then told him one of my regrets: that more than twenty years after the Black affinity group was founded, it still existed. Darren looked surprised and asked me why; after all, the company often bragged about having such groups, holding them up as examples of ExxonMobil's responding to employees' needs and concerns. I said the fact that such groups were still needed showed that substantive changes had yet to be made. Employees in those groups still felt that they were "other."

As always, Darren listened intently and took my words to heart. But he disagreed. He's a systems guy. The system worked for him and largely works for ExxonMobil. Like many others at the company, I had known Darren would rise to the very top years before it happened. He was smart and focused, with a vision for where he wanted to take the business and the ability to articulate it. He was both principled and performance driven. In a company crawling with high achievers, he stood out. He also looked the part: tall, square-jawed, and, like every CEO before him, white.

Darren argued that the corporation's role is to put the right systems into place, oversee them, then hold the leaders accountable to make sure that in time they get results. He wanted me to suggest strategies that could work within the system to make it better. I was telling him that the system wasn't working at every level—that it worked for some people but not for all.

Darren challenged me on every point, just as he had done when I'd come to him with a proposal to merge all the logistics operations across the company into one organization. He wasn't dismissing me. He was asking me to convince him. At times, our discussion turned full-throated. We broke eye contact only when one of us plucked something off a plate. When I'm in a room, I usually notice everything. But I couldn't tell you anything else about that restaurant other than what went on at our table. It was as though we were the only people there.

"You know me and my record, Jimmie," he finally said, looking straight at me. "When I say something is going to be achieved, it's going to be achieved. Watch me."

And true to Darren's word, progress has been made. In the years since I left ExxonMobil, African Americans have been promoted higher than ever before. The leadership row I'd pointed out almost two decades earlier was still nearly all white and male. But there were more women and African Americans reporting directly to the presidents in those seats.

Three hours in, the salesman in me—the teenage kid who'd knocked on a thousand doors to peddle more encyclopedias in one summer than anyone else—knew what every salesman knows at some point: I wasn't going to close. Darren and I chatted for another thirty minutes about topics completely unrelated to race, then shook hands, wished each other well, and headed out.

His driver, expecting Darren much earlier, had waited out front the entire time. Darren slipped into the back of the black sedan and was whisked off.

I stood there for a moment to contemplate the night, alone except for the ever-present company of my six-year-old self.

I ARRIVED AT DALLAS NATIONAL early the next morning, hoping to beat the heat. The course was pristine. It reflected little of the rugged north Texas landscape surrounding it, its Tom Fazio design more rolling and lush than flat and stunted. The zoysia grass fairways were as barbered and well tended as any I'd seen, as if they'd been rolled out by the sheet and rated by the thread count. Even in the wilting dog days of July, each spongy blade acted like its own fairway microtee, propping up every shot.

I was hosted by a longtime member at the request of a friend: a local physician who is part of a group of thirty-two successful African American professionals I play with at Kiawah every year in what we call the Black Jacket Tournament—an affectionate if pointed send-up of Augusta's green jacket. The tournament is an excuse for us to gather and talk about careers, politics, family, and the state of African Americans in business and government. It's played over three days using a scoring system that awards points for each hole rather than counting the number of strokes during each round, theoretically making it more equitable for higher handicappers.

To the winner goes the coveted Black Jacket. To the loser: an acrylic case containing a pair of pink stiletto pumps that must be displayed prominently in his home or office for the next calendar year. As you might imagine, everyone focuses more on avoiding the pink pumps than on winning the Black Jacket.

The men I played with at Dallas National were curious about my dinner the night before. We discussed our similar experiences coming up through the professional ranks, the slights and oversights and even the misreads. We were trying to fit into a world that wasn't originally designed with us in mind. The biggest challenge was often the question prompted by our mere presence: Are these guys competent?

They weren't surprised by the different conclusions that Darren and I had reached about how progress could be accelerated. Our refrain was by now an overworked jingle: we've come a long way, but still have a long way to go.

After we finished our round and promised to see one another again next fall at the Black Jacket Tournament, I jumped into my rental and headed toward Tulsa, where the next morning I'd play Southern Hills Country Club. The skyscrapers of Dallas receded in my rearview mirror. I soon crossed the Red River into Oklahoma, where I whizzed past miles of the same unbroken string of tiny but not teeny, run-down but not ramshackle wood-framed houses I'd seen on my earlier trip through Oklahoma.

I still found it fascinating that shacks just slightly above my shack in the Sawmill Quarters—remote but not godforsaken—were still inhabited.

"WHAT ONE PIECE OF ADVICE would you give me on playing this course?" I asked the security guard at the gates of the Southern Hills Country Club.

His response was short and to the point: "Stay out of the bunkers. They're deep."

I caught glimpses of the gigantic craters as I drove beneath the overhanging oak and maple trees, climbing toward the clubhouse. Eleven courses into my quest, the entryways to America's most coveted country clubs still inspired awe.

J.J., the Flint Hills president, had followed up on his promise to arrange for me to play the course. J.J. was good friends with Cary Cozby, better known as Coz, the head PGA professional at Southern Hills. J.J. put that friendship to the test by asking him to arrange for a stranger to play the expansive Perry Maxwell design that had hosted multiple PGA Championships and U.S. Opens.

Coz got two members, John and Doug, the president and chief lending officer of a string of local banks, to host me. Both took the morning off to guide me around the cavernous bunkers and creeks that bisect and line the fairways and across the contours of greens with breaks so subtle they're practically imperceptible to the unaided eye.

In the spirit of Charles Dickens, my round was the best of nines and the worst of nines. I started the front nine with two humiliating double bogeys, an embarrassing display of missed fairways, shanks, and topped shots. But John and Doug were much too polite to give any hint that they might be thinking "We took the day off for *this*?" Doug said the opening two holes at Southern Hills were two of the toughest in golf and that the course would get easier. I could only hope.

As a child, I was ashamed of my family's poverty, uncomfortable wearing pinstripe overalls with nothing on underneath, and humiliated by the biscuits and syrup in my lunch bag when the other kids had sandwiches. In comparison, you wouldn't think playing golf poorly with others should stress me out. But everything is relative; I was embarrassed nonetheless. My first par didn't come until the sixth hole. My front-nine score—an eleven-over-par 47.

Doug and John seemed unbothered by my poor start, despite the fact they both shot in the low forties. I was reminded of a truism my friend Dennis had taught me when I began playing: other golfers don't care about your score as long as you play fast.

Dennis was an up-through-the-ranks engineer at the Beaumont refinery when I was a manager there. We met on the eighth hole of the Henry Homberg Golf Course at Tyrrell Park, and our relationship got off to a tempestuous start. Dennis, fiftyish at the time, was a self-avowed redneck with a bristly mustache playing with a coworker also named Dennis. I was playing with Kevin Hobbs, one of my opponents in the Bout in the Bluegrass at Valhalla.

Kevin and I were playing so closely behind the two Dennises that day that they called us up to join them. Once we got to the tee box, I unintentionally stood too close to Dennis as he prepared to hit his drive. "Could you please move?" he shouted at me. "You're in my line of sight."

It was only my third or fourth round of golf, so I wasn't yet familiar with all the nuances of golf etiquette.

Dennis warmed up to me after I told him I was just learning to play. Over the next few months, we ran into each other on the course several more times. Our rounds turned into golf lessons, with him teaching me much about the game. Over the years, our relationship transformed into an unlikely friendship between two guys on opposite ends of the organization chart at ExxonMobil. I'm pretty sure I was Dennis's first and only Black friend. Years after I'd moved on from Beaumont, he and his wife stayed with Erika and me at our home in Charlottesville while they were traveling through Virginia touring Civil War sites. Had we not been brought together through golf, our friendship probably wouldn't exist. And I've never forgotten his admonishments not to linger over shots or dally between them—to at least play fast when you're not playing well.

I rediscovered how to swing the club on the back nine at Southern Hills. Solid ball contact seemed to appear from nowhere. Golf is a mental game, and I often think its biggest challenge is dealing with the course between your ears. If you can hit a drive 250 yards straight down the fairway once or twice, why can't you do it every time? You're clearly physically capable of doing it. The rest is all in your head. I wasn't doing anything different on the back nine than I had on the front, but now I parred the tenth hole with a beautiful approach shot that soared over a tree, carried a giant trap guarding the front of the green, and stopped dead twenty-five feet from the cup.

The diminutive par-three eleventh green, with sand looming menacingly along almost every inch of its perimeter, offered no forgiveness for errant shots. My 155-yard tee shot spun to a stop just three feet right of the cup—leading to the first of my two birdies on the back nine. As embarrassed as I was about my poor play, I didn't give up on my game. I finished the back nine with a very respectable 39. John and Doug had gotten a glimpse of what it meant to never give up and seemed genuinely impressed with my turnaround. Golf is only a game, but they had no idea how emblematic of my life's journey those eighteen holes of shame, embarrassment, challenges—then triumph—had been.

In the two weeks since I'd dropped Jordan off at Duke, I'd traveled to Kohler, Erin Hills, Indianapolis, Atlanta, Houston, Dallas, and finally Tulsa—reconnecting with old friends and making new ones. Eleven courses in, I'd played golf between the tall pines of Augusta; in the shadows of the former Confederacy; within sight of the Tulsa and Dallas skylines; near the wheat fields of Kansas, the horse farms of Kentucky, and the dairy farms of Wisconsin—all of it a sampling of America's rich and diverse tapestry.

CHAPTER SIX

MERION

This is what kindness does. . . . Each little thing we do goes out,
like a ripple into the world.

—Jacqueline Woodson

"Why would you want to do such a stupid thing?"
That was a first.

I had just told the affable guy chipping balls next to me in the short-game practice area at the Merion Golf Club just outside Philadelphia about my yearlong quest to play America's hundred greatest courses. His blunt response was not unreasonable. We were engaged in what had become a familiar introductory dance for me. The fact that he dismissed what I was pursuing out of hand didn't faze me a bit.

I've cold-called strangers since I was a kid. I sold mail-order flower seeds when I was a young boy. A week after graduating from high school, I caravanned to Dallas with a crew of other teens to sell magazines. On the five-hour drive, our adult handler taught us to pitch potential customers by telling them that we were earning points toward a college scholarship. As I listened, it became clear to me that the scheme was not much better than indentured servitude, akin to the way Boettcher's Mill had operated during my youth. I did the math. Most of the money I earned would be taken to cover hotel and meal expenses. And then there was the line about the college scholarship. I never figured that one out. To me it was just a lie. So to prove a point, I sold a bunch of cold-call subscriptions the day after we arrived solely by appealing to people's interests. One woman was gardening in her yard when I walked up. She invited me in for lemonade. As we sat on her sofa, I showed her how *Better Homes and Gardens* could give her gardening and decorating ideas. She said, "Sign me up." The next day I bought a ticket for a Greyhound bus back home to Houston.

A year later, when I was nineteen, I peddled *Collier's Encyclopedia* sets throughout Houston to earn money for college. I set out each evening, as instructed, right before dark. That was when families were either starting or finishing dinner. First I'd scope out neighborhoods for telltale signs of young children: swing sets, a Big Wheel parked under a porch, stuffed animals scattered around a yard. We canvassed apartment complexes filled with young professionals—it was a few years before they'd be dubbed "yuppies"—and neighborhoods lined with starter homes.

I wasn't merely selling those people twenty-six-volume encyclopedia sets; I was selling them their children's futures. Once I got in the door, I'd make my hour-long pitch centered on the idea of educating those children to give them a leg up on—or preventing them from falling behind—everybody else's kids. With infants crying, TV sets blaring, and laundry scattered around their living rooms, that was what spurred parents to write me a $700 check on the spot.

Of course, plenty of families turned me away. It taught me a lesson that I've used in life, in work, and on my quest: "no" is not terminal. I'm not afraid of it. There's always another customer, another opportunity, right around the corner. I applied the same skill set to my golf journey. Whenever I showed up at a course, I'd "read the room" the same way I'd read a neighborhood, scanning the crowd for people wearing shirts and sweaters emblazoned with a logo of one of the top golf clubs. Then I'd chat them up, hoping that they were a member. It was the same kind of dance I'd used to sell encyclopedias. I wasn't selling golf; I was selling them my dream.

I didn't want to tell the golfer practicing next to me at Merion that my quest was about more than golf; that it was about whether America was still a land where people would help others achieve their dreams. If I revealed the full purpose of my quest, it might influence whether he'd offer to help me. I hadn't relied on emotional manipulation when selling magazines, and I certainly wasn't going to during my quest.

So instead I told him, "I'm doing it because of the challenge."

"You should have talked to me first," he shot back. "I would have told you to only play the top fifty because the bottom fifty aren't worth all that travel. I've played several of them. But since you're doing such a stupid thing already, I might as well help."

And there it was, that American spirit. John Sokol, the chairman and CEO of one of the nation's leading specialty insurance companies, had been drawn into my dream. He lived in Columbus, Ohio, and was a member of all four Top 100 clubs there: Muirfield Village Golf Club, Scioto Country Club, the Golf Club, and the Double Eagle Club. He was obviously a generous guy; he'd brought three friends to Merion using a round he'd purchased at a charity auction. He took my email address and said he would get back to me in September with dates to come to Columbus to play all four courses. I'd closed another sale.

My three-month stint selling encyclopedias spanned June through August in 1978. The very first door I knocked on was unlike any I would encounter during the rest of that long, hot summer. When the door of the ground-level apartment swung open, I was eye to eye with a tall, white, broad-shouldered man in a white dress shirt with the sleeves rolled up. He acted fidgety, with one hand wrapped around the doorknob and the other behind his back. I didn't suspect anything until I saw a reflection in a mirror on the wall behind him: the hand he'd kept hidden was gripping a pistol.

I tried to remain calm. I then saw another figure reflected in the corner of the same mirror, a woman curled up in the fetal position on the couch, looking afraid for her life. I ditched my opening spiel. The man made it clear that he wasn't interested in whatever I was peddling, and instead of countering with one of my rehearsed comebacks, I calmly nodded in agreement. The moment he shut the door, I fled. I spotted a pay phone in a convenience store parking lot across the street and called the police. I told the dispatcher I thought a woman's life could be in jeopardy.

I didn't go back to see what happened, but the dispatcher told me the police were on the way. I headed to another apartment complex and spent the rest of the night banging on more doors.

The summer turned out to be ridiculously profitable: I made $15,000 in those three months (about $60,000 in today's dollars), more than any other *Collier's Encyclopedia* salesman in the country. I earned more in that brief time than my mother had made in any two years combined. I rented my own apartment, just north of downtown. I bought my first car, a brand-new burgundy Monte Carlo, with $500 down. I was making big bucks. No one in my office could believe I had come back after my harrowing first night, and they were even more surprised when I quit at the end of the summer to start school at the University of Houston.

My eye was on a bigger prize than a payday.

I FELT NERVOUS ON THE first tee at Merion. As I stood over my ball thinking about how desperately I wanted to hit a good drive, an eerie silence fell over the group of men sitting around the table on the terrace beside the tee box. Merion is a serious place for serious golfers. The membership take their traditions, and the rules and customs of the game, deadly seriously—I say that with respect. Members watching other golfers tee off from the terrace is one such long-standing tradition. Allegedly there was once a member who would look on waiting for someone to hit a mulligan, so that he could scold him.

As I addressed the ball, the sound of glasses clinking behind me stopped; silverware ceased scraping against plates; conversations paused midsentence. It felt as though the world had stopped to allow me my moment.

Talk about pressure!

My ball took flight, zoomed along the right edge of the fairway, then headed toward the bunker inside its left-to-right bend toward the green. It dropped right in. The hole was 340 yards, and I was left with only 95 yards to a back-right pin topped with one of the club's signature red wicker baskets—a more benign Merion tradition. I looked at the bunker lying in wait a few paces to the right of the pin and decided to play it safe, hitting my lob wedge to the front of the green. It also didn't hurt that the loft of my lob wedge would more easily clear the steep face of the bunker I was in. I focused on hitting the ball first rather than the sand. Unfortunately, I hit too high on the ball; it hit the lip of the bunker and bounced back into the sand.

I gathered myself, thinking back to all those sand shots I'd hit in the practice area while waiting for Malcolmn, my host, to arrive. I asked my caddie, a high school kid from the neighborhood, for my sand wedge. No more playing it safe. I dug my shoes into the sand and took dead aim for that red wicker basket on the back-right portion of the green. Propelled by the most perfect of bunker shots, the ball flew high, dropped seven feet to the right of the flag, and stopped dead. I rolled the putt in to save par.

A drive that flew over the fence along Ardmore Avenue on the par-five second hole, followed by a tee shot that kicked into the deep bunker off the right side of the green on the par-three third, took the wind out of my sails. I've heard it said that the first six holes at Merion are a drama, the middle six are a comedy, and the final six are a tragedy. Somehow I experienced that entire gamut on the first three.

Over the next five holes, after I'd finally calmed my swing, I tried to get Malcolmn to talk about his membership at Merion. I asked if he'd been invited to join the club during the period when golf's leading governing bodies were pressuring clubs that hosted tournaments to diversify their membership. It wasn't something he cared to reflect on. Not now. He preferred to talk more about how much he appreciated the camaraderie between the members and the respect for traditions at the club.

Malcolmn, a paragon of the financial industry and an avid golfer, had been a trailblazer. He has stood at the crossroads of two of America's last bastions of white male dominance: golf and Wall Street. Few top clubs admitted Black members until the PGA, which was itself under pressure to diversify, forced them to. There were also very few Blacks on Wall Street in the early seventies when Malcolmn went to work in fixed-income sales at Goldman Sachs as a freshly minted MBA from the Wharton School at the University of Pennsylvania.

My industry, oil and gas, also employed very few Blacks when I started in the mideighties. I didn't take up golf until mid-2004. A short time later, I joined my first country club, the Club at Glenmore, in Keswick, Virginia, just outside Charlottesville. We lived in a gated golf club community. There wasn't much of an application process; if you owned a home you were invited to join the country club. It was the twenty-first century, but I still got the sense that some of the golfers I played with were merely tolerating me.

I played regularly with a great group of guys that included one of three other Black members at the club. But eventually I joined another group that went out very early on Saturday mornings. I soon discovered that some of its members were outright racist. They oozed an air of superiority out of every pore, not just as golfers (I was a beginner) but also as people. I felt that they resented every moment I was out with them—as though I were a stain. They made offhand comments stereotyping Blacks as lazy, criminal, and not very bright. I think they did it to run me out of the group. Out of defiance, I exercised my power to be included. I kept showing up. The power was mine, not theirs.

I began the back nine at Merion with a renewed sense of hope. My drive slipped through the daunting, narrow alley of trees off the front of the tenth tee box and landed in the fairway. Then it trickled into the rough where the fairway makes a hard left turn toward the green. After a shanked approach shot and a two-putt bogey—drama *and* tragedy—we walked toward the eleventh tee, where Malcolmn pointed to a rock with a plaque commemorating Bobby Jones's completion of the Grand Slam on that hole in 1930. Coming into Merion, Jones had won the U.S. Open, the British Open, and the British Amateur Championship. He completed the Grand Slam by defeating Gene Homans 8 and 7 for a victory in the U.S. Amateur Championship.

Malcolmn noted that every year on September 30, after a club tournament, members don tuxedos and stroll to the rock across Ardmore Avenue to toast Bobby Jones and his achievement. It's yet another of Merion's valued traditions.

My walk in the footprints of legends neared its end as we approached the eighteenth tee. My young caddie pointed to an American flag on a pole in the distance. "That's your target," he said. My ball flew past the trees on the left and over a ravine before taking a short hop and coming to rest beside a plaque that marked the spot where Ben Hogan had hit his legendary 1-iron to within forty feet of the pin during the final round of the 1950 U.S. Open. He two-putted to make par and tie Lloyd Mangrum and George Fazio for the lead. He went on to defeat them the next day in an eighteen-hole playoff to capture the title.

His improbable win came sixteen months after a gruesome car crash that, by all accounts, should have taken his life, marking the culmination of one of the greatest sports comebacks in history. That 1-iron shot from a little over 210 yards out to the eighteenth green, with a mesmerized gallery looking on, was memorialized in a photograph by Hy Peskin. I'd seen the photo framed in the clubhouse at several of the top courses I'd already played. What is it about that shot that so completely captures our imagination? Is it the triumph of a warrior over adversity, or that thing that brings us back to the game again and again—the pursuit of the perfect shot, the one that comes off just as we envision it?

As I looked down the fairway toward the final red wicker basket, I asked my caddie to capture the moment with my camera. There was no gallery or championship on the line, except for the one I imagined. I took my 3-hybrid back with a full turn, twisted my hips, then let the club drop down as if it were swinging itself, sending the ball soaring toward the pin. It faded and dropped into the rough five yards short of the bunker off the front-right portion of the green. My pitch over the sand rolled to six feet below the pin. I hovered over the ball, a white speck on a large green, and imagined that, like Hogan, I was putting to tie for the lead, rather than the 90 for the day that a par would bring. A firm stroke sent the ball rolling toward the cup. It fell in, and in my mind I heard the crowd go wild. I removed my hat and waved.

Hogan had faced great challenges, but he had never quit. I'm no Ben Hogan, but on a warm summer afternoon at the Merion Golf Club in Ardmore, Pennsylvania, where the rough is thick, the greens fast, and the breaks subtle, his journey and mine intersected—if only in my dreams.

———

EARLY THE NEXT MORNING, I caught a glimpse of the sun-splashed Manhattan skyline as I approached the Baltusrol Golf Club in northern New Jersey. For once, word of my quest had preceded me: the spirited attendants at the bag drop next to the club's massive brown-and-cream Tudor clubhouse told me they'd heard about it. An Atlanta golfing buddy of mine had asked his Baltusrol-member friend to arrange for me to play the first simultaneously constructed dual courses in the country, both of which were in the *Golf Digest* Top 100.

At the onset of the Roaring Twenties, a young, not-yet-legendary course designer named A. W. Tillinghast did something no one had done before: he tore up an existing course—already considered among the nation's finest—and rebuilt it while carving out a neighboring eighteen-hole layout at the same time. The resulting venue has since hosted seven men's and two women's U.S. Opens, two PGA Championships, and a half-dozen men's and women's U.S. Amateur Championships.

My 7:10 tee time didn't allow me to do much more than race down the narrow hallway in the clubhouse to the locker room, change into my golf shoes, and rush back outside. I was in the first group to go out that morning, and my caddie and playing partner, an intern from the Mississippi State University PGA Golf Management Program, were already waiting for me.

The caddie, Brian, a young Latino with the height of a jockey and the calves of a rugby player, told me it was his job to keep me and Beau moving so we didn't hold up any members playing behind us. Though a member had arranged for my round, I wasn't playing with one, and the last thing any caddie wants to do is to annoy members on the course.

At the start of our round on the Lower Course, Brian made it clear that I needed to trust his guidance. "I'm going to manage your game so you can get around the course in as few strokes as possible," he said. I appreciated that. The game is easier when you play from the fairway, of course, but there are times when you can play from the rough and still make pars and birdies. But why make the game harder than it already is? Why not just let my caddie manage my game?

On each hole, Brian handed me the club he thought I should hit and told me the line to hit it on. He advised me when to play conservatively, as on the tight 435-yard third hole, when he made sure I took an easy swing and didn't try to muscle it down the fairway—a sure way to play my way outside it. He smiled slyly when my smooth swing delivered a ball that flew past the drive hit by the young stud playing with me, landing in the center of the fairway.

Other times, Brian encouraged me to play more aggressively, as when I asked if I should lay up on the fifth hole after my drive sailed into a bunker to the left of the fairway. I wanted to avoid another huge sand trap off the front of the green. "No," he told me, "you got this shot. Just keep your head down."

Brian clearly understood that golf is mostly about believing—the same kind of belief that had fueled my pursuit of one dream after another. I caught the ball cleanly. It carried the bunker and dropped on the green before rolling to ten feet below the flag.

I quickly learned to believe in Brian. I had to. Of the hundred courses on my list, I'd played only three before I started my quest. Baltusrol wasn't one of them. And I didn't research the courses before stepping onto them, wanting instead to experience them as they unreeled before me, like a movie I was watching for the first time. In those circumstances, having a caddie like Brian made a huge difference.

Then Brian noticed the torn, dingy golf glove on my left hand. "You playing all one hundred courses with the same glove?" he asked.

He'd called out the lingering cheapskate in me. Though I was willing to spend whatever it took on things that mattered to me, I was pretty frugal about the things that didn't. Yet when those things were pointed out to me, I'd be instantly embarrassed—not by my cheapness but by the fact that somebody had noticed. It's an involuntary response that goes way back. In the eighth grade, my reading teacher often brought me her son's hand-me-downs. I was grateful, but I was embarrassed by the fact she recognized that I needed them. I knew my clothes were dirty and tattered and torn, but knowing that others could tell only made the embarrassment cut deeper.

Even decades later, as a retired executive spending the day on one of America's most opulent golf courses, my immediate response to a friendly rib about my torn glove was to reach sheepishly into my golf bag and pull out a new one.

———

As we strode down the fairways of this legendary course, I asked Brian, whose family had come to New York from Puerto Rico, how long he'd been caddying. He told me that over the past fifteen years, he'd earned enough from carrying bags to start a couple of businesses, including janitorial and delivery services. His next words echoed my own boy-hood dreams: "I want to make a better life for my kids."

I smiled and grabbed a cold, crisp apple from a barrel Brian pointed to just past the seventh hole. But just as I bit into it, the best caddie I'd had so far looked over his shoulder and saw that the members who had teed off just after us earlier in the morning were only a hole and a half behind. He told Beau and me to pick up the pace—all business. I made a point of speeding up. The members tailing us never got any closer.

On the way to the final tee, both Beau and Brian pointed to a plaque commemorating Jack Nicklaus's two U.S. Open wins at Baltusrol. By that point on my journey, plaques marking golfing feats had become as ubiquitous as the Civil War markers that dot the South. Nicklaus's first win there had come in 1967, the second in 1980. I told them how the plaque on the final hole at Valhalla had inspired me to hit a spectacular drive from the rough to set up a reasonable birdie attempt. (As a different kind of "inspiration to all golfers," there's a plaque on the eighteenth tee at Rancho Park Golf Course in Los Angeles that marks the hole where Arnold Palmer shot a 12 at the 1961 Los Angeles Open; later asked how he could have possibly shot a 12, Palmer cracked, "I missed a short putt for an eleven.")

As we walked side by side toward the bridge over the creek cutting across the eighteenth fairway, Brian pointed to another Nicklaus plaque. That one marked the spot where Jack, one stroke ahead of Palmer and with an opportunity to tie Ben Hogan's U.S. Open scoring record, hit his own famous 1-iron shot from 238 yards out to within twenty feet from the pin. He drained the putt to win the tournament and tie Hogan's record.

I finished our morning round with an 88. This time, after my final stroke, I didn't remove my hat and wave to an imaginary crowd.

My playing partner had shot under par.

AFTER PLAYING THIRTY-SIX HOLES ON two championship courses, finishing one stroke better on the Upper Course, I left New Jersey exhausted. Three hours later, I watched the sun drop over the Alleghenies. With more than two hours of driving left—I was headed to Ligonier, Pennsylvania, where I'd play Laurel Valley Golf Club the next day—I exited the freeway at the first McDonald's sign I saw after crossing the Susquehanna River on I-76 and grabbed a burger, fries, and a Coke for my first meal of the long day. I hadn't made any sleeping arrangements, so while inhaling my tray of food I googled hotels near Ligonier. All I found was a Ramada Inn.

Even in the dark, it was clear that the aged, three-story Ramada had seen better days. The red-carpeted room was spacious and clean enough, but the bedsheets looked so old that I couldn't tell whether they'd been washed. I'm sensitive—maybe hypersensitive—to that kind of thing. When I was twelve, my family lived on the first floor of a dilapidated duplex in La Marque. It was so roach and rat infested that my siblings and I slept with our heads under the covers to shield us from the flying roaches that emerged the instant the lights went out, all the while trying to keep our feet covered to avoid nibbles on our toes by the rats. Throw in the bugs swimming around in our sink and bathtub, and we had an army, air force, and navy of pests and rodents. On that muggy summer night in Pennsylvania, I was more concerned about bedbugs than flying roaches. I slept fully clothed on top of the covers rather than under them.

I awoke early the next morning to overcast skies. A short drive through the bucolic countryside brought me to the entrance of the Laurel Valley Golf Club at the base of the Chestnut and Laurel Ridge Mountains—Arnie's Place. Palmer had learned the game growing up in Latrobe, a dozen miles away, but he had founded Laurel Valley with a group of investors in 1959, just as his career was taking off. It became his home course.

It was one of the lower ranked of the Top 100 clubs, so my head pro at Cherokee was able to arrange a tee time for me with one of the assistants at Laurel Valley. Yet my admiration for Palmer far outweighed the course's ranking. I drove past the tall cedar trees along Palmer Drive and made my way to the clubhouse, where I was told that there was a club tournament in the afternoon. To accommodate it, there would be a shotgun start that morning—everyone would tee off at the same time at a different hole to make sure that more golfers would get through their rounds before the tournament started.

Accompanied only by my caddie, Adam, who'd worked at the course for more than a decade, I started on the thirteenth hole. For a linear engineer like me, not starting on the first hole on the course was a mental challenge. I've never been able to enjoy a round as much when starting on any hole other than the first. Golf courses are designed with an eye toward the progression from hole one to hole eighteen. There's a flow.

But it was what it was. As an unaccompanied guest, I couldn't complain.

It was another early start for me, and each step I took left a footprint in the dew blanketing the tee box. I wondered how many footprints Arnold Palmer had made there in the early-morning dew as he stepped onto the tee box to hone his patented lash of a swing with its exaggerated high finish.

I put a tee into the ground in between the blue markers, which played 6,800 yards, and off we went. The gray sky—some might say the classic Pennsylvania summer sky—seemed to deepen the green of the fairways, the rough, and the trees they ran between. On our walk to the sixth hole of the round—the course's eighteenth hole—Adam told me that Ben Hogan had taken the same path in 1965 on the way to his last hole of his final PGA Championship. He said that Laurel Valley had gotten the tournament only after Palmer had convinced the skeptical club leadership to step in when the original site backed out. Palmer played in the tournament but wasn't competitive. Hogan wasn't, either, finishing nine strokes behind the winner, Dave Marr. I was impressed by Adam's knowledge, and humbled by the privilege of playing Merion, Baltusrol, and Laurel Valley, all so rich in golf history, over three successive days.

The lush course, with its soft fairways and receptive greens, seemed to play much easier than its rating. I was cruising with no other golfers in sight; I guess everyone else was playing in the tournament that afternoon.

Golf can be counterintuitive. With the hole cut only a few paces from the bunker off the right edge of the green, I was undeterred. I aimed dead for the flag and missed right. The ball dropped into the deep bunker, leaving me short-sided. Despite the short distance between my ball and the cup, I had to swing hard, hit the sand between the ball, and accelerate through the shot. Unlike my fairway bunker shot on the first hole at Merion, where I'd needed to hit the ball first, then barely skim the sand, this time the clubface would never touch the ball. The ball would ride out of the bunker on a bed of sand. That would make it spin and stop suddenly. I knew I'd executed perfectly when I heard Adam yell, "Go in!" I raised my head and saw the ball sitting on the lip of the cup. I stood in the bunker watching for a long ten seconds, hoping that gravity would pull it in. The ball stayed frozen. Adam picked it up and I recorded my par.

Hubris and its cousin stubbornness reared their heads on the course's sixth hole—my twelfth. After two straight pars, I let my ambition exceed my skill. In the hope of setting myself up to go for the green in two, I swung big—Arnie big. The ball sliced even bigger and landed behind several trees. With undiminished confidence, I tried to hit over them rather than taking my medicine and pitching under the branches and back into the fairway. The double bogey and shame that followed were a stark reminder that big ambitions can be easily destroyed by lack of humility.

As my round neared its end, the trees along the eleventh fairway provided the perfect frame for the distant mountains. I told Adam I wouldn't let big ambitions cause me to play the final par five as stupidly as I had played the two preceding ones. After a drive into the first cut, Adam said, "Let's get this right." He handed me my 9-iron to lay up about 130 yards from the pin. The ball flew 10 yards farther than we expected, but I choked down about an inch on my pitching wedge and put my approach twelve feet right of the pin. Adam pointed to the line. I pushed the ball, wasting my birdie opportunity, but I was impressed with how committed Adam was to helping me score well on the course where Arnie had once roamed.

My shirttail hung outside my belt as we walked to the final hole of my round—the twelfth. The wear and tear of seventy-two holes of golf, four different hotels, and hundreds of miles of travel over the past few days had finally hit my fifty-eight-year-old body like a ton of bricks. With a slower gait, drooped shoulders, and a head that wasn't as high as normal, I had neither the strength nor the inclination even to stop and tuck in my shirt. I still hadn't seen another golfer on the course. I just let it hang. After all, I was at Arnie's place.

Adam pointed to a small white building with a large red door and six colorful seals attached to its sides. "Five of those seals are related to the Quakers," he said, "but the sixth one has the names of the club's original founders."

As we got closer, I noticed Palmer's name among them. Adam explained that the other founders had tried to convince Palmer to leave the PGA tour to become the club's head pro. He had declined. I wondered aloud what professional golf would have been like had the King decided differently.

I never met Palmer or even saw him play live. Yet like golfers everywhere, I felt as if I'd lost a friend when he died in late September 2016. I was in Atlanta, watching a football game at home, when an alert announcing his death flashed across the screen. Why did it have such an effect on me? Palmer came to prominence while I was still living—still surviving—in the Jim Crow South, when golf was still something *they* played, not *us*.

But for many fans of the game, Palmer transcended both them and us. Though he didn't directly break down racial barriers, he helped erase the line between country club exclusivity and muni course populism. For him, golf was about people; he connected with people and connected people with golf. Arnie's Army wasn't so much a tribe as a movement that anyone could join. It was an Everyman's club. Danny Yates, my Augusta National host, had played with Palmer later in his career at the Masters and said that what had blown him away most was that Palmer had remembered the name of everyone who had approached him, asking about their spouses and children. He'd seemed to know something about every one of them. He wasn't a perfect guy, but despite his flaws he was authentic. And he genuinely loved people. I was touched by that, and when he died, it was as though a part of the game had been taken away.

My final putt of the round at Laurel Valley dropped in for an 84. It was my lowest score so far.

I WAS SCHEDULED TO FLY from Pittsburgh to Dulles, then connect with a flight back to Atlanta. I called an audible and changed my ticket to a departure directly from Washington. I wanted to stop at the Flight 93 National Memorial in Shanksville to pay my respects to those forty brave American souls whose spirit of never giving up, even in the direst circumstances, had prevented unknown horrors on a day when every American's dreams were attacked.

In a twisting, winding way, 9/11 always made me think of my mother. When I was in college, interning in Maryland, years before the attack, I wanted to give my mother an experience outside of the life she lived. So my siblings and I bought her a plane ticket to the nation's capital. I showed her all the sights and then took her on to New York City. My lasting memory of that trip is of Thelma "None" James walking through the World Trade Center—in her fluffy pink slippers. She was never not herself.

I'd never been to Shanksville. The site is profound in its simplicity—a low, white-marble Wall of Names; a ninety-three-foot-tall tower (still under construction at the time) containing forty wind chimes representing every lost passenger and crew member; the open field that is all that remains of the hemlock grove damaged by the crash. As I stood reading the names of the dead on the wall, there weren't a lot of other people around. But it wasn't long before we'd all connected with one another in silent acknowledgment of what we'd come there to honor. I talk to everybody wherever I go—that should be clear by now—but I didn't say a word to anyone there. Glances and nods were enough to unite us in feeling.

We were simply Americans in that place, come to honor other Americans. The men and women on that flight didn't go away quietly, meekly; in the face of the biggest adversity anyone could encounter, they chose to charge. To meet their fate head-on.

That's really never quitting.

CHAPTER SEVEN

BANDON

What's meant to be will always find a way.

—Trisha Yearwood

Eight years into my climb up Exxon's ladder, one of my engineering buddies, with whom I played basketball and flag football in after-work leagues, decided he'd had enough of my nonstop nerd routine. While breaking down the previous night's game over lunch, he told me that my reading list, dominated by government labor, energy, and economic forecasts, was a real conversation killer. He said I needed more to talk to people about than my seemingly bottomless knowledge of every number in the universe.

He was right.

So one day he brought me a bag filled with novels by Tom Clancy, Scott Turow, John Grisham, Robert Ludlum—thrillers with the kind of detailed dives into specialized fields like law and the military that engineer-types tend to eat up. I hadn't read much fiction since college, but his gesture got me back into it. One of the first books I pulled out was *The Firm*.

Not long afterward, on a slow Sunday morning, as I approached the gate at the half-empty Dallas Fort Worth International Airport for a flight back home to Houston, I spotted a striking young woman sitting there with her nose in the same Grisham novel.

"Oh," I said as I passed her, "I just read that book."

It was the perfect opening, just as my colleague had intended. The woman and I talked about how much we both liked the story, how it set up one impossible-seeming situation after another at what felt like breakneck speed. Our conversation moved on to our reasons for being in Dallas. I was returning from a meeting of the National Society of Black Engineers, a group that focuses on improving the recruitment and retention of African Americans and other minorities in industry. Erika had grown up just outside Dallas and had come back for the weekend to attend a friend's wedding. She was interning at American Express in New York, a short break before she defended her PhD dissertation at the University of Michigan.

We didn't have time for much more than that before we boarded the plane. She sat a row behind me, and I turned around at least once to ask her where she was in the book. After landing, she told me she was headed to her gate "for New York," and I went off to the parking garage.

I ran into a colleague about halfway there. We talked for a while before it hit me: I hadn't even tried to get the woman's name or phone number. I just did what I always do, which is be the guy who talks to everybody. There's a clumsy, Inspector Clouseau–like quality about me that I've long since come to terms with. It has its advantages; for one, it played a big role getting me onto courses throughout my golf odyssey. But my determination and problem-solving ability usually made up for my occasional bouts of cluelessness.

Forty-five minutes into my conversation with my work colleague, the things I'd noticed about her sank in. She'd left an impression: smart, engaging, genuine, and certainly attractive, with lemon-drop eyes and a bright warm smile. My engineer's brain also noted that her facial features were symmetrical, unlike mine.

So I spun around in the hall that led to the airport garage, stepped back through security (it was pre-9/11), and checked the gates for flights to New York. There was no sign of her anywhere. But making good use of my compulsive attention to details, I also checked flights to Newark. I noticed that one had left earlier, taxied onto the runway, then returned because of engine trouble. I spotted Erika waiting at the gate to be assigned a new plane.

I made my move—in my artless but honest way. "You know, Newark is in New Jersey, not New York," I told her as she looked up.

When I tell that story to friends, most say they would've been done with me right there. But not Erika. As she'd explain, "You're so funny at trying to be funny."

Six years later, we were married.

Two years after our wedding, during the summer of 2001, as Erika and I stood high above the Columbia River Gorge before making our way down the Oregon coast, she surprised me with a positive pregnancy test she'd been saving for that very moment, to let me know we were about to become parents.

The Oregon coast has held a special place in my heart ever since.

———

THREE HUNDRED MILES SOUTH OF where we stood on that glorious day is one of the sport's real wonderlands: Bandon Dunes Golf Resort. The four eighteen-hole resort courses that made it up when I played, each by a different designer, are all ranked in the top two-thirds of *Golf Digest*'s Top 100. There's no place like it—no place with as much pure, time-honored, concentrated golf. With two courses unwinding atop dunes and beach grass, one routed through an inland coastal forest, and another an homage to the origins of golf course architecture, all smack in the middle of nowhere—a four-hour drive from Portland, seven from Seattle, nine from San Francisco, twenty-three from Denver—it's a must-play destination for golf idealists. Its draw is likened to baseball's mythical Field of Dreams: build it, and they will come.

The notion to build it belonged to Mike Keiser, a golf nut who made a fortune from an environmentally friendly greeting card start-up. He sold the business in the late 1980s and shifted his focus to developing links courses modeled after those in the United Kingdom, the sport's motherland. (One at Bandon is a "template course" that replicates the most distinguished holes from various British courses and strings them together in a single layout.) The truest links courses literally "link" the land to the sea on largely natural routes that don't include trees or water, except for whatever sea churns off to the side. The undulating fairways are fast and firm and the ball runs a long, long way, requiring a more earthbound approach than "parkland" courses, with their tree-lined, lawnlike fairways and meticulously barbered greens. As the English pro Justin Rose put it, "When the ball's in the air, every golf course is the same. It's when the ball hits the ground and what it does there that distinguishes them." When playing links golf, it's what the ball does on the ground that usually matters most.

Under cloudless skies on my first full day at the resort, I struck the ball well—low and accurate—on the Bandon Dunes and Pacific Dunes courses, both of which unfurl along rugged cliffs that plummet toward the Pacific. It's as breathtaking as it is terrifying. All of it—the course, the dramatic scenery, my ball striking—was more than I'd hoped for, especially after meeting my nineteen-year-old caddie and assuming that I'd be left pretty much on my own.

When Thomas introduced himself as my caddie, I was immediately skeptical: slight, nerdy, virtually swallowed up by his two-sizes-too-big white overalls, he admitted that he didn't play the game. Yet he quickly dispelled my concerns with accurate reads on the greens and wise guidance. Over forty-eight holes, he helped me avoid most of the prickly rough, tall fescue, and bunkers—not to mention the raging ocean—that peppered the courses.

Thomas explained that he had started working at Bandon to qualify for a college scholarship awarded to high school students who caddied and excelled academically. He was using that scholarship to study business a couple hours up the road at the University of Oregon. I sensed that he might not have been able to attend college without the scholarship, and I let him know that I'd also relied on academic scholarships.

I initially attended the University of Houston and majored in architecture. I'd been drawn to the profession for the silliest of reasons: to follow in the footsteps of two television characters on shows I watched during my early, impressionable years. Mike Brady, the patriarch of *The Brady Bunch*, and Wilbur, the owner of the talking horse in *Mister Ed*, were both architects who appeared to love their jobs and their lives. Their circumstances resonated with me because I'd always been drawn to math and building things, like those small-scale cities I erected with cast-off wood in the Sawmill Quarters. But while studying dimensions, space, and the aesthetics of buildings at the U of H, I realized I was more interested in the steel beams and structural systems that keep the buildings standing. After a year, I transferred to Prairie View A&M, a historically black university northwest of Houston, and changed my major to civil engineering.

At the time, Prairie View had a strong reputation for producing successful African American engineers, graduating more of them than any other school in the country. During my four years there, professors not only taught me theories and applications of math and the basic sciences, they also served as role models for what it meant to be a responsible Black man in America. Prior to college, I'd had just one African American male teacher—for sixth-grade math. At Prairie View, I studied derivatives and integrals in calculus under the dapper Freddie Frazier, who lectured with the cadence of a Baptist preacher. He was quick to say, "I'm gonna flunk you!" to any student who came to class unprepared.

In thermodynamics, Dr. Rogers flunked me during a semester I earned straight A's in every other class. I made the highest scores in the class on his tests, but they were still below passing. And since I worked evenings and weekends selling fridges and stoves at Montgomery Ward, I couldn't attend the tutoring sessions in which he allowed students to correct their tests and earn better scores. I repeated the class and made an easy B.

Physics with Dr. Thomas was just as exacting. He told us during our first class that the only people who could earn an A were Sears, Zemansky, and Young—the authors of our textbook. He said the best that even he could earn was a B and that the brightest students in the class should feel fortunate if they earned a C. He then said that everyone else should just assume they were in "Introduction to Physics I" because they'd be repeating the class the next semester. I escaped with one of those scarce C's.

Despite their eccentricities—I can't forget Dr. Doctor, whose son, Dr. Doctor, Jr., also became a professor—all of those men were exceptional teachers and my first examples of Black male professionals. They wore suits, had families, and did research for companies outside academia. They not only helped me become a capable engineer, they prepared me for a professional world filled with challenges and tough consequences when you didn't meet them.

They taught us how to be engineers—how to look at problems and add value. If somebody asked during a lecture whether the material was going to be on a test, Dr. Frazier would declare, "I'm giving you an FF— I'm going to flunk you twice!" He'd then explain, "Nobody's going to pay you to solve problems that have answers in the back of the book. Those have already been solved. You're learning to solve problems that aren't even known yet."

At Prairie View, I could focus solely on becoming an engineer without having to deal with racial bias. The professors created a comfortable environment for learning while ensuring that we understood that after graduation, we would enter a workforce where people would likely doubt us because of the shade of our skin and the school we had attended. That was why they were so hard on us.

That was why they threatened us with FF's.

PLAYING BANDON TRAILS, THE THIRD course, with Thomas on my bag, required a long shuttle ride inland from the resort's main area. We rolled into a wilderness of tall evergreens and shifting dunes. The absence of the Pacific's ceaseless roar seemed to be the only difference between the first hole at Bandon Trails and the opening holes on the two courses I'd played the previous day. But from the perch on the second tee, with distant mountains bursting into view, the course turned transportive. Sounds of wildlife filled the crisp air; they were so random and piercing that they almost seemed piped in, the way CBS had once piped in bird sounds during its golf telecasts to make them sound realer. It didn't get any realer than this. Man's hand was at a minimum. Bill Coore and Ben Crenshaw's design felt almost like a wide, playable hiking trail. Bandon Trails' sense of calm took me back to when solitary walks and exploratory romps through the piney woods of East Texas had provided a youthful refuge from a world in which I sometimes struggled to find my place.

Thomas's voice cut through the mellifluous background melodies and jolted me back to the present. "You can take ten yards off the distance since it's downhill."

As we walked down the wide-open sixth fairway, Roy, the big boss among the three copper salesmen I'd been paired with, told me that their golf outing was in recognition of his team's performance as the top sales force of the year. "We invest a lot in our people," he said. "We think that when they feel appreciated and respected, they return that appreciation and respect to our customers."

I understood the wisdom of that people-first approach early in my own career. It was integral to who I was and who I wanted to be. Yet as I worked my way up through the company, I occasionally lost my sense of that. It took more than eighteen years at ExxonMobil for me to finally feel that I belonged there. I remember the moment precisely. Late one night in 2002, as I sat at my desk in a corner office of our sprawling head-quarters nestled among the trees in Fairfax County, Virginia, I looked out through glass walls onto the vacant trading-room floor, where earlier in the day my team had solved a complex logistics and regulatory problem. I sat in the dark by myself for a long time as a powerful sense of belonging washed over me.

Those cold winter nights during my youth, sitting next to a wood-burning heater, learning to read by the light of a coal-oil lamp, were a distant memory. Somewhere along the way, I had begun to run as hard as I could, chasing one dream after another. And on that night, after almost two decades at ExxonMobil, it no longer mattered to me that my colleagues had grown up in families more traditional than mine and attended more esteemed schools. The box on my birth certificate marked ILLEGITIMATE was irrelevant. I finally felt that I belonged just as much as they did.

Yet that fear of not belonging was soon replaced by a fear of not performing well enough to remain among the highest achievers. I dealt with that new fear by driving my folks harder and harder—at times inappropriately so. Once, unsatisfied with his work, I accused a subordinate—a lifer who'd worked his way through the ranks from entry-level wage employee at a refinery to management—of being either incompetent or a liar. It was a blindsiding, out-of-line reaction to his fumbling a simple task. He'd made a mistake, and instead of merely reprimanding him or talking to him about how he could perform better next time, I humiliated him. My words broke his spirit.

I have very few regrets from my career.

That's one of them.

NOT LONG AFTERWARD, I HAD an epiphany. In late September 2005, a month after Hurricane Katrina ravaged New Orleans and much of the Gulf Coast, Hurricane Rita raged through Beaumont, Texas, near the Louisiana border. It devastated the city and did tens of millions of dollars' worth of damage to the ExxonMobil Beaumont refinery, where I oversaw maintenance and project execution. My teams were responsible for repairing the damage so that the refinery could get back to producing gasoline, diesel fuel, and jet fuel. It was an all-hands-on-deck moment. I and several others spent a month straight at the refinery, living the entire time on a riverboat moored at the dock.

A week or so into the repairs, I walked into the small shop-floor office of one of the managers and found him weeping at his desk. He'd just gotten off the phone with his daughter, whose roof had been ripped apart in the storm and who was now living with her family in a house without power and not much of a roof. Framed photos of her and other family members were displayed everywhere. His eyes red with tears, he looked helpless—a father torn between two responsibilities. His daughter was turning to him in her biggest moment of need, while I was requiring him to lead a team as it worked nonstop to get the refinery back up and running. I suddenly understood more fully the level of sacrifice people were making to put the company's priorities ahead of their own. They deserved our respect more than we deserved theirs. I was in awe of them and ashamed of myself.

I don't know if I would've experienced that epiphany without the life I'd had. The moment I came upon that middle-aged family man sobbing at his desk reminded me—*re*reminded me—how real life can get for most people. So much of what we occupy ourselves with is insignificant; so often we're in our workspaces creating problems to solve, with artificial targets and deadlines. If we started back up a day later, it would have an effect, but the world would keep turning. For people dealing with water coming through their roofs but not their faucets, however, the world had crashed to a complete stop.

I remember how hard life can be. I understood the dilemma that man was struggling with; I'd seen my mother do the same for years. I knew it would be easier for me to make the decision for him than for him to make it himself. "Right now, you're no good to your daughter, yourself, or us," I told him. "So please, go take care of your daughter."

A weight lifted from him in an instant. His problem wasn't solved, but it suddenly seemed solvable.

In that moment, it was the right thing to do—for both of us.

———

THE FOG THAT DRAPED THE course's coastal wilderness like fine, damp linen had finally burned off by the time I reached the thirteenth hole. Up to that point, I'd hit more fairways than I'd missed. Yet on the course's most generous driving hole my shot sailed right and dropped in the rough behind a cluster of cedars.

"Just get it back in play," Thomas advised when we arrived at the ball, nestled where the hole's dogleg bends left toward the green. "You'll have less than a hundred twenty yards to the pin."

It was sound advice—the only advice, really, exactly what even the most experienced caddie would offer. But I'd spotted a small patch of blue, fog-free sky through an opening in the trees about the size of a batter's strike zone. I studied it for a minute, then for a minute more. I walked around the trees to study it from a whole other angle.

"See that opening?" I finally said to Thomas, pointing to the crack in the trees. "It's in line with the flag and at the exact launch angle of my pitching wedge. If I can get the ball through that opening without hitting anything else, it has to land next to the flag."

I pictured the shot in my mind's eye—the clubface striking my ball, the ball clearing the trees and dropping onto the green—as clearly as any vision I'd ever had. Thomas stared at me as if I'd gone crazy. He didn't say it, but he had to be thinking, "How is a guy who just missed the widest fairway on the course going to finesse a shot through a tiny gap high in the trees?"

Good question.

I'm glad he didn't ask it.

Straddling the ball, steadying my legs, lightening my grip, I swung without hesitation, doubt, or fear. I was all in. I looked up just in time to see the ball arc through the opening like a called strike without so much as grazing a branch or a leaf. Unable to see where the shot landed, I held my follow-through as if posing for a portrait, then glanced over at Thomas, who had a better view from where he was leaning on my bag just beyond the trees. He stood there in stunned silence until, still staring, he said, as much to himself as to me, "Looks like it's next to the pin."

As we hustled toward the green together, I suddenly spotted something small and round and white. It had stopped three feet left of the hole. "Sometimes, Thomas," I said, as much to myself as to him, as we strode toward the pin, "we just have to believe it and go with it."

Thomas didn't say a word. But I'm guessing he thought what anyone would've thought: "And sometimes we just get lucky."

He was probably right.

It wasn't the first time I'd felt lucky in Oregon.

CHAPTER EIGHT

OAK TREE NATIONAL

The things you do for yourself are gone when you are gone,
but the things you do for others remain as your legacy.

—Kalu Ndukwe Kalu

I met Melvin Floyd on the third hole of the North Course at Cherokee Town and Country Club in Atlanta during the summer of 2015. I'd just hit a 3-wood from the right rough, 235 yards out, hoping to get the ball close to the front of the green. Seconds after the ball cleared the crest of a rise in the middle of the fairway, blocking my line of sight, I heard someone yelling from somewhere off in the distance, "It went in! It went in!"

I rushed to the top of the hill. An exuberant caddie in a white shirt and khaki shorts was jumping up and down beside the green. His childlike excitement energized me and touched something deep. I didn't know his name or his story, but before my next round at Cherokee, I asked the caddie master to assign the young Black man to my bag. He quickly became known around the club as my caddie; some of the other caddies referred to him as my son. I became a father figure to him, just like the men who had been a father figure to me during my youth.

I soon learned that Melvin had had a troubled past. He'd been arrested a couple of years before I met him while transporting what he thought was a dead body across state lines. His story was that he had been threatened by two men who said they'd kill him unless he drove their car to Alabama. He never told me how he had gotten mixed up with such dangerous characters, but that was his story and he stuck to it. He said they had set him up. They had reported the car as stolen. When the police pulled Melvin over in Alabama, they found a bloodied man, barely holding on to his life, in the trunk. The man's two sons were eventually arrested and charged. Melvin received probation but wound up with a criminal record. I don't know the full story of Melvin's involvement, but I do know how fast the quicksand of poverty and crime can suck an unlucky young man down and drown him.

During the many loops we made together at Cherokee, I listened to his stories about learning golf through First Tee, a program for increasing minority participation in golf, and his dreams of a career as a golf instructor, a club pro, or a golfer on one of the minitours. I suspected that his biggest dreams might be beyond his reach, but I wasn't about to tell him that. I didn't want to be like the social worker who had told me that my dreams were unrealistic. I know firsthand that people can achieve the improbable, and I don't think we should impose our limits on someone else's perception of their potential.

Melvin and his twin brother, Kelvin, had started caddying at Cherokee as young boys, maybe twelve or thirteen. A member of the club had met their mother and learned that they loved golf. As a favor to her, he had brought them to Cherokee so that they could earn money caddying. Melvin told me that he and his brother felt loved by the members who had seen them grow into young men. And as best I could tell, he was right. Several members had tried to help them build a better life over the years. They had collected money and purchased a car for them, found job opportunities for them, and given them advice when asked. One member once told me that Melvin and Kelvin had protected his disabled son from bullies at the middle school they attended together.

Cherokee kept Melvin and Kelvin out of trouble, it was their refuge from the streets of West Atlanta, where they saw the same types of drug crimes and violence that I had seen when I lived in the projects during my own teenage years.

I began to spend time with Melvin away from the club; we played golf together on local courses, we shared meals at restaurants. He even dropped by my house a couple of times. But one day at Cherokee he exchanged words that were considered threatening with one of the staff. He was barred from the club's property; there was a concern he might turn violent. I advocated on his behalf for a different outcome, but I think the club leadership thought the risks were too high. Their decision brought him to tears.

Over lunch at a café near the club, Melvin told me that because of his probation, he had no place else to go to earn a living. A month or two later he called me from the county jail. He had been arrested for some parole violation. Though Kelvin stayed out of trouble and improved his life, the hundreds of hours I spent with Melvin didn't seem to change his. I felt as though I'd failed him. We still talk occasionally, and I believe there is still hope for him. Like me, he's not a quitter. I offered him money; he refused it and said, "I don't need money, I need a job."

Cherokee had been Melvin's refuge from a world of trouble since he was twelve. Joe's shoeshine shop on Fourth Street in Texas City was mine. That was where I went when I was ten and had to choose between wandering the streets alone or the potential trouble I could get into by hanging out with my brother and his mischievous friends.

Sixth Street, the commercial center of Texas City, became my playground. I would visit local shops to browse the toys and clothes and books, wondering who the people were that could afford such things. Eventually, I started selling newspapers for the local afternoon rag, the *Daily Sun*. I would stand on the corner of Sixth Street and Fourth Avenue near the local drugstore, yelling out whatever the headline above the fold on the first page trumpeted.

One day as I crossed Fourth Street on my way to Sixth Street, I stopped to chat with a fortyish double amputee sitting in a wheelchair outside his shoeshine shop. I was curious as to what had happened to his legs. Joe had lost them in a battle during World War II. After our first chat, I returned often to listen to his stories.

Soon after, I started helping at his shop, a single room slightly smaller than the bedroom in the shotgun house that we lived in at the time. I'd sweep the floor and arrange loose items in a neat stack. He'd give me a dime or two for my labor. His stories were real and interesting to me. He told me about life in the army as a Black man during the war, how segregation had been as strong among those who saved the world from Nazism and its racial hatred as it was at home. I really didn't understand what Nazism was at the time. His voice seemed emotionless when he told me how Blacks had served mostly in menial jobs but were proud of the elite Black fighting forces such as the Buffalo Soldiers and the Tuskegee Airmen. He said, "President Truman eventually ended the segregation in the military, but we came home to face the same discrimination we left before we went off to fight."

Back in the late sixties, I was Melvin, and Joe was me. He helped me understand that you always have a choice between giving up and fighting on. He had chosen to fight on. Like my mother, he never complained about his condition; he just dealt with it the best he could. He also taught me to shine shoes and set me up with a shoeshine box. Soon I was earning a quarter for every pair of shoes or boots I shined, plus tips, during my weekend strolls past the bars along Texas Avenue and Sixth Street. The bars were filled with men, white men, who worked in the nearby refineries and chemical plants. As the sun went down, they'd shed their work clothes and put on their best boots to have a drink and dance the hoedown with the local girls. Money I earned shining shoes and selling newspapers helped put food on the table after my stepfather abandoned us.

Melvin put food on the table by becoming an excellent caddie during his years at Cherokee. He would have appreciated how well I was playing at Oak Tree National in Edmond, Oklahoma. When I was playing alone with him on my bag, he often said, "Mr. Jimmie, you play your best golf when it's just the two of us, and your game gets worse the more people you play with." He was right.

I'd flown halfway across the country to play Oak Tree. Pete Dye built it in 1976 with the aim of creating the most difficult eighteen holes on the PGA Tour. He stretched the distance of the course and made the fairways and greens fast and firm. I got off to my best start ever with nothing but pars and birdies over the first four holes. There were no caddies at Oak Tree and only one other group on the course, a foursome. So I played alone. There was no one, not even Melvin, to share the glory of my spectacular start. I eventually finished the course with my best score yet on my one-year golf odyssey. I was just one stroke shy of the goal I'd set of breaking 80 on a Top 100 course.

CHAPTER NINE

OAKMONT

Keep every promise you make and only make promises you can keep.

—Anthony Hitt

I stared out at the storied course with its sprawling Tudor Revival clubhouse from the back porch of Pro's Cottage on the grounds of Oakmont Country Club outside Pittsburgh.

The view from the guesthouse adjacent to the eighteenth fairway was a long, long way from the view I'd had from apartment 62 in building G, the four-bedroom that seven of us crowded into at a public housing compound in Hitchcock, Texas.

Most of the other families in those projects lived there for the same reasons we did: too many kids and not enough money. We were the poorest of the poor, a fact underscored by the black iron fence that ringed the property. Amazingly, we viewed those who lived in the houses just outside the grates as wealthy, though our notion of "wealth" in Hitchcock was wildly misguided. The Burton kids, for instance, who lived a couple blocks outside the fence, rarely failed to note that they lived in "*the* two-story"—emphasis on the *the*. In a neighborhood filled with cramped bungalows, theirs was the lone multistory, single-family dwelling, if a modest one at best.

Economics weren't the only factor that made life hard in what was formally designated the Missionary Independent Village. (We simply called it "the Village," composed as it was of families bound together by scarcity.) Health, especially complications of obesity, was a source of struggle for many folks. Our food came primarily from an overpriced convenience store. That was really all there was. With our choices limited, we often subsisted for long stretches on rice and beans. Meat was a rare luxury, unlike when we had lived with my grandparents in the country, where we had grown or raised or killed much of what we ate, then worked it off fetching water or clearing brush.

Yet for us kids, the Village was more than an address of necessity. It was teeming with young people, and my siblings and I instantly made friends; at one time or another, I found myself inside most of the Village's sixty-four units. Building G, one of seven yellow-brick rectangles, was in the back, and from our apartment's second-floor window I could spy everything that unfolded in the courtyard below. I spotted football games as they formed on the grass between the buildings and raced out to join. I listened for the clack of domino tiles being slapped atop makeshift tables on the cement patios, and just as I'd done in the Sawmill Quarters, I showed up every chance I got to try to outduel the elders.

I also saw tragic events unfold.

One afternoon, I watched a kid die. I first heard the furious footsteps of a teenager I knew as he vaulted down the cement stairs in a neighboring building. I didn't realize it, but he was sprinting for his life in a mad dash for cover behind a brick barrier that hid the dumpsters in front of the complex. He made it about halfway across the courtyard, where we'd tackled each other a thousand times, before another kid chasing him fired a gun. Foolishly, I followed the shots and arrived in the courtyard to find Boogie lying there, bleeding and still, a lifeless footnote, probably to a drug deal gone bad.

We lived there almost three years because the rent was dirt cheap. We were evicted before my senior year of high school because we couldn't afford even that.

Standing alone outside Pro's Cottage, I inhaled the warming western Pennsylvania air. A breeze floated off a bend in the Allegheny River, not far away. At that moment, I wasn't thinking about the Village. Not exactly. But one way or another, every thought I had was informed by life in those projects and the countless other homes I'd had to abandon while growing up. The distance I'd come was only amplified by every exclusive course I played.

Sometimes, as on that morning, the contrast pulled the air right out of my lungs.

―――

THREE DAYS EARLIER, I'D GOTTEN a call even the most ardent golfer can only dream about. "Jimmie, can you play Oakmont on Sunday and Monday?"

Bill Teberg, the commercial real estate exec I'd played with at Augusta National, was on the other end of the line. It was a last-minute chance for me to join some of his JLL colleagues on an overnight golf outing. When you get an invite to a place such as Augusta or Oakmont, even at the last minute, your response has to be an emphatic "yes." You deal with the consequences later.

For me, one such consequence was potentially breaking a promise I'd made to Jordan a year earlier. I'd said I'd take him to Dragon Con, the annual pop-culture convention held in Atlanta that attracts comic book and sci-fi enthusiasts from across the country. The event didn't mean much to me, but it meant the world to my fifteen-year-old. More significant, however, was the matter of keeping my word. I'd grown up with a stepfather who had rarely kept his.

I was already scheduled to fly from Atlanta to Denver to begin a stretch of golf across Colorado and Nebraska from Monday through Thursday. Now I had to push those rounds back to Tuesday through Friday. That meant I'd have to find a way to get from Sand Hills Golf Club, my final course that week, back to Atlanta on Friday night. It wouldn't be easy. Sand Hills is in middle-of-nowhere Nebraska. The closest major airport, Denver International, is 320 miles away, about five hours by car. The last flight to Atlanta would depart Denver at 5:40 that evening. I'd have to finish my round before noon to make the flight. But I told Bill I was in for both days in Pittsburgh. I'd just have to figure it out.

I was the first to arrive at Oakmont's five-bedroom guest cottage that Sunday morning. The folks I was meeting trickled in over the next hour. Our host, J. C. Pelusi, a middle-aged director at the company who still carried the physique of his football-playing days as an All-America line-man at the University of Pittsburgh, treated us to lunch on the clubhouse veranda. It felt like Augusta all over again, sitting around a table with a bunch of guys who knew one another but none of whom knew me.

I didn't bring up the Village or any of the other childhood stops that had prompted my deep breaths earlier; course by course, I was getting used to making random small talk with groups of random people. I didn't have a choice. If I didn't do that, the rest of the year would be unbearable, my quest almost impossible.

———

THE EXPANSIVENESS OF THE COURSE that has hosted more U.S. Open championships than any other is visible from the first tee. It's certainly more visible than it used to be. More than ten thousand trees had been removed from Oakmont's grounds since 1993 to restore the course to the original less lush, links-style vision of Henry Fownes, a local steel mag-nate and scratch golfer who had sculpted it from open farmland at the turn of the twentieth century. The removal had reversed the trend of tree-planting beautification programs that had swept through golf courses sev-eral decades earlier, including at Oakmont, whose members cringed when a golf writer described the course as "an ugly old brute." The restoration of playability and the uncovering of its original crevices and contours inspired other top courses to follow suit. Personally, I think classic courses should preserve the intent and playability of their original designers, yet I so often find my own voice in the serenity of fairways carved through the wilderness, even if they're more difficult to play and more costly to maintain.

After a decent drive, my approach shot on the first hole landed a little short. An embarrassing shank then sent my chip shot scurrying along the ground to the right of the green. Shanking a golf ball is like stubbing your toe getting out of bed: not much makes you feel stupider. I told Seth, my industrious caddie, that I needed to hole out my next chip to maintain my string of first-hole pars over the last few courses I'd played.

"Chip it straight at the flag," he told me.

Easy for him to say. Everyone looked on as my shot landed softly on a line halfway to the hole, then watched with mounting disbelief as the ball rolled right into the cup. I don't know who was most surprised: my playing partners, my caddie, or me.

On our way to the next tee, I was stunned to find that the Pennsylvania Turnpike, the notorious superhighway roaring with speeding cars and eighteen-wheelers, sliced right through the course. It felt like the ultimate intrusion—not quite paving paradise to put up a parking lot, but close. Walking across one of the two bridges that straddled the Turnpike, Seth told me that a railroad had originally cut through the old course; the Turnpike had later been built along the same route.

Seth had grown up in Pittsburgh, then left for college before returning to teach seventh-grade geography. Teaching middle school has always struck me as a nearly impossible challenge.

"What's it like to teach seventh-graders?" I asked him.

"Probably the same as when you were in middle school," he answered, grinning. "The girls are starting to get interested in boys and the boys are still trying to figure out what to do about it."

My memories of middle school were more complicated. It was a bleak time for Black people in my little town of La Marque. Though *Brown v.*

Board of Education outlawed public school segregation in 1954, it wasn't until the early seventies that our school district got around to integrating. Whites protested and resisted attending schools with Blacks. Blacks resented their schools being shuttered and having to be bused across town. There were rumors of riots at the junior high school up the road from my middle school. There were also threats of students there bringing the rioting to our campus. I even heard a rumor that the junior high principal had been tossed out of a second-floor window.

We were all scared. Some parents kept their kids home.

Fortunately, no trouble came to my school. Still, it was the first time I experienced deep hatred. The NO COLORED signs in downtown Huntsville, the whooping and hollering by drunk college kids on Friday nights, and the racial epithets of the white kids up the hill in the Sawmill Quarters had all felt more like bad traditions—like hazing. It's inexplicable, even unimaginable, to anybody who didn't live through it, but to many of us who did, and who felt incapable of initiating change, it's what we mean when we say, "It's just the way things were back then." But this felt different. Times had changed. The world was supposedly moving forward. The explosion of racial hatred felt like a more intentional, last-gasp remnant of America's original sin. Many of the white parents and their kids wanted nothing to do with us, then or in the future. They didn't think white kids should be going to school with "dumb niggers."

Those years were also challenging for me in more personal ways. I had two pairs of polyester pants and a couple of cotton shirts that I alternated wearing the whole school year. That was it. We used vouchers from the county welfare office to buy our school supplies, but they didn't cover the white T-shirt and shorts required to take part in gym class. Every day during the sixth grade, my routine was the same: I walked into my PE teacher's office, bent over, put my hands palms down on his desk, and braced myself as he delivered three swift swats with a wooden paddle. It was supposed to be punishment for not participating in the class, but it felt like one more act of retribution for being poor.

So although teaching middle school was probably as difficult for Seth as it had been for my teachers, his students' experience was likely quite different from mine.

Amid that darkness and pain, however, there were silver linings. From first grade through fifth, all of my teachers were women. In sixth grade, however, I had Mr. Calvin, my first Black male teacher. He was tall, handsome, and middle-aged, sporting a full head of black hair streaked on the sides with gray. If there had been Black role models on TV at the time, they would have looked just like him.

In the classroom, Mr. Calvin made math practical and fun. As a kid who had nothing, I lived vicariously through the problems he gave us. I took pretend trips to restaurants—I'd never been to one—and then calculated how much the bill would be for our meal after a 10 percent tip. I put up pretend Christmas lights while determining the angle to lean the ladder against our fanciful two-story house. It was the same in social studies, where I imagined traveling to cities across America or around the world where the people we learned about lived. I was fascinated by how different their lives were in all those distant places.

It was during those years—despite the anxieties of desegregation; despite being swatted for not having enough money to buy gym clothes—that the seeds of my love of math and my yearning to explore America and beyond were sown.

MY GOOD FORTUNE ON THE first hole at Oakmont followed me to the third as I avoided one of the most famous sand hazards in golf: the "Church Pews." The nearly football field–sized bunker—about a hundred yards long and forty yards wide—contains a succession of twelve narrow, grassy berms arranged like pews in a small country church. As if that weren't enough, the Pews are cut into the rough between the third and fourth fairways, ensuring that you face them twice.

I didn't avoid them the second time. As a matter of fact, I did exactly what I told myself not to do as I stood on the fourth tee box and stared them down: I hooked my drive. The ball dropped between the last two berms, coming to rest against the base of the final four-foot-tall pew. As a kid, I had often spent all Sunday, from morning to night, in one church service after another; I had no desire to spend that type of time in Oakmont's equivalent. I chipped out sideways.

Every great golf course needs a short risk-reward par four. Oakmont has two, the eleventh and seventeenth. The eleventh plays only 330 yards, but it's bisected diagonally by a dry creek that will eagerly blow up your scorecard if you go for the green and fail to carry it. The seventeenth is guarded by par-killing bunkers and fescue. I laid up on the eleventh and birdied it. I went for the green on the seventeenth and was grateful for the double bogey.

I played Oakmont again on Monday but was forced to cut the afternoon round short to make it to Denver that night. The two JLL managers in my foursome that afternoon—one of whom ran operations in Detroit, another of whom led a team in Cincinnati—told me to reach out if I needed help with any of the clubs near them.

I'd come to Oakmont to join strangers on a last-minute invitation. Now more courses on my list were clicking into place.

———

I SPENT THE NIGHT IN Denver, then drove to Beaver Creek in the morning to visit and play a casual round on a local course with my longtime friend and former colleague Gary Pruessing. We'd known each other long enough that I remembered when his white hair had been blond.

We'd met while I was still an engineer at the Baytown refinery. By the time I'd been promoted to my first supervisory position, he was leading the technical organization there. While attending a seminar together on diversity at the Houston Business Roundtable, an association of refining and chemical companies, we had a frank discussion about some of the challenges that Black engineers faced trying to build a career at Exxon. Gary confided in me that there were managers who didn't think Blacks were smart enough to be engineers.

Very few of the hundreds of engineers working at the refinery were Black, and Black managers were essentially nonexistent—maybe two or three out of more than a hundred. During my first week, I had been caught off guard when another African American engineer, who'd been with the company for six years, had walked into my office. He sat down across from me at my desk and asked where I'd gone to school. When I told him, he said I was probably at Exxon as a token minority since I'd attended a historically Black college. He went on to tell me that he was there on his merits because he'd attended a prominent predominantly white university.

Gary was white, but he seemed to understand the challenges faced by those of us who were in a place where many people thought we didn't belong. His moment of uncensored truth endowed me with a level of trust and respect for him that remained throughout my career. It also kick-started a deep and enduring friendship.

I left Gary's house the next morning long before sunrise to make my 7:27 a.m. tee time at Cherry Hills Country Club back in Denver. Gary would join me later that afternoon at nearby Castle Pines Golf Club.

The Cherry Hills head pro had agreed to host me after getting a call from J.J., the president at Flint Hills who'd promised me help a couple of months earlier. The most celebrated course in the Rocky Mountain West, Cherry Hills is best known to many for Arnold Palmer's vintage charge during the final round of the 1960 U.S. Open. Trailing by seven strokes, he drove the green on the short par-four first hole—at an elevation of 5,300 feet, the ball sails there like almost nowhere else on tour—and birdied it, as well as the three holes that followed, to score a blistering 30 on the front nine. He eventually overtook Ben Hogan, who sent balls into the water on the final two holes, to capture the championship. I didn't drive the green on number one, but I did make par, increasing my string of opening-hole pars to four. Several double bogeys followed while I watched Jacob, the intern playing with me—who, like Dylan, the intern I'd met at Valhalla, attended Sam Houston State—make perfect turns and balanced swings. He did what good golfers do: made a difficult game look easy.

Jacob suggested that I relax and slow my tempo; it's the simplest but best piece of advice—in golf as in life—99 percent of the time. I did as he said and easily made par on the next hole. Jacob smiled ever so slightly when I plucked my ball out of the cup. I think he took pride in how quickly his tip had paid off.

My approach shot over a pond to a front pin on the seventeenth green hit the bank, then trickled down into the water. As Hogan had done after hitting his approach into the same pond during that 1960 U.S. Open, I slipped off my shoes and socks, waded in, and splashed my ball onto the green. Jacob and our caddie got a good laugh when I sloshed back up the bank, soaking wet. I was just happy to get the ball onto the green. Hogan hadn't, and it had cost him the tournament. The only thing at stake for me was pride, and I'd long ago gotten past caring about looking ridiculous on a golf course. If you can't make a difficult game look easy, make it look tolerable, no matter what it throws at you.

━━━━

I ARRIVED AT CASTLE PINES later that afternoon and immediately sought out Zack Anderson, the club's new head pro. He had agreed to host me when I had called the week before and explained what I was up to. I'd hoped never to directly ask anyone to host me, but although I was already set for Cherry Hills Country Club, Ballyneal Golf and Hunt Club, and Sand Hills Golf Club—the nearby courses I'd knock out that week—I hadn't found anyone to help me with Castle Pines. Zack agreed to let me play, though he joked that he had one condition: "I get to play with you."

He also said I could bring a guest to fill out our group. I invited Gary, which made it a threesome.

I felt every one of my fifty-eight years from our perch high above the first fairway, overlooking rows of yellow poppies with the Rockies towering in the distance. Zack allowed that he was tired, too; he and his wife had welcomed their first child into the world twelve weeks earlier. He laughed when I said I'd take it easy on him.

My string of opening-hole pars came to an unceremonious end at Castle Pines. I made a double on the first hole and a triple on the second. Meanwhile, Gary played like a pro, hitting fairways and greens, and the sleep-deprived Zack swung his clubs as gracefully as Jacob had that morning. I finally got lucky and made a forty-foot putt to save par on number three, but I feared it was going to be a long afternoon.

From the moment he opened his mouth, it was obvious that our forecaddie, Paddy, was from Boston. I reeled off a string of neighborhoods and towns—Peabody, Worcester, Dorchester—with a pronunciation only someone who'd spent time in Beantown could muster. (Erika and I lived in Boston for a year while she was a visiting professor at the Harvard Business School.) Dressed in white coveralls, Paddy smiled as though he'd found a new soulmate.

On the elevated ninth tee at Castle Pines, an opening in the adjacent trees provided a clear view of the imposing square stone that gives the city of Castle Rock its name. Perched atop a volcanic rock formation that towers over the surrounding landscape, it really does look like a fortress. It's breathtaking. I got my second wind and finally hit another good drive. Soon my putts started to drop for pars. Gary continued to play well, and Zack's swings continued to look effortless, which reminded me that I had picked up the game too late in life to ever have a swing that grooved and natural—no matter how often I played or how many lessons I took.

My eyes popped wide open when we came to the twelfth hole: its wide fairway was complemented by a blaze of red, yellow, orange, and violet flowers near a waterfall that spilled to the left of the green. We caught it all just before the bright blue sky went gray.

The clouds turned dark after I birdied fourteen, and the skies opened up on the fifteenth hole. I was surviving on adrenaline anyway, as was Zack, so we called it a day after each of us made par.

I wasn't taking any chances. My improved play on the back nine had clearly angered the golf gods.

———

THE NEXT DAY UNFOLDED UNDER blue skies. Twisting through grass-covered dunes three hours northeast of Castle Rock, numbed by the drive's monotony, I rolled over a hill to suddenly find, rising in front of me like a mirage in the desert, a golf course like nothing I'd ever seen. Luxurious, rippling fairways flowed like rivers through knolls carpeted with golden fescue that waved in the breeze like wild wheat. It reminded me of my first visit to the Grand Canyon, where no pictures I'd seen, or descriptions I'd heard, had prepared me for what wind, water, and time had created. The Ballyneal Golf and Hunt Club was not created by God, just by someone who might have thought he was. How could something this spectacular be at the end of such a humdrum drive? I stepped out of my rental car and gazed at the masterpiece built by Tom Doak, whose minimalist design philosophy sounds a lot like my own outlook on life.

"We play the ball as it lies," Doak has written. "The minimalist's objective is to route as many holes as possible whose main features already exist in the landscape, and accent their strategies without overkilling the number of hazards."

The owner of Ballyneal grants onetime opportunities for nonmembers to play the course if he finds their request compelling. I had spoken with the club's director of golf, who had told the owner about my pilgrimage. The owner found my story captivating enough to allow me to play.

My caddie, a twentysomething named Travis, had come to Nebraska to be closer to his daughter. He skillfully guided me around the Mulligan Course, the club's newly opened par-three layout, so I could loosen up while an assistant pro looked for a member to pair me with.

Between shots, Travis told me that he and his daughter's mother had met in one of the neighboring states but had never been married. She had moved back to Nebraska and married somebody else. I wondered silently if his daughter's birth certificate branded her with a scarlet "I" as mine had done to me. I like to think that as a society we've grown past that. The box marked ILLEGITIMATE on my birth certificate was a burden that filled me with a sense of inferiority and shame. For most of my early life, innocent questions about my family made me want to disappear. I would turn mute and hope that no one asked me about my parents directly. I eventually came to realize that how I lived my life was more important than how it had started. My hope was that Travis's daughter would come to understand that earlier in her life than I had.

I also prayed that her stepfather wasn't the monster mine was.

The assistant pro soon found a member who was delighted to have me play with him and his brother. Gary Albrecht was a charismatic lawyer from Denver. He also worked with the Colorado Golf Association to help disadvantaged youths pursue better lives through a caddie and leadership program at CommonGround Golf Course, the group's Doak-designed public course in Aurora, outside Denver. Most of the kids in his program were minorities. Gary was the embodiment of what I was traveling across the country to find: someone who truly cared about and supported the dreams of others.

Gary immediately pointed out that there are no tee markers at Ballyneal. Instead, you tell your caddie what distance you want to play, and he points you to a spot to tee off. It's a way to add your own touch to Doak's canvas of natural, twisting contours routed through wildflowers, weeds, and dunes.

Doak eases you into the course with a short and easy first hole, then pounds you with a monstrous 460-yard par four along a narrow fairway dotted with bunkers off its edges. He follows that with a 125-yard downhill par three, which, on that beautiful Thursday afternoon, looked to me like the golf equivalent of sacred ground.

Travis and I agreed on a sand wedge. It was the perfect club: my ball landed on a slope just left of the flag, and we all stared in silence as it slid toward the cup. Making a hole in one was probably the most challenging of all the goals I had set for my Top 100 quest. My heart pounded as the ball closed in on the cup. It took a brief peek into the hole before continuing along the edge and stopping ten inches past. Close but no cigar.

On the way to the green, Gary told me a story about a friend's hole in one. Initially, I only half listened, too disappointed by my near ace to care about somebody else's moment of glory. But I perked up when he said that his friend, Tom, who had been forty-four at the time, had been diagnosed with stage IV cancer. Tom had played while tumors were growing throughout his brain and spine. It would be his final full round of golf.

They were playing at Glen Falls Country Club in upstate New York with two of Tom's other friends. As they approached the first par three, Gary talked about it being the day they needed an ace. Nobody came close to making one on that hole, nor on the two par threes that followed. The final par three, it turned out, was the course's last hole.

I was hanging on Gary's every word. That last par three was playing exactly 136 yards—they all noted that 136 was the number on the house where Tom had grown up. The coincidence was hard to ignore. Gary and the other two friends hit their shots onto the green. As Tom stood over his ball, Gary called out, "Okay, everybody, think one. *Think one!*"

Tom's short-iron shot looked great from the start. Nobody moved or said a word. The ball landed on the green with the others before releasing to the hole. It tapped the flagstick, then stopped dead on the lip of the cup. Still silence. A split second later—a lifetime in golf—it slipped in.

Everybody erupted in cheers.

Eighty-one days later, Tom was gone.

I fought back tears as I tapped in for a birdie. Gary's story made the hole far more memorable than it would have been had my own ball dropped in for an ace.

Throughout the back nine, Gary and his brother reminisced about their childhoods, bantering about their scuffles while sharing bunk beds in a bedroom crammed with their three other brothers. I told them they had been lucky to have multiple beds. When my mother and siblings and I had lived with her sister and five children in Needmore, six of us had been pressed together into a single bed like canned sardines—three with our heads at the head and three with our heads at the foot. I had spent most of those nights trying to keep my sister's feet out of my mouth.

We all laughed. In the farthest corner of northeast Colorado, only a dozen or so miles from the Nebraska line, it was liberating to share a childhood story and not feel like an imposter in a world so different from the one where I had grown up.

———

AFTER DRIVING TWO AND A half tedious hours through the flattop land-scape of central Nebraska, I finally saw the terrain give way to rolling dunes blanketed with sunflowers. My only signal to stop was a small wooden sign that read SAND HILLS GOLF CLUB—there wasn't a club-house or golf course in sight. I shouldn't have been surprised; with its fair-ways and greens placed only where the topography deemed they fit and the bunkers shaped—and continuously reshaped—by the wind howling across the dunes, this far-flung layout has been called by *Golf Digest* "un-doubtedly the most natural golf course in America."

Unfortunately, golf took a back seat that morning to my day's real priority: playing the course in less than three hours. If I missed the last flight from Denver to Atlanta, there wasn't any other way I could get across the country before the sun came up the next morning.

During the years my stepfather had lived with us, my siblings and I had often waited hours for him to get home to take our family someplace he'd promised: a cousin's house, Galveston's beach, the park. Inevitably, he'd show up drunk long after it was too late to go anywhere. Then he'd yell at my mother. She'd scream back. In our tiny house, his voice thundered. Arguments usually ended with him hitting her as my siblings and I huddled in the next room, Jen's arms wrapped around all of us. Despite those beatings and that chaos, having a father figure around remained for me the closest thing to normal we had. When Frank didn't show up, it only served to remind me that we weren't normal at all.

I want my kids to understand that it's normal to keep your promises, normal to do what you say you're going to do. It was imperative for me to get back to Atlanta in time to do just what I'd said.

So I basically played Sand Hills to punch my ticket. I didn't even look for anyone to play with that day. I just wanted to get around the course as fast as possible.

I joined Riley, my caddie, after I finally found the first tee beyond the dirt and the dunes, near Ben's Porch, a way station with restrooms, drinks, and a grill. The starter, Cameron, who had been alerted to how rushed I was, promised that he'd have a burger waiting for me after my round.

I reminded Riley of my deadline and then teed off. We sailed through Sand Hills' winding fairways, mostly avoiding the spongy rough, tall fescue, and scraggly bunkers. We played the front nine in less than an hour and a half and didn't catch sight of the group ahead of us until the fifteenth hole. They'd been moving pretty fast themselves. With four holes left, playing at a pace that guaranteed we'd finish in time, I told Riley I wanted to slow down to try to break ninety for the first time that week. I needed to par at least three of the final four holes and not blow up on any of them. I got lucky on fifteen when I missed the green to the left but chipped on and made my putt to save par. I then made a pain-free par on sixteen.

Even with the slower pace, we caught the group in front of us on the seventeenth hole. They saw us waiting and motioned for me to play through. Having a gallery on the short par three added a little drama to my push to finish strong. But my soundless iron let me know I'd struck a good shot. The ball hit the green and stopped twelve feet below the cup. The four-man gallery applauded. My two-putt par ensured that I'd break 90 even if I bogeyed the final hole. I parred it and finished with an 88.

As I hurried past Ben's Porch, Cameron handed me a cheeseburger wrapped in aluminum foil before I dashed to my car. Thirty minutes outside Denver, I called National and told the agent I'd be coming in hot; I'd have no time to park. I explained that I needed to get home to keep a promise to my son.

"We'll have someone waiting outside the terminal," she said.

We made the exchange like a car swapping drivers during the legendary 24 Hours of Le Mans race.

I phoned Erika as the plane pushed off the gate to let her know I'd be home in time to take Jordan to his event. When I had been his age, I had just hoped that my stepfather wouldn't show up drunk and beat my mother. Jordan just hoped that I'd find a decent parking spot and not embarrass him around his friends.

It was a small but profound marker of how much I'd succeeded. That was what my kids' lives turned on now—not hunger, not danger, not abandonment, but Dragon Con. They would understand something that it had taken me far too long to see and that no amount of money could ever buy them: keeping your word is normal.

CHAPTER TEN

CANYATA

Wilderness gave us knowledge. Wilderness made us human.
We came from here. Perhaps that is why so many of us feel a strong
bond to this land called Serengeti; it is the land of our youth.

—Boyd Norton

We called it "the country." Mount Zion was an unincorporated settlement just a few miles west of downtown Huntsville, yet it felt a world away. There were no WHITES ONLY signs posted around Mount Zion. There were only Blacks.

The few named roads in Mount Zion bore the monikers of the families of the landowners who lined them, such as Archie Road, named for Ernest Archie and his clan, and Murray Lane, named for a family whose house was one of the nicest in the area. There were fewer than ten other families nearby, but each had enough land that only one other house was visible from my grandparents' porch. Each family's property was set apart by barbed-wire fences, "gaps," and ruts carved out of the dirt with a grader to keep each household's cattle from moseying into somebody else's pasture. Everyone shared the same phone line, though each phone had its own distinct ring. Calls were connected by an operator at a switchboard that generated the cadence of the ring of the family being called. There were no commercial enterprises in Mount Zion, no stores or repair shops or grocers; folks mostly raised their own food, sewed their own clothes, birthed their own babies. They did their own house and car repairs. If they needed help with something, they called a neighbor.

I spent almost every boyhood summer out there with my grandparents. Their world was endlessly wild and intriguing and thrilling and scary. It was rolling prairie, thick in spots with red oaks and sweet gums and thorny bushes, opening into pastures pocked with daisies, low cactus, hoof prints, cow dung. Pigs, deer, foxes, snakes, armadillos—they all thrived. Birds squawked or sang with a clear, urgent purpose—to warn, to mate. Tadpoles roiled the water in the metal bucket I hauled back from a nearby pond so we could wash our clothes or bathe. For drinking and cooking, we drew water from the well or caught rain as it ran off the house's tin roof.

I spent a lot of time out there by myself, but I never felt alone. Under Texas's high blue sky and fast white clouds, with heat that rarely dipped below ninety degrees, I whooped and shooed cows up and down the cuts and ravines, like a cowboy on a twenty-yard cattle drive. I couldn't believe my good luck whenever I came across a pile of junk—old cans, jars, busted toys, a car part—hidden under thick, overgrown brush. I tried to imagine who it had all once belonged to and why it had been discarded. The toys didn't look any more unusable than the ones I played with or improvised every day.

It's not a leap to suggest that one of the reasons I love golf so much is because the open fairways and deep, tree-lined roughs often take me back to the world I immersed myself in while roaming across those boundless East Texas prairies. Propelled by fond memories of my boyhood treasure hunts in "the country," I will search through bushes and deep rough for an errant golf ball forever.

I HAD CANYATA GOLF CLUB all to myself. That's almost a given there. The club has no members, no professional golf staff, no caddies—just a course superintendent and his grounds crew. Set off State Highway 1 in central Illinois amid corn as high as an elephant's eye, Canyata is the semiprivate playground of a steam boiler and auto-racing magnate named Gerald Forsythe. Plenty of fanatical golfers have never heard of the place; it hosts fewer than two hundred rounds a year.

Forsythe originally intended to build three holes on his farm—a par three, par four, and par five—for his family and friends to enjoy. But the practice layout quickly grew to nine holes and then to eighteen after the course architect, Michael Benkusky, convinced Forsythe that he had the potential for a singular creation in the middle of nowhere. Only four years after it opened all eighteen holes in 2004, Canyata (a Kickapoo word for "backwoods") became a perennial Top 100 course.

Though the course comprises more than three hundred acres, I still rolled right by it. By the time my GPS announced, a couple of miles after I'd passed the entrance, that I'd arrived, I was already somewhere around the back of the course, surrounded by endless farmland. I surely wasn't the first to get lost. The course is hidden by design.

"Mr. Forsythe wanted to block off everything from around the property," Benkusky has said of the design, which includes holes that can't be seen from the holes that run right beside them. "We started building mounds (from the dirt dug to create the lakes) and kept building them higher and higher around the edges of the property."

I finally called the guy whose Chicago-based golf management company oversees Canyata and who had arranged my reservation, and he quickly guided me back to the narrow road that leads past a pasture of llamas to Forsythe's house. Mike Boudreau, the course superintendent, met me in the adjacent parking lot. There's no clubhouse or pro shop, but there is a little log cabin with lockers and free snacks—"free" in that they were included in my $750 greens fee.

I was the only one on the course that day, and I asked Mike to join me. He was prepping for a large group coming to play the next day but said he'd catch up with me on the back nine. That gave me two hours of solitude in paradise. The man who, as a boy, had never had a bed to himself, let alone a room, now had a world-class golf course with no one on it but him.

I usually play briskly—following my earliest piece of golf advice: play fast if you can't play well—but I moved across Canyata deliberately, taking in every sight and sound, feeling in harmony with nature during the silences between strokes. Once again, I was my six-year-old self—sporting golf shoes, riding a golf cart, but still thrilled to be roaming that wild land alone.

Hole after hole, I watched my ball sail over the pristine morning dew. Then, with my foot pressing gently on the accelerator, I'd slow roll my cart between the greens and the next tee box. On the third hole, a 203-yard downhill par three with water backing the green, my ball landed so far from the cup that I had time to pick up my camera after hitting my putt and snap several shots of the ball rolling straight for the pin—which it hit, leaving me an easy par.

The next hole struck me as Benkusky's best work. The pond, the contours of the deep green fairway, the placement of the bunkers, and the overall length of the 440-yard hole—a secluded pasture filled with golf adventures—were at once stunning and intimidating. It continued like that for the next five holes, where the only footprints in the dew-covered fairways were my own.

Mike joined me at the turn. As I reset my tempo after playing alone for nine holes, I watched him birdie almost every hole and wondered out loud if he was just that good or if he had set up the pins that day to favor his game. He told me that no matter where the flags are, you still have to get the putts to drop. His wise words reminded me of all those evenings I had spent selling encyclopedias: no matter how well I presented my sales pitch to the families who let me into their homes, I still had to close the deal.

On one of the holes, needing to make a twelve-foot putt to extend my string of four pars in a row, Mike offered to help me with the read.

He gave me the line; I stroked the putt and watched the ball roll into the cup. We smiled at each other. I realized that he knew the contours of those greens as well as the lines in the palms of his hands—as well as I had known the gaps and ravines and fences on my grandparents' farm.

Between Mike's birdies and my pars on Canyata's soft fairways and hospitable putting surfaces, I learned that Mike's son and Kevin Hall, the first African American to play golf for Ohio State University, had been on the same college team. I'd first heard of Kevin, who had lost his hearing at the age of two because of meningitis, when he had received the Charlie Sifford exemption to play in the 2017 Genesis Invitational, an annual PGA Tour event held at the Riviera Country Club in Los Angeles. The exemption, granted each year to one minority golfer, is named in honor of the first African American to play on the PGA Tour. Sifford had been blocked from playing on the tour by its Caucasian-only clause, which wasn't rescinded until the early sixties, when the California attorney general threatened to prohibit Tour events in the state as long as the clause was in effect. Sifford's journey has been an inspiration to many, including me; a statue of him as a boy stands on the front porch of our vacation home on Kiawah Island.

At the end of the round, Mike told me to play as many holes as I could fit in on that mid-September day. But eighteen were enough for me.

I'll never forget playing the front nine alone without ever feeling lonely.

———

The next day, after driving from the cornfields of Illinois to the banks of the Milwaukee River, I felt as if I'd been beamed into a whole other place: a bygone era of privilege and power.

The Milwaukee Country Club exuded all of that. I walked through a locker room outfitted with a saloon-style bar, polished-wood tables, and rows of dark lockers set beneath a vaulted ceiling with rafters of solid exposed timber. It felt like the kind of place where, back in the day, local power brokers would meet to hash out deals in a haze of cigar smoke—a place where someone who looked like me would have been unwelcome. It was the kind of place where I had previously felt uncomfortable.

But now I didn't feel out of place. A couple months earlier, I had been on pins and needles virtually everywhere I played. I was either a guest playing alongside complete strangers or playing unaccompanied. Either way, I felt like an interloper. I had the looming sense that one mistake or inappropriate move, on or off the course, would doom my quest. Word of any miscue—not replacing a divot, bringing up some awkward incident from my past at the wrong moment—would spread instantly over the elite-list transom and I'd be branded as a guy you didn't want to invite.

Being Black only magnified my apprehension. Over the course of my quest, apart from four clubs where I was hosted by Black members and two others where Black friends joined me, I only saw one other golfer at any of the private clubs I played who looked like me. Needless to say, I didn't blend in. If I made a mistake, it would be on full display.

By the time I showed up at Milwaukee, however, I'd been in that situation frequently enough that I'd gotten used to it. I felt at ease, despite the club's exquisitely throwback trappings. There was nothing to justify my skittishness.

I also got onto the course the way I'd hoped to navigate my way onto my list's harder-to-play venues: via an unforced mix of serendipity, six degrees of separation, and buy-in. It was classic I-know-a-guy-who-knows-a-guy, set into motion by a stranger who seemed to be as eager to see me succeed in my quest as I was.

It all started on the driving range at Prairie Dunes, where a few months earlier I had started talking with the guy hitting balls in the slot next to mine. As we aimed our shots toward a lone tree at the end of the open field, we rambled for a minute about where we were from and what we did. It turned out that Kurt, from Austin, had an uncle who'd worked for ExxonMobil. I recognized his name immediately; we'd worked together closely for years in Virginia. And just like that, in the middle of the wheat fields of Kansas, another stranger and I found our link. When I told Kurt what I was up to, he stopped his practice routine, said, "I have someone you want to meet," and walked away. A few minutes later, he returned with a friend named Mike who wanted to know everything about what I was attempting.

"You have a staff arranging all of this for you?" Mike asked.

Before I could open my mouth to tell him I didn't, Kurt jumped in with "Yeah. You and me."

This strategy of relying on strangers, which I'd worried was too ambitious after the coolness of my round at Kinloch, was now starting to unfold as beautifully as the petals on a blossoming rose. Mike asked which courses I was having the most trouble gaining access to. I told him that after talking to everyone I knew who had any connection to Wisconsin, I still hadn't found a member for the Milwaukee Country Club—in fact, I still hadn't found anyone who'd heard of it, with its small, clubby membership.

Mike smiled. "I have a friend whose brother is a member," he said, and with that we exchanged contacts before he went off to the first tee.

Pat, the energy executive and member Mike introduced me to, met me in the clubhouse. We shared the instant comradery of strangers linked by a common friend, common profession, and common pastime. Then Pat introduced me to the other two guys in our foursome, and it turned out that one of them, Danny Whigham, was a club champion at my club back in Atlanta. How had Milwaukee seemed so tough to get onto?

Members of Milwaukee Country Club have to start their rounds on the tenth hole when they bring a guest during peak hours. That was already going to throw my linear brain off, but then I agreed with Danny's suggestion that we play from the tips—7,100 yards—on that mesmerizing course running through a bucolic valley along the Milwaukee River. I figured I'd played well from 6,800 yards at Canyata the day before, so why not go for it? Well, there were at least two reasons I should've thought of: I'm not that good and don't hit the ball a mile, for starters. I spent the next four hours overswinging on fairways dotted with large, shallow bunkers and elevated greens protected by slightly deeper ones. Trying to match Danny's long, straight drives and pin seeking approach shots was an exercise in futility.

Rarely had I put in so much effort for so little return. When I was eight years old, I had walked what felt like miles upon miles, knocking on countless doors. I was peddling packages of flower seeds I'd ordered from a company that advertised on the back of a Superman comic book. I sold every package it sent and earned a prize. But that, too, turned out to be an exercise in futility. I never got my prize. My stepfather, Frank, was supposed to take the money I made and convert it into a money order to send to the seed company. He never did. When I finally asked him about it, he told me we needed food more than I needed that toy. I have no idea whether he actually spent the money on food—I sincerely doubt it—but I was devastated and started crying. That set him off: he called me a sissy and beat me with a fan belt he had lying around from an old car. For the next week, I wore long sleeves to school to hide the welts left by the hard rubber when I tried to block his enraged whipping with my skinny arms.

A year and a half later, Frank disappeared. He simply abandoned us. My mother reported him missing to the police, but it was two years before he resurfaced. I remember him standing in the living room of our shotgun house trying to explain his disappearance to the man who had been his best friend. The friend held a gun in his jacket pocket as Frank told him that I had caused problems between him and my mother. That was what he called the conflict between my mother and him over the beatings he had given me. Even then, I could not conceive of a grown man blaming a child for his actions, yet I carried the pain and guilt of that burden with me for the rest of my childhood. Eventually, it became part of my motivation to do better so that I could do better for my mother and siblings.

As comfortable as I finally felt at the Milwaukee Country Club, I didn't share those stories there.

As we stood on the tee box of our final hole, a guy with a tan, boyish face stepped swiftly in our direction before he called out to me, a little out of breath, "Are you the guy playing the country's top one hundred courses?" When I nodded yes, he asked if I had a host for Olympia Fields Country Club near Chicago. I didn't. He handed me his card. "You do now," he said. "The guys in the golf shop told me you were here. Call, and I'll host you."

<hr>

ARCADIA BLUFFS GOLF CLUB IN Arcadia, Michigan, is one of the twelve resort courses in the *Golf Digest* Top 100 rankings. Though I was starting to build momentum in gaining access to private courses, I was still relying on resort courses, where I could play as a single, for opportunities to meet new contacts. Playing as a single was how I'd gotten on at Milwaukee, and I made the drive from there around the bottom of Lake Michigan and north to Arcadia—with a weekend stop in Chicago for a rendezvous with Erika to celebrate her forty-eighth birthday—to see if I could repeat my luck.

As had happened at Blackwolf Run a couple of months earlier, the group I was paired with when I had made the reservation a month earlier had canceled. But this time there was no two-hour wait for the next pairing opportunity. I was immediately put with a group already on the first tee. I had no time to warm up or wait for the caddie who had been assigned for my original tee time.

Fortunately for me on that mid-September day along Lake Michigan's eastern shore, my life and David Enderby's converged. Standing outside the pro shop as I headed to the first tee, he needed a loop, and I needed a caddie. The starter introduced us. He grabbed my bag, and we hurried to join three guys about half my age teeing off from the tips. I put my ego in check and moved up to the tees that were playing from 6,900 yards.

David proved his prowess as a seasoned looper on the very first hole as he guided me to an easy opening par along a treacherous fairway lined with straggly bunkers carved into fescue-covered mounds. His read on my birdie putt was precise. He traced the line my ball should follow. I rolled it along that exact line, but it stopped one revolution from falling into the center of the cup.

The neatly manicured third fairway snaked past a plethora of small but cunning bunkers before appearing to fall into the deep blue sea; hidden from sight, there was another hole between it and the shore. The illusion was stunning. As David expertly guided me along the fairways cutting through the bluffs along the shore, he asked if I was planning to play Oakland Hills Country Club, just outside Detroit. I nodded. "I grew up caddying there," he said. In fact, when he was sixteen, he had caddied for a golfer who had played a practice round there with Arnold Palmer before the 1972 PGA Championship. Back then, tour players were not allowed to bring their own caddies. They had to randomly draw local ones from a hat.

David had also seen Jack Nicklaus hit a 1-iron in 1977 while he was caddying for another golfer at Jackie Gleason's annual tournament at Inverrary Country Club in Florida. I felt honored to have a looper on my bag who had caddied on the tour, one who had met the King and the Golden Bear, no less! David became a regular on the tour in 1976. The most notable golfers he caddied for were Craig Stadler, during his first event on the PGA Tour; Jim Thorpe; and Calvin Peete. At the time, most pro golfers had Black caddies, so it was unusual to see a white caddie carrying the bag of one of the few Black golfers on the tour. David told me he had caught grief from both sides. White caddies had given him a hard time for carrying a Black man's bag. Black caddies had said he was taking a job from them.

David's response to both: "The money spends the same."

Each nine on Arcadia Bluffs has the uncommon setup of three par fours, three par threes, and three par fives. The fifth hole—the third par five on the front nine—is the longest and most challenging of them all. The fairway has more than fifteen bunkers, including one that runs from about a hundred yards out from the green to its front edge. For a duffer like me, it's the stuff of nightmares. But thanks to David's skillful club selection and shot guidance, two swings and a putt after hitting to one of the scariest fairways on the course, I walked off the green with a birdie. David's expert advice and PGA Tour caddying stories had a soothing effect on my game. The threesome we were playing with seemed to fade into the background. It was as though it were just the two of us.

I'm not a very coachable person, especially when the coaching comes from people who are critical rather than constructive. I was ridiculed so often growing up because of how big my dreams were that I came to trust my own judgment above almost everyone else's. During our time together walking the fairways on Arcadia Bluffs, David earned my trust.

After my approach shot on the eleventh hole landed on the steeply sloping green, then rolled back, stopping just off the front edge, David said, "I need you to hit a Willie Nelson." Befuddled, I asked, "What in the world is a Willie Nelson?" Golf is full of names for shots. There's the Linda Ronstadt—my ball blew by you ("Blue Bayou"). The son-in-law shot—wasn't quite what you wanted, but it'll do. Or the mother-in-law ball—looks good leaving. Now David explained the Willie Nelson: "You need to get the ball as high as you can."

After the round, as David was cleaning and artfully arranging my clubs in my bag, he asked, "Do you have a host for Oakland Hills?"

I told him someone was working on it.

"They don't need to," he responded. "You took care of me today by giving me a loop, so I'm going to take care of you." He told me to expect a call from someone at Oakland Hills that evening.

Sure enough, I got a call that night from Leo Savoie, the club's past president. Leo told me that he and David had been childhood friends and caddied together as young boys at Oakland Hills. Without my even asking, he said he'd be happy to host me and a couple of buddies.

Professionalism. Class.

And more important for my task at hand: momentum!

———

SIXTY-FIVE HUNDRED OF THE MOST terrifying yards in golf. That's how I would describe Crystal Downs Country Club, located in the northernmost part of Michigan's Lower Peninsula. My host, Brent Rector, a retired Grand Rapids lawyer and USGA rules official, seemed to take great pleasure in the toll the sloping fairways, diabolical greens, and pesky fescue took on my pride. I four-putted the first green. Brent had warned that I should leave my approach shots below the hole since the greens at Crystal Downs slope from back to front. I did. Then I watched the ball roll back down to my feet after my first putt failed to reach the cup. My second putt rolled past the cup and stayed, leaving a fast downhill third putt. And so it went, hole after hole.

After playing two Alister MacKenzie courses—Augusta National and Crystal Downs—where I had struck the ball with my putter more than with my driver and irons combined, I wasn't feeling too fond of short courses defended by devilish greens. The most unusual of them all was the severely undulated seventh green at Crystal Downs, which looked as though it had been built atop a giant kidney bean. As a college student, an engineer, and an executive, I've solved some complex problems over the course of my life, but figuring out the line for my birdie putt on that par-four seventh hole was beyond my capabilities.

Brent, seeing how perplexed I looked, said, "Watch this." He proceeded to hit a ball along the slope on the left side of the green, another along the slope on the right side, and yet another down the center. All three balls ended up directly in front of the hole. I took the center route and watched the ball meander toward the hole. It still took me two more putts to find the bottom of the cup.

And then there was what Brent referred to as the "Seventy-six Trombone hole," so called because the ideal tee shot on the narrow, winding, tree-patrolled fairway, which slopes drastically from right to left, was one that landed near a sprinkler head marked with the number 76—the number of yards it was from the green. It was also a takeoff of Meredith Willson's *The Music Man*, in which seventy-six trombones led the big parade. A drive to any other position in the fairway leaves an almost impossible shot to one of the most severe back-to-front sloping greens on the course. My tee shot landed within a few yards of the sprinkler head. My high, arcing approach landed twenty feet right of the pin.

Didn't matter. I four-putted for a double bogey.

All I could do was laugh at myself as I sat under the clear blue Michigan sky with Brent and his guest for a postround drink. I think Alister and I will have a little chat when I make it to that great golf course in the sky.

Golf and life are hard enough without being extra.

CHAPTER ELEVEN

PLAINFIELD

More and more, when I single out the person who inspired me most,
I go back to my grandfather.

—James Earl Jones

I was struck by the gentleness of the elderly man who lifted the golf bag from the trunk of my car in front of the colonial clubhouse at Plainfield Country Club in bucolic Middlesex County, New Jersey. His smile disarmed me. While we chatted before I went inside, he told me he'd found peace and purpose greeting golfers at the bag drop after he'd lost his wife of many years.

My grandfather, Jesse James, lost his wife nine years before he died, and he found a similar peace and purpose serving others.

Pa Pa was the most consistent male role model in my life. In fact, to my young eyes, he was much bigger than life—tall, slim, and dark, with giant workingman's hands that seemed to engulf whatever they held, including me. His baritone could fill any room; despite having had only a third-grade education, he read the Bible to himself every day—aloud, softly. My earliest memories are of him strumming a guitar and warbling gospel songs with me on his knee, looking up at the kindest face I knew.

He was a model husband: a hardworking provider and his family's spiritual leader. He loved his wife and was never threatened by her strength; he considered her his equal, a pioneering notion for the time and place. He helped her with whatever needed doing, regardless of whether it was considered a "man's job" or a "woman's job": washing the dishes, hanging clothes to dry. (The only chore my grandmother did unfailingly: cook his meals.)

To those who listened to him on Sundays speaking from the pulpit of the church he had built and from which he took no money, he was Elder James. But to his family, he was just Pa Pa, as salt of the earth as they come. Having lost a child, he had a way of feeling other folks out and making them feel better about themselves, as if that helped heal his own ache.

My sister Jen remembers a heart-to-heart she had with him on a train to California after our grandmother passed. He told her that after his daughter had died at twelve, he and our grandmother had prayed for another girl—and then Jen was born. He loved her like a daughter. At the time, Jen had just gone through a divorce; his words comforted her and boosted her self-worth.

That was my strong, indominable, gentle grandfather.

During the years between my grandmother's passing and his own, he found solace as a caretaker for an elderly white couple, although they were about the same age as he was. When I visited during those years, I'd take him on drives along the dirt roads of Mount Zion, where he had spent most of his life and where I'd spent so much of my boyhood.

During one of those drives, as my car kicked up dust and he and I gazed at the land that had once belonged to his ancestors, Pa Pa shared a family history passed down to him by his grandfather. He said that his father's father, Tiny Profit, had fled France after arriving from Africa and killing a man in a fight. (Rumor had it that the man had been decapitated.) Tiny had hopped on a ship to Central America and eventually made his way to East Texas, where he had fallen in love with an enslaved woman named Tankie.

As he possessed neither the means nor the legal standing to buy her out of bondage, their first child, a son, bore the last name of Tankie's master. The son's full name, whether by error or intent, was recorded in birth records as James James.

When news of the Emancipation Proclamation finally reached Texas, more than two years after its signing, Tankie was freed, and she and Tiny married. They had five more kids, but it was their first child, who by then everyone called Jim, who became my great-grandfather. Pa Pa said that Poppa Jim was a frugal man who had tried to do right by others, although it was also rumored that he'd killed two men. Everyone in our family held Poppa Jim in the highest regard, including my mother, who named me after him.

I was the thirteenth grandchild of Pa Pa and Jamama, which is what we called our grandmother, born Malentha Othella Jones. She was the seventh and last child of John Henry Jones, half Irish and half African American, and Mary Hayward Jones, a mix of African, Caucasian, and Cherokee. For me, one detail of that tangled heritage always jumped out: my mother's parents, their parents, and their parents' parents were all married. Three generations after slavery, it was I who had a birth certificate that bore the word ILLEGITIMATE.

Half a century later, that illegitimate thirteenth grandchild of Jesse and Malentha stood beside the sixth hole of his thirty-fourth Top 100 golf course. I'd hit an impeccably silent 8-iron on Plainfield's 141-yard, par-three sixth hole and watched as the ball arced over the surrounding traps, landed on the wavy green, plopped like a single raindrop a few feet from the hole—then rolled to within an inch of it.

Another almost ace that wasn't.

For a moment, I was stunned and elated, savoring the thrill of a nearly perfect shot. Then the magnitude of what I'd chosen to do hit me. After all the miles and random encounters and fairway saves of the first thirty-four courses, I still had almost twice that many left to play. The weight of it felt enormous. My dream suddenly became a job, and the job became a burden.

As for all those ancestors of mine? I'm guessing that they would've been disbelieving, proud—and put out by my first-world griping.

———

PLAINFIELD HAD BEEN A LAST-MINUTE addition to my whirlwind trip north. For almost five months, I'd played every course as scheduled. Then, days before I was supposed to play the Country Club of Brookline, near Boston, my host suffered a season-ending shoulder injury. I reshuffled the end of my week on the fly. I swapped out the Country Club on Friday with Long Island's Bethpage Black Course at Bethpage State Park, a move made possible because it was my list's only public course, and replaced Bethpage Black on Thursday with Plainfield, thanks to the pro at my club in Atlanta. I'd still finish my weekend trip in Ohio, only now I'd be flying there from New York instead of Boston.

It turned out fate hadn't finished messing with me. A major accident on the New Jersey Turnpike turned what should've been a one-hour cruise into a three-hour crawl. My playing partners and I finally rolled through the gates of Hudson National Golf Club in Croton-on-Hudson, New York, an hour past our tee time. With sunset looming in less than four hours, we worried that we wouldn't make it to what some consider the most picturesque holes on the course, a Fazio design perched on a plateau along a bend in the Hudson River.

The clouds were fluffy and white when we finally set out around three o'clock. Our caddies warned that we'd have to play at an exceptionally fast pace to have any chance of finishing all eighteen holes.

Time wasn't our only foe. About halfway through the round, a single dark cloud appeared directly over our heads. A minute later, it unleashed a downpour as we scurried to find shelter. The twenty-five-minute delay virtually ensured that we wouldn't get to the final holes before dark.

By the twelfth, the setting sun made it difficult to see Fazio's deep bunkers with raised faces or where the greens' false fronts turned flat.

By the fifteenth, with the sun below the tree line, our caddies wanted to call it a day. But my partners, whom I knew only through a common acquaintance, insisted that we finish the round for my sake. They seemed as committed to my quest as I was.

We reached the 225-yard downhill par-three sixteenth as darkness swallowed the course. Somehow, we all managed to card a par. It was too dark to read the seventeenth green, so we hit our balls as close to the cup as we could, tapped in, then raced in complete darkness to the final tee box.

Lit only by starlight, our caddies parked themselves in the middle of the eighteenth fairway, sure that it was the safest place to stand while we hit our drives. They were right. Mine was the only ball we found. We all hit our approach shots from that spot and miraculously found all four balls on the green.

Fickle fate.

———

TWO WORDS THAT HAVE NEVER crossed my lips: "my dad." Yet standing in the parking lot at Bethpage State Park in Farmingdale, New York, one of the two strangers I'd asked about the process for getting on the course uttered those words almost every other sentence. The bond between Drew and his father, Tim, was as obvious as it was ironclad.

Tim, a former naval officer who worked for a defense contractor, lived in Connecticut. Drew, a scratch golfer, worked in insurance in Atlanta. Their trip to Bethpage was an annual ritual and a tribute to the course's cult status. It was all about golf, comfort be damned. The two of them planned to sleep overnight in their van, parking in the lot's first slot to ensure that they got the morning's lead-off tee time. A ranger would show up between 7:00 and 7:30 to issue numbered wristbands; the lower the number, the earlier you'd go out. Tim said that if I got there by 6:30, I'd likely get a time close to theirs.

I left my hotel before sunrise. When I got to Bethpage, the first twenty parking spots were already taken. I backed my car into the twenty-first slot and walked down to see Tim and Drew. Bethpage has five courses, and not everybody plays the Black Course. It's the most famous and most popular but also the most challenging. When Tiger won the 2002 U.S. Open there, he was the only player to finish under par.

I returned to my car to wait my turn, but Tim showed up a few minutes later and invited me to join him and his son in their slot and go out with them in the first group—an unexpectedly generous offer. They'd slept all night in a cramped van. I'd slept in a nice hotel bed.

On an asphalt lot at the Bethpage State Park Golf Course, aka "the people's country club," we strangers had become fast friends.

A warning greeted us in big black letters near the first tee: "The Black Course Is An Extremely Difficult Course Which We Recommend Only For Highly Skilled Golfers." The once private, now public course laid out among tall trees, ponds, and streams in the middle of a 1,500-acre state park is indeed a demanding one. Its lengthy fairways and deep bunkers placed strategically around pristine greens aren't easily navigated. Thick fescue bordering the fairways makes it virtually impossible for any ball lodged there to reach the green in regulation. But for once, I kept most of my shots in the fairway and avoided the deepest bunkers.

I finished with an 87—a duffer's rebuke to the warning sign that had greeted us.

CHAPTER TWELVE

PIKEWOOD

Many people will walk in and out of your life, but only true friends
will leave footprints in your heart.

—Eleanor Roosevelt

The Golf Club in New Albany, Ohio, is a private, men-only club. For a long time, that meant white men. That may be why, for decades, no one thought it might be inappropriate to tie a hangman's noose from a tree on the course.

One of my playing partners pointed from the sixteenth-hole tee box toward an aging oak next to the challenging par three's green. "That," he said, "is 'the tree.'"

It was only the second time during my quest that I'd played with all Black golfers. I'm not sure that "the tree" would have been mentioned otherwise. Michael Redd, a former NBA player who had grown up in nearby Columbus and starred at Ohio State University, told me he wouldn't have joined the club if the noose hadn't come down. A white member tried to justify its presence. He said the hole was deemed so hard that people had often joked they wanted to hang themselves after playing it. That sentiment was formalized by Fred Jones, the founder of the Pete Dye–designed course, when he had the noose strung up in the early 1970s after carding a series of disastrous scores on the hole.

Michael didn't care. The symbolism made it unacceptable regardless of the intent. I agreed. To me, it was no different from displaying the Confederate flag. No amount of historic relevance can wash away the hatred and evil it represents. I suspect that decent people of any race understand that. It's unclear what effect Michael's stand before joining had on the club's decision, but the noose quickly disappeared.

Sometimes racial slights are the result of unthinking insensitivity. I believe that was the case at the Golf Club. But there are times when slights are driven by obvious hatred, and they make even innocent intentions like those behind the noose more problematic.

Early in my career, when I worked at the Baytown refinery, someone began posting unequivocally racist flyers on hallway walls throughout the eight-story office building, casually referred to as the "White House" because of its bright white exterior. No one had a problem with calling the building the White House. The problem was the flyers with racist epithets. Some depicted Black people as monkeys.

Employees throughout the building, who had believed that there had been enough progress to make the workplace more accommodating to everyone, were embarrassed, even ashamed, by the anonymous flyers. Black employees saw them as a lingering sign that some people still thought we shouldn't be there. Management was incensed and secretly placed cameras throughout the building to catch the perpetrator.

Soon thereafter, I witnessed firsthand how decent people deal with intentional racial slights. While waiting for visitors in the lobby of the White House early one Monday morning, I noticed the refinery's top manager, Ben Markham, standing by himself next to the receptionist's desk, eyeing each arriving employee who passed him. Finally, when a senior engineer stepped through the building's glass entrance, Ben walked right up to him. I knew the engineer—a tall, slender guy—but not well. I had interacted with him a number of times on various projects. He'd never displayed any outward signs of racism. And until that moment, no one had considered him a suspect.

"We know it's you," I heard Ben say as he escorted the engineer straight out of the building. "We have you on tape. We have no room here for people like you."

Ben earned my unwavering respect that day. Without fanfare or spectacle, he took the matter into his own hands—as swiftly, efficiently, and forcefully as possible.

Just eight years earlier, when a coworker had shown me his grandfather's Klansman's hood as we inspected a tower inside the same refinery, I had simply nodded my head and continued on without another word. I had reacted similarly when a supervisor began daily meetings by placing a box of rocks that supposedly represented my intelligence in the middle of the conference table. I didn't feel comfortable raising those issues with anybody at the time because I didn't think anything constructive would come of it. The most likely outcome: I'd be labeled a troublemaker.

Over time, however, as the company hired more Black engineers and made a concerted effort to address issues around diversity and sensitivity, things started to improve. When an issue came up, it wasn't simply dismissed or chalked up to someone being a malcontent. It was handled.

Ben's approach that Monday morning in the early 1990s signaled to me and others throughout the White House that the type of harassment and racism I'd once accepted and dealt with on my own would no longer be tolerated.

That was leadership.

———

THERE IS A SEASON FOR everything, and October was my season for reunions.

John Sokol, the guy I'd met three months earlier in the short-game practice area at Merion, outside Philly, came through with his connections, as promised. In addition to hosting me at the Jack Nicklaus–designed—and redesigned and, in the case of some holes, re-redesigned—Muirfield

Village Golf Club, it was he who arranged for Kevin Reeves to host me at the Golf Club. Kevin, an electric power marketing exec at BP, and I met as strangers that day, though something familiar about him nagged at me. When he said he was former military, I dismissed the sensation that we'd met before; I figured it was just his standard-issue Black male officer look—tall, clean-shaven, low-cropped haircut, ramrod-straight posture—that rang a bell. It wasn't until that evening, when he and his wife had me over for dinner at their house, that it hit me: twenty years earlier, Erika and I had briefly spoken to them during a mutual friend's wedding at a country church in Rocky Mount, North Carolina. It's a small world, and golf shrinks it even further.

It was Kevin who had invited Michael Redd, along with Charles Patton, a friend he'd once worked with, to join us. Not only was it one of the rare rounds I played with Black golfers, it was also the tallest foursome I'd ever played in. Michael stood at six foot six, Kevin at six foot five, and me at six foot four. We made Charles look like a shrimp at six feet even.

Michael and Kevin took advantage of their height, bombing high-flying drives over the long waste areas sprinkled throughout the course. My height didn't help much; I was always fifty yards behind them. The Golf Club course contains every element you'd expect in a Pete Dye design: wooden timbers embedded in the bunker slopes, a red boxcar bridge, and short par fives that force even long hitters to lay up lest they succumb to the hazards, the curvature of the fairway, the waste areas, the fescue.

Beginning with Crooked Stick, the first course to earn him national acclaim back in 1964, to the Dye Course at White Oak, an aptly named Florida layout he designed before his death in 2020, Dye used at least one of these features in virtually all his designs. The round at the Golf Club played like a Pete Dye tribute course.

My most profound reunion came in the middle of the month in Morgantown, West Virginia, the night before I played Pikewood National Golf Club.

It had been a decade since I'd seen Carole Dobrick. Now past eighty, she was as sprightly as I remembered her, if moving a little more deliberately. Her smile broke through the years and warmed my heart. I'd met her and her husband, Joe, not long after I turned twenty. They were financial supporters of the Fellowship of Christian Athletes (FCA), a nonprofit sports ministry.

I've never been very religious, but faith has always been an important part of my life. My faith was formed early while attending church all day on Sundays, from just after sunrise to well past sunset during the summers my siblings and I spent in the country. We'd head out early with Pa Pa and Jamama, leaving their house for a three-mile hike—shooing cows as we crossed open fields, attracting ticks on the narrow path through the woods (we couldn't pick them off until the next morning), arousing neighbors' barking dogs. We'd finally arrive at our destination, the Galilee Church of God in Christ, just in time for nine o'clock Sunday school.

We'd close out the day around 10:00 p.m. after Pa Pa's baritone floated from the pulpit throughout the little building atop deep, loud chords that vibrated from the musicians' instruments—organ, guitar, bass, drums—during his evening sermon. We kids, dead tired, would pile into the back of some deacon's truck for the ride back to Pa Pa and Jamama's tiny house. We'd bed down together on the floor on pallets of the multicolored patchwork quilts Jamama made from clothing too old and worn out for us to wear.

I'm not much of a churchgoer these days, but those Sundays full of scripture grounded me in a faith I still carry.

Carole and Joe's donations helped make my work with FCA possible and allowed me to draw a paycheck. They also practically adopted me. I ate at their kitchen table and traveled with them to FCA meetings all over the DC area. Carole and Joe didn't have kids, but they treated me like a son. They weren't some rich benefactors; they were ordinary folks who taught high school and coached in nearby Rockville, Maryland, and believed that helping kids was the ultimate expression of their faith.

Joe and Carole were white. Yet race never played a part in our relationship. Often during my childhood and young adult life, when I was alone with whites, they would tell me that I was not like other Blacks. For some reason they thought I would take that as a compliment. To them, I was different because I "spoke well" or I was "smart" or I was "ambitious." To them, that meant I wasn't "Black"—that I was just a colored white person. To me, it was one of the most identity-erasing acts someone could commit.

Whenever I tried explaining just how racist I thought the statement was, hoping I might inspire people to confront their biases, I was almost always disappointed. Instead, I found that most people clung desperately to their preconceived stereotypes like a rock climber holding on to the edge of a cliff. Not once in all the time I spent with Carole and Joe did they say anything so ridiculous and insulting. They always accepted me for who I was. They showed me that people could support the dreams of others simply because they, too, believed in those dreams.

Back in 2006, when we lived in Charlottesville, I drove Erika, her mother, and our two kids across the Shenandoah and Allegheny Mountains to Morgantown so they could meet two of the people who had influenced my abiding faith in the innate goodness of people.

Now, the evening before my round at Pikewood, Carole and I sat in a booth inside an Italian restaurant near my hotel. We mostly reminisced about working together with Joe, whom Carole had lost years earlier, to influence the lives of young, mostly Black athletes nearly four decades before. I often wonder how the lives of those young men turned out—whether we had made a difference. We visited schools in poor, often desperate neighborhoods all over the city, but there was one kid in particular at Spingarn High School—a massive redbrick structure that was the last segregated school built in DC before *Brown v. Board of Education*—whom

I wished I'd kept up with. He reminded me of the boy I'd been: an average football player, bright and disciplined but also unsophisticated and humble. I'd lost track of him after I graduated from college and immersed myself in my career at Exxon.

Who knows: maybe I'd passed him during one of the rounds along my quest. Maybe we'd even played together. It wouldn't have been any more unlikely for him to be there than it was for me.

───────

THE MORNING AFTER MY DINNER with Carole, I found myself at a place some consider heaven.

The course was designed and built atop limestone deposits by two local mining executives and golf enthusiasts. It was their first and last course. I've been fly-fishing once in my life, on the Bighorn River in Montana. I whipped my line through the air like a conductor directing an orchestra and, over the course of the day, hooked eighteen trout. I've never been fly-fishing again. So I get why John Raese and Bob Gwynne stopped after building that one golf course: it's hard to improve on perfection.

Pikewood is the hardest course that you or anyone else is likely to play—as unabashedly tough as it is aesthetically pleasing. It seduces you with its beauty while simultaneously destroying your score one swing at a time. It's also long; the shortest tee boxes play over 7,000 yards. Some of the greens appear to have boundless edges that fall into vast valleys. A cascading waterfall accents the par-three fifth hole, and the eighth hole, with a fairway that wraps around a gorge, is so bold that John and Bob named it "Audacity." When I tried to cut off too much of the gorge there, I carded an eight.

My host at Pikewood was a member named David Smith, a turbocharged businessman who drives fast cars and loves expensive boats. Together we spent the morning taking what some afficionados call "The Greatest Walk in Golf."

It took me 105 brutally scenic strokes to finish the round. When friends asked how I had put up such a dismal score, the worst I put up all year, I borrowed a quip from Arnold Palmer: "I missed a short putt for 104."

As the years go by, every one of those 105 strokes will likely fade from my memory—well, most of them, anyway—but I will never forget my reunion with Carole Dobrick. She and her late husband's approach to life helped instill in me the belief that I could rely on the kindness and generosity of others to complete the yearlong odyssey that led me to West Virginia and beyond.

ON THE LAST DAY OF October, I dropped Jordan and Alexandra off at school, then made the two-hour drive from Atlanta up Interstate 75 to Ooltewah, Tennessee, a tiny enclave just east of Chattanooga. On the biggest candy day of the year, it seemed appropriate to be meeting up with Marshall Brock, a descendant of one of America's biggest candy magnates. A friend of a friend had asked him to host me at the Honors Course, a club built to celebrate and honor amateur golf.

Marshall's great-grandfather purchased a small candy company outside Chattanooga in 1906 and transformed it into one of the largest candy businesses in the country before it went public and was later purchased by the Brach Corporation. It had taken three generations to build the family fortune, and over the course of our round, Marshall shared that he was worried that his generation might be the last to fully enjoy it. What began as a day of golf with a stranger evolved into a day of reflection on the lives of two southerners who'd traveled from opposite ends of privilege to an intersection of divergence.

Marshall, almost two decades younger than I, told me he'd lived a privileged life. I later discovered that his ancestors included soldiers in the Revolutionary and Civil Wars, US senators, a cabinet member, and a college president. I offered some of the details of my impoverished upbringing: the shacks we lived in, the tattered clothing I wore, and how we hunted and grew our own food out of necessity. Our paths met at an unlikely junction: Marshall worried that future generations of his family wouldn't have as much privilege as his generation, and I worried about building a solid foundation for my descendants.

Marshall seemed to be at a personal crossroads, wanting to make his life and those of his children, and his children's children, more meaningful. A life in which purpose was more significant than money.

I returned to Atlanta that evening. As my neighbors dropped Halloween candy into Jordan and Alexandra's trick-or-treat bags, I couldn't help but worry about their future. Though they were born into a life of privilege and opportunity, I wondered if they would truly appreciate what they have and work hard to make the most of it.

Growing up, I was given only about 10 percent of what I needed and had to work hard for everything else. In contrast, my children have been incredibly fortunate. They have gotten not only everything they've ever needed but also most of what they've wanted.

Obstacles and difficulties in life are inevitable. It's hard for me to know just how much to protect Jordan and Alexandra from the kinds of challenges and indignities I faced in my own childhood while allowing them to deal with enough adversity to develop their resolve. I'm sure every parent faces this dilemma, but it is even more poignant when you come of age in the world I was born in and raise children in the world I now inhabit.

Ultimately, we want our kids' lives to be the outcome of their own efforts and choices.

CHAPTER THIRTEEN

OAKLAND HILLS

*If you're in the luckiest 1 percent of humanity, you owe it to
the rest of humanity to think about the other 99 percent.*

—Warren Buffett

There are only so many ways to arrange grass, sand, water, and trees, and after playing nearly forty of the country's most desirable courses, I found that some layouts started to lose their novelty.

I love the thrill of experiencing something fresh and original. As a kid, I'd feel it in the most unexpected ways. The first time Frank took us to the beach in Galveston was one of those moments. I can still feel the grit of the sand between my toes, the rhythmic beat of the waves as they broke and washed ashore, bubbling up at the end like laundry detergent suds. I jumped up and down and whooped and hollered as wave after wave crashed against my skinny body. You would have thought I'd discovered water.

I also discovered parts of Frank on those trips. Or rediscovered parts of him. There were rare times—during a sober moment—when we'd get a glimpse of the playful, joking, candy-carrying man who arrived at our overcrowded house in Needmore to court my mother.

Although those moments with Frank wouldn't last long, they gave us kids a chance to see what our mother had originally seen in him. The day at the beach ended as the sun went down, the sea smell still clinging to us and precious new memories etched in our minds.

———

I WAS UNINSPIRED BY THE Inverness Club in Toledo, Ohio. After my playing partner, Ron Thompson, a Kiawah Black Jacket buddy, and I putted out on the second green, we searched everywhere for the third tee box. It wasn't there—or at least it wasn't where it was supposed to be. The Donald Ross–designed tract was undergoing a major renovation—holes put in by George and Tom Fazio in the late 1970s were being restored to Ross's 1920s design—so even though Ron had played there before, he wasn't sure where to go. He turned the cart left, then right, then back-tracked until we figured out which route made the most sense.

It put a new perspective on everything. I'm not sure we played the holes at Inverness in the right order, but we did play all eighteen.

I spent that night in Toledo with Ron and his wife, Cynthia, which gave me a chance to admire their immense collection of African and African American art from around the world. About a decade my senior, Ron had grown up in Detroit at a time when automotive companies dominated but few management opportunities existed in the corporate world for African Americans. That was why he followed the trail of his father and his father's friends, who owned and operated dry cleaners, auto repair shops, funeral homes—businesses that served the Black community. Necessity was their mother of invention. He and Cynthia became entrepreneurs. They bought a company in the eighties that manufactured railcars for irregular and heavy freight, then expanded it to build special shipping containers for the military. Eventually they sold it and bought another company that made unibody car components.

I was never drawn to starting my own business. When I graduated from Prairie View, the corporate world had cracked open just enough for me to become more interested in seeing if I had what it took to climb the ladder. To his credit, Ron eventually did both, parlaying his career as a successful business owner into seats on major corporate boards, including Chrysler, McDonnell Douglas, and the financial services company TIAA, where he was chairman.

We both understood how fortunate we were. Sitting around the Thompsons' kitchen table, Ron and I talked about policy proposals that the government could implement to address income and wealth inequality. It's a topic we discuss a lot during the Black Jacket tournaments. Having struggled through poverty myself, it's hard to see others live through it and not wonder how we can eradicate it.

Ron believed that we should guarantee a basic income for anyone living below the poverty line. I told him that when I'd lived among the affluent residents of Chevy Chase, Maryland, during my college internship, I'd seen for the first time the contrast in how the wealthy and poor interacted with money. Poor people seemed to see money as something they worked for. Rich folks saw it as something that worked for them. I told Ron that I thought it would be better to provide the poor with capital assets, such as a portfolio of stocks that would grow in value and generate an ongoing income, rather than just giving them payments—something not too different from what the GI Bill had done for soldiers when they put a dollar down to buy a house.

What's really needed, I said, are policies that create conditions that will empower the poor to solve their problems on their own. If you want people to pull themselves up by their bootstraps, you can't make it so hard to have boots.

My mother didn't want to be on welfare. Bad choices and unfortunate circumstances left her with few options. She used food stamps from the early seventies until my youngest two siblings were the only ones left at home, but she received a welfare check for only a couple years after Frank left—until she could be trained as a nurse's aide and get back on her feet. And for three years during my teen years, we lived in government-subsidized housing.

I believe that most people want to be independent, as my mother did. We were grateful that the government provided a safety net for us when we needed it. But it came at a price. Dealing with case officers was often demeaning, even dehumanizing. It was as if they used our hunger and need for shelter as leverage to control parts of our lives. We couldn't buy certain foods with our coupons. In the projects, there were restrictions on who was allowed to stay with us, even if it was a family member spending the night or other kids sleeping over for a couple days. Managers could enter our apartment day or night without notice or permission.

It was our decision to surrender those choices for the guarantee of food and shelter. But there were times when it felt as though we were looked upon like the inmates in the prisons around Huntsville.

Poverty was our prison.

RON ACCOMPANIED ME TO OAKLAND Hills Country Club north of Detroit, where David Enderby, my caddie from Arcadia Bluffs, had gotten Leo Savoie, the club's past president, to host us. During their teens, David and Leo had been caddies and busboys together at the club.

I, too, was once a busboy, at a breakfast-and-burgers joint in Houston, but perhaps for different reasons from those of Leo and David.

It was my first real job. Prior to that, I'd made money doing odd jobs around people's houses, mowing lawns, shining shoes, selling newspapers. I tried to get real, clock-punching jobs, such as sacking groceries at supermarkets or stocking shelves at a hardware store. But like the captains of industry who wouldn't hire African Americans for leadership positions, local merchants weren't interested in hiring boys who looked like me— colored and wearing worn-out clothing—even for basic jobs.

During high school, I discovered more options. I kept stats for the basketball team and called them in to the local dailies. I became the yearbook's lead photographer, toting the school's fancy single-lens reflex camera everywhere I went. I sold pictures from school sporting events to the same newspaper I'd hawked on a street corner when I was ten.

The newspaper even bought a photo I snapped of a body floating in a ditch along the railroad track I crossed on my way to school. I vividly remember sitting in the school's darkroom in shock, staring at the images coming into focus in a tray of chemicals under the red glow of the safelight.

The reality hit me like a ton of bricks. I wondered how the man had died and if he'd left a family behind. The picture appeared on the paper's front page, above the fold, with my name credited as the photographer.

The money wasn't much, but with it I opened a savings account at the local bank. The few hundred dollars that piled up there by my senior year helped pay for my cap and gown and my graduation photos and invitations.

When Leo had said he'd host me at Oakland Hills, he'd added that I could bring along a couple friends. In addition to Ron, I invited Ken Koupal, one of the JLL executives I'd played with at Oakmont. Before I called him, Ken had been trying to find me a host for Oakland Hills.

The South Course at Oakland Hills has a storied history in championship golf. Arnold Palmer, Gary Player, and Jack Nicklaus, who are often referred to as the sport's "Big Three," all won championships at Oakland Hills. Its narrow, rolling fairways, lined mostly with maples and oaks, and its difficult greens had earned the course its nickname: "The Monster." Ben Hogan had called it golf's greatest test.

Monster or not, one thing I loved about the course was the way, from each tee box, it was all right there in front of me—no deception, no trickery. It was as if Donald Ross was saying, "Here it is, deal with it."

The fifth hole, the toughest on the course, is a perfect example. The tee box is offset to the left of a gently rising fairway that slopes back down to the level of the green about midway to the flag. The fairway is lined with trees, heavily on the left and sparsely on the right. Three bunkers dot the rough just ahead of where the fairway descends toward the green.

The challenge was clear: to navigate the harrowingly narrow fairway while avoiding the trees on the left and the bunkers on the right. The only question: Could I do it?

I couldn't. I bogeyed the hole.

I arrived at the final three holes needing to par at least two of them to end my string of scores over 90, which I'd shot at Scioto, the Golf Club, Muirfield Village, and Inverness. I made par on all three to shoot an 88.

I'd played two Top 100 Donald Ross courses on back-to-back days, and the experiences couldn't have been more different. Oakland Hills felt fresh and unique. Inverness just left me wondering what it would be like after the renovation.

———

THREE DAYS LATER, I FLEW into Chicago under threatening skies. Medinah Country Club, just west of the city, is home to three courses, and Course No. 3 is the most celebrated—home to three U.S. Opens, two PGA Championships (both won by Tiger Woods), and a 2012 Ryder Cup so ridiculously memorable that it was dubbed the "Miracle at Medinah."

First laid out in the Roaring Twenties, then redesigned several times since, Course No. 3 is appropriately challenging. Yet there were stretches where I felt as though I were just repeating the same hole. Too many of the fairways followed straight and narrow lines sandwiched between thick groves of trees. All but one of the par threes play over the same pond.

The clubhouse, however, was something else, unlike any other I'd seen: a redbrick, green-roofed 120,000-square-foot building that blends (according to Medinah's website, because how else would anybody know?) Byzantine, Oriental, Louis XIV, and Italian architecture. It's jaw-dropping.

Just as memorable: the locker room attendant and my caddie.

Fito, a Mexican immigrant, seemed sincerely interested in every golfer who entered the locker room. He asked guests he'd seen before about their kids. If somebody forgot their golf shoes (as I certainly have once or twice), he'd find a pair for them to use; or if their shoes were soaked—as mine were after our round in the cold, lingering mist—he'd blow-dry them before putting them into a bag. He did it all with grace and seemingly without effort, and always without being asked. He had come to America and carved out a niche; many club visitors claim he is the best attendant anywhere. Watching Fito work is part of the Medinah experience.

Rudy was also a Mexican immigrant, as well as a person with special needs. He walked with a severe limp and rarely spoke. Yet he lugged two bags and tracked down every ball for eighteen cold, wet holes—without a whimper or a complaint. Even I moaned about how cold it was.

Fito and Rudy were both hard workers living their version of the American Dream.

I DON'T THINK WORKING HARD is a talent. I think it's a choice. Throughout school and my career, I accepted that there were people smarter and more talented than me, but I was determined never to be outworked.

During a Christmas break in college, I wanted to buy gifts for my family. So I went to a Houston mall and filled out a half-dozen applications. No one would interview me.

By the time I got to Montgomery Ward, a now-defunct department store, I'd had enough. When a woman there told me they'd call if anything came up, I insisted that they interview me on the spot. She said that no managers were presently in the store. When I asked who'd handle an emergency, she allowed that the toy department manager was around but that nobody wanted to work there during Christmas—too chaotic with so many hyped-up kids running around.

"It pays, right?" I asked.

The toy department manager interviewed me, and I got the job. For two weeks, I worked my butt off. Like Fito, I treated every customer as though he or she were the most important person in the world. The manager, Mr. Dabney, was so impressed that he offered me a job in the major appliance department, which he also ran. I took him up on his offer when I returned to school that fall.

I later learned that there was a long waiting list of store employees who wanted to work in appliances because it paid a commission. But Mr. Dabney moved me ahead of them all. And since I was a student, I could work only nights and weekends—prime time for selling fridges, stoves, washers, and dryers. Like the encyclopedias I peddled as a teenager, they were big-ticket items best purchased with husband and wife both present.

The clerks who were passed over let me have it almost daily: "Here comes college boy again, waltzing in after we worked all day."

I didn't let it faze me. I knew I'd gotten my opportunity because I'd made sure that no one ever outworked me—just like Rudy and Fito.

I was less successful on Medinah's Course No. 3. I hit just one fairway and four greens in regulation. But I still shot a respectable 87. I've played a lot better and scored worse, and vice versa. It didn't seem fair, but that's golf—and life.

———

THE NEXT DAY, I LANDED in New Jersey to play Somerset Hills Country Club.

By then, I'd played courses designed by Maxwell, MacKenzie, Nicklaus, Coore and Crenshaw, Doak, and a host of others. But as I stood on the second tee, I was still unfamiliar with the concept of template holes, which A. W. Tillinghast, who designed Somerset in 1917, brought from one of his pilgrimages to Great Britain. Yet I instinctively understood the genius of Somerset's par-three second.

The hole featured the usual Tillinghast bunkers, positioned just short of the green but close enough to distract from the true hazard: the trap guarding the putting surface off the front left. The green itself was small and sloped severely from right to left, with no safe areas for shots that missed their intended target. If you missed the green off the tee, your pitch and sand shots would have to be dead accurate to make par.

The hole's shape is called a Redan. After playing other courses with template holes, both during and after my quest, I labeled Tillinghast's second hole at Somerset Hills the best Redan in golf.

By the time I reached the eleventh tee box, I felt as though I'd wandered onto a different course. The front nine's flat, sweeping fairways with shallow bunkers had given way to undulating fairways carved between the trees.

I emerged from the tree-lined fairways and a deceptively sloping green on the par-three sixteenth to a blind tee shot on a wide-open seventeenth fairway. I ended the back nine in a setting that looked like the front nine—wide-open fairways bordered by fescue.

As I changed my shoes in the locker room, a tall, self-effacing gentleman walked up and said, "I finally caught up with you!"

Reynold Nebel, a retired corporate lawyer and member of the most underrated course on my list, had arrived at the club shortly after I'd teed off. Someone had told him about my quest, and he had proceeded to chase me for his entire round in the hope that we could play together. He treated me to lunch instead.

We hit it off, and after my quest, he joined me on the board of a nonprofit I helped start called the Caddie School for Soldiers. Its mission was to help veterans work through PTSD by taking them to St Andrews in Scotland for a month to train to become caddies.

We've been friends ever since.

CHAPTER FOURTEEN

PEBBLE BEACH

A joyous life is an individual creation that cannot be copied from a recipe.

—Mihaly Csikszentmihalyi

In the early nineties, I read a book by Mihaly Csikszentmihalyi, a Hungarian American psychologist. The book discussed the concept of "flow," a state of being in which you're so focused, prepared, relaxed, and undistracted that the boundary between mind and body collapses; you do something exactly how you want to do it without really thinking about it. Today folks call it "being in the zone."

Csikszentmihalyi, who as a kid was interned in a POW camp during World War II, believed that happiness doesn't just happen, that it wasn't the result of circumstances or luck. It comes from within, from appreciating what you have and not fixating on what you lack. My mother taught her kids to practice the same thing that Csikszentmihalyi wrote about when she told us that things "are what they are," that you need to work through whatever challenge you face and find your joy in trying to overcome it. That wasn't bumper sticker logic—it wasn't "Turn that frown upside down"; it was the belief that you shouldn't bemoan what you don't have and can't control. Instead, you should live in the present, be confident in your choices, and concentrate on the process. Happiness will follow.

Being poor wasn't fun. Absorbing the blows of my stepfather's fists or his lashes with fan belts, tree branches, and whatever else he could find wasn't fun. Being laughed at and bullied in school wasn't fun. Being evicted from our rat- and roach-infested homes wasn't fun. Becoming immune to hunger pains wasn't fun. Wearing flip-flops to class because that was all I had wasn't fun.

Yet even though I smiled with closed lips to hide a broken front tooth we couldn't afford to repair, I still found joy in my life—an exhilarating sense of peace. I felt it when I let go of my concerns about things I didn't have and embraced my appreciation of the things I did. Clouting that deformed doll's head with a discarded piece of lumber for a home run or marching around a dirt road on homemade stilts left me in a state of unexplainable bliss. In moments like those, I was "in the zone," despite the collapsing shacks, unspeakable outhouses, and shamefully segregated living arrangements that surrounded us.

Long before I read Csikszentmihalyi's book, the belief that joy can come from one's state of mind rather than one's circumstances resonated with me.

ON A CLEAR AUTUMN DAY, I experienced on a golf course what I'd experienced in life: I found my "golf flow" on the Shore Course at Monterey Peninsula Country Club.

Getting there involved a five-hour flight from Atlanta to San Francisco and then two more hours of driving down the 101. I was tired and hungry. It didn't feel like a day when I'd reach peak performance on a golf course. That sense of foreboding was underscored when the club's head pro warned me that the greens had just been aerated—punched with tiny holes and filled with sand to loosen the soil and promote good turf growth—and that the driving range was closed. Stiff as I was, I'd have to start my round without a warm-up.

From the first tee box, high above the fairway, I looked beyond the trees and caught a glimpse of the Pacific Ocean. Despite my weariness, the sight of the ocean had a calming, restorative effect. I hit a decent drive. But after my caddie and I descended to the fairway below, trees hid the view of the water, and whatever calm I'd felt evaporated. I bogeyed the first hole and double-bogeyed the second.

When I stepped up to the tee box on the short par-three third, however, I heard waves washing ashore. I set up and took dead aim at the flag. There was plenty to warn against that. Trees protected the green from breezes off the ocean to the right, and seven bunkers encircled it. Yet I did something almost impossible for a control freak like me: I let go of my thoughts, my fears, my innumerable calculations, and just swung the club.

The ball sailed high and true, plopped onto the green, bounced twice, then rolled to within fifteen feet of the flag. It was an easy par. So were the pars that followed on three of the front nine's remaining holes—each with a stunning view of a whitecapped Pacific that surged toward 17-Mile Drive, the winding two-lane that cut between the course and the coastline. Unlike in Oregon, there were no cliffs, just uninterrupted views of a rocky beach and a mist that hung like low-lying cloud cover above the roiling waves.

The view from the eleventh tee stopped me cold. Beyond the windswept cypress, the waves crashing over the rocks, and that mist over the water, two of the peninsula's three other top courses, Cypress Point Club and Spyglass Hill Golf Course, were literally in my sights.

Also in my sights: my goal of breaking 80 on a Top 100 course.

I swung, I gaped at the view, I gulped the salt air—it was all one and the same. No matter what club I chose on any hole, the ball landed right where I wanted it to. If I couldn't shoot under 80 that day, I might never do it. I birdied ten and eleven, then made my way through the following seaside holes tapping in one par after another.

For once, golf was not just a nice way to spend a day outside or a challenging diversion; for that one extended moment, *golf was easy.*

As the sky over the bay behind me burned gold, rose, and coral, I hit my final drive of the day. It was a fine enough shot, but with the wind in my face and my body suddenly buckling under the weight of fifteen hours of being awake, I plunked my approach shot into a bunker.

On the final hole of a day that had started in Georgia and ended in California, I made bogey. Yet for the fifteen holes that preceded it, I'd found the elusive "flow." I finished with a 76.

I missed a short putt for 75.

———

THOUGH MIHALY CSIKSZENTMIHALYI'S ELUSIVE FLOW enabled me to find joy in the things I had rather than fixating on the things I didn't, my childhood was marked by a single absence that almost changed the course of my life: a mere dollar.

The same school whose rules got me paddled in gym class every day also held back students who owed it money. I misplaced a library book. By the time I found it, I'd racked up a dollar in late fees. As we broke for summer vacation, I was told I'd have to stay in sixth grade for another year if I couldn't pay the fine.

Every day that year when I got home from school, I'd flipped on a light switch to make sure we still had electricity. If we did, I would go outside to play. If not, I'd do my homework before it got dark. I think I got A's in every class but one—PE—but none of that mattered if I didn't come up with a dollar to pay the library fine.

Today, a dollar seems like almost nothing, but back then, every penny mattered. I didn't have a hundred pennies to give the school. So I borrowed an uncle's lawn mower and begged a neighbor to let me cut her grass. She said no until I told her I'd charge only a dollar. I crisscrossed her yard for what seemed like forever, pushing that little red mower under the hot Texas sun. It was the hardest dollar I ever earned. I paid the fine. My life stayed on track.

That experience ensured that I'd never forget the value of a dollar. When I'd called Pebble Beach Golf Links to reserve a tee time, I'd learned that it required a three-night stay at one of their on-course accommodations to secure a guaranteed start. The cheapest room available was more than $1,000 a night. No matter how many more dollars I've accumulated since the lack of a single bill almost changed the trajectory of my life, a thousand of them will always be a lot of money to me.

I decided to take my chances with the waiting list. When I was a kid and one dollar seemed like more than four thousand, I had faith that I'd find a way to make it from sixth grade to seventh; this was golf's version of that same belief. I booked a room at the Marriott and left the rest to fate.

THE MORNING AFTER MY MIND-BLOWING, free-flowing round at Monterey, I arrived at the Pebble Beach pro shop before sunrise. The starter put my name at the top of the list for alternates; I'd be first in line if someone on the filled-up tee sheet canceled. While hanging out at the shop, I met the first Black assistant pro I'd seen at a Top 100 course, Norman Blanco. He was a Louisiana native and graduate of the University of Maryland Eastern Shore, the only HBCU in the country with a PGA Golf Management program.

Norman told me that he knew of only one other Black assistant pro at a Top 100 course: "Burley Stamps at the Riviera Country Club."

Burley, who played basketball most of his childhood, fell in love with golf at thirteen after hitting a bucket of balls at a range with his father, who was a member at a local country club. That allowed him to follow the same path as most white PGA pros: he got his certification working under a PGA professional at a private club.

It is worth noting that African Americans make up less than 1 percent of the 29,000 PGA of America members—the men and women who give golf lessons and sell apparel at most courses around the country.

Most African American PGA pros are groomed and employed at municipal courses, concentrated in urban areas with significant populations of African American golfers. In contrast, many white PGA pros come up through the ranks in a close-knit network of elite clubs. Although there was no longer a "Caucasian only" clause in the PGA bylaws, few Black PGA professionals had breached the most exclusive clubs in the country by the time of my quest.

After waiting around for five or six hours to see if anyone canceled, I gave up on getting onto Pebble that day. If I teed off after 1:30, I probably wouldn't finish the round before sunset anyway, missing the spectacular final couple of holes while still paying full price. So I drove over to nearby Spyglass, another of the resort's Top 100 courses, and grabbed one of its open tee times.

Spyglass is often labeled the best course never to have hosted a major, yet every time I called about tee times, there was always one open. So I assumed that it must not be that great. It blew me away. I caught sight of the ocean on the first tee and promptly hit the best drive of my life, a three-hundred-yard poke that landed in the center of the wide downhill fairway.

I still had "flow." I finished before dusk with an 84.

I returned to the pro shop at Pebble Beach the next morning, right around sunrise, to see if there were any cancellations. Again, nobody dropped off the list.

I'm an optimist. I expect things to work out more often than not. During my senior year at Prairie View, I participated in a national technical paper contest held at the University of New Mexico in Albuquerque. My paper focused on research I'd done during my internship at the National Bureau of Standards, using ultrasonic waves to measure residual stresses in stainless steel. I was competing with students from some of the country's top universities—MIT, Purdue, Georgia Tech—but like Tiger Woods every time he showed up at a golf tournament, I still expected to win. My classmates had different expectations. They were just happy we had been invited to an event with such distinguished schools. As one earnestly remarked, "Jimmie, you have the best chance to bring recognition to Prairie View. Hopefully you can get a third place for us."

I prepared for hours on end. I practiced my presentation over and over in front of a mirror. I tried to think of every possible question the judges could ask. When I finally presented my paper, I felt confident that I'd done my best. My classmates thought so, too, but were still pessimistic. Prairie View A&M University was but a humble David in a contest full of Goliaths.

My classmates' doubts only intensified when someone else's name was called for third place at the award ceremony. I was relieved; I wouldn't have to settle for third. After the name of the second-place finisher was called, my palms turned sweaty in anticipation. Then, after a dramatic pause, the lead judge called out, "And first place goes to Jimmie James from Prairie View A&M University." The whole room stood and applauded.

I believed that I could win. And because of that belief, I put in the work necessary to do it. It's hard to put your all into something when you don't think it will pay off. I believed I could earn that dollar to pay my library fine. That was why I didn't accept no when the homeowner first rejected my offer to cut her grass. I believed I could win that technical paper contest at the University of New Mexico. That was why I wasn't discouraged when my name wasn't called for second or third place.

And as meaningless as it was compared to the starker, often life-and-death challenges I'd faced growing up, I believed I would play all of America's hundred greatest courses in a year. That was why I had faith that I would somehow get a tee time at Pebble Beach without a reservation. When I basically said as much to the assistant pro behind the counter that second early morning, he responded, "Give me a minute."

He pulled up the tee sheet for the next day, studied it, then said, "There are two slots available tomorrow. I'll keep an eye on them, and if they aren't filled by midnight, I'll make sure you get one." When I showed up the next morning at the crack of dawn, he told me I was set to go off at 11:15.

There's nothing magical about believing. It simply motivates you to put in the effort to make happen what you believe is possible.

———

I DON'T THINK PEBBLE BEACH Golf Links is a great course. I think it's a storied track with eight awe-inspiring holes that every avid golfer should experience—plus ten middling-to-decent ones. And unlike Augusta National, Pebble is a public resort course, so dreaming to play it isn't merely a fantasy. You control whether you're going to play Pebble. It's your decision. You pay, you play, simple as that. I just didn't want to pay the price it was asking for a guaranteed reservation.

So I went with the flow.

Pushing the first tee into the sacred ground of an iconic course should stir a range of emotions: excitement, gratitude, a fear of making a fool of yourself. I felt all that at Oakmont. I felt it at Merion. I felt it in spades at Augusta. I didn't feel anything special on the first hole at Pebble. The tee box is wedged between the pro shop to the left and residential villas to the right. It felt commercial and frankly a little cheesy. I wasn't excited or nervous when the starter called out my name. It all seemed affected.

That cloud of disappointment didn't lift as I made my way around the first three holes. The fairways were flat, characterless, and largely unkept; unrepaired divots dotted stretches that were trampled and worn.

That all changed as I passed the hedges beyond the fourth-hole tee boxes. Behind me was an unremarkable course with poorly maintained turf. Before me was a picturesque fairway with views of whitecaps washing against a rocky coastline that threads its way into the horizon. The difference between what I'd just played and what unfolded in front of me was the difference between going to a zoo and going on a safari. Everything I'd expected to feel on the first tee but hadn't—excitement, awe, dread—now hit me. This was the real deal.

But the fourth hole was only a prelude of what was to come. The view of the not-so-distant mountains from the fifth green, juxtaposed against a cliff falling into the Pacific, erased any ho-hum memories I had of the first three holes. It's where the course catches its own flow, where golf and the edge-of-the-world panorama become one. For a sightseer, it was breathtaking. For a golfer: chilling.

It only gained momentum from there. The right edge of the par-five sixth-hole fairway sweeps along another cliff so stark and dramatic you almost wish there were a guardrail. The hole's architect knew exactly what he was doing: trying to avoid the bunkers to the left, I hit my drive to the right. It landed in the fairway but harrowingly close to the don't-look-down drop-off.

Days in the country during my boyhood summers were filled with adventure and wonderment. Nights were something else. They were pitch black except for the stars and maybe a random, distant headlight. In the trees' scraggy silhouettes, I imagined monsters and mythical beings, who'd later visit me in my dreams or in the stories my older sister told us kids as we huddled together in the dark, bullfrogs croaking from an unseen pond. Her most vivid tale—the one that haunted us long after the sun came up—was about our mother sending us to a store in town to buy liver. That was the plan until we got there and spent all our money on candy. When we realized we couldn't go home without liver, we ran to a nearby cemetery, dug up a grave, and took a liver from a corpse before heading back home. We forgot about the dead guy until he crept into our house under the cloak of darkness to get his liver back. The story scared us to death no matter how many times my sister told it—Freddy Krueger had nothing on Liver Man!

But even Liver Man wasn't as scary as the sixth hole at Pebble Beach. I was nearly shaking in my FootJoys as I addressed my steep uphill second shot over the edge of the cliff. I'd have to send it out over the water and hope it curved back to land. Amid all that sky and sea, your sense of scale gets distorted. From where I stood, nearly three hundred yards away, the ample green looked infinitesimal.

I wanted to ask my caddie the question Jordan had asked me when I took him on his first amusement park ride: "Dad, you sure I'm ready for this?"

He was six. I was fifty-eight.

My caddie sensed my anxiety. I was that obvious. He handed me a 3-hybrid and essentially recommended flow: "Just make a good swing, and everything will be okay."

I felt as though I'd escaped the grasp of Liver Man when the ball landed safely in the fairway, ninety yards from the pin.

What followed is maybe the most recognizable hole in golf: the preposterously short par-three seventh. It ends on a tiny peninsula jutting out into the waves, with a postage stamp–sized green buffered from the cliff, the bay, and the rocks by a pair of traps. From the tee box, it's a seductively harrowing postcard.

The hairiest part is what you can't see: the wind. It can range from a breeze to a gale, and the only predictable thing about it is its unpredictability. The hole plays less than a hundred yards with a forty-foot drop, but clubbing it can be a crapshoot. Sam Snead once putted from the tee to avoid a wicked wind. (It's said he was the only golfer that day to make par.) A club pro once made a hole in one with a 3-iron.

We civil engineers have an array of principles at our disposal to determine the effects of multiple types of simultaneous stresses on steel, but there are no such concepts in golf. I had to lean on my own experience and that of my caddie to pick the right club. I was torn between a lob wedge, which is my eighty-yard club and would get me to the front of the green, or a sand wedge, which usually travels ninety yards and would either stop close to pin high or roll off the back. There was hardly any wind. After talking it over with my caddie, I decided it was better to be short than long and possibly wet. I wound up short—and in a front bunker. I carded a bogey. I was grateful for the vista and the adventure but walked away with a better understanding of why professional golfers struggle so much with club selection on that hole.

Pebble's last two holes didn't disappoint. The par-three seventeenth has a long but shallow green protected from the water by bunkers cut into high mounds. The eighteenth fairway curves slightly right to left along the rocky coastline, like the last leg of golf's yellow-brick road. Both holes etch an indelible impression in the golfer's mind of the magic and splendor of America's most familiar and famed seaside golf course.

Done with my round but in no rush to leave the peninsula, I capped off the day on nearby Carmel Beach. I watched continental America's last sunset of the day, stepping along the sand and rocks and water until the stars popped out. I didn't want the week to end. I knew that the level of play I'd experienced—"the flow"—wouldn't last forever. I'd be lucky if it carried over to my next round. But that week, at least, it all clicked. Fate came through. Again. All I'd done was what I'd learned to do early on in my life: trust myself and trust the process. That's where I've always found real happiness. The fact that everything turned out as well as it did was a bonus.

I lingered there as long as I could.

CHAPTER FIFTEEN

CONGRESSIONAL

Reach high, for stars lie hidden in you. Dream deep,
for every dream precedes the goal.

—Rabindranath Tagore

On my first flight ever, I threw up.

At age seventeen, flying from Houston to Washington, DC, on Eastern Air Lines, my stomach got queasy. The more I tried to hold it in, the worse it got. I pushed the call button above my seat for the stewardess—what flight attendants were called in 1977—and she pointed to a bag in the seat-back pocket. I grabbed it and let loose. Nobody was more relieved than I was when we landed, except maybe that flight attendant. At least my classmates got a good laugh at my expense.

We'd come to the nation's capital to participate in Close Up, a program that gives high school students an inside look at how our government works. From the minute I heard about the program, I was determined to take advantage of the incredible opportunity it presented. My family couldn't afford it, but Close Up gave a scholarship to one student in need from each participating school. I knew I was the neediest student at Hitchcock High, but even so, I didn't assume that I'd get the scholarship.

My mother instilled in us a belief that people are kind and generous, but she also taught us that living in poverty didn't entitle us to anyone's generosity. She was grateful for the government checks that kept us afloat after Frank deserted. We all were. But when a new government program offered the opportunity for job training, she jumped at it. She trained as a nurse's aide, then took a job cleaning bedpans and mopping linoleum floors at Autumn Hills Convalescent Home. If you account for the taxi fares to and from work that ate up more than half her earnings—she never learned to drive, and there was no public transportation—it paid less than her welfare check. But to my mother, having a job was about more than money; it was about finding her own way to take care of us, even if it didn't change our standard of living. I was committed to following her example and finding a way to pay for Close Up on my own.

The savings I'd accumulated doing odd jobs didn't come close to the four hundred dollars I needed. Besides, I still had to pay for graduation-related costs, including my cap and gown and senior portrait. So I did one of the things I'd always done: knocked on doors. But instead of selling seeds or lawn care services, I sold my enthusiasm for going to our nation's capital. I asked for one dollar from each house until I collected what I needed for the trip.

Starting early on a Saturday morning, I walked the route I took every day to high school to reach the town's middle-class white neighborhoods. At each door, I shared my story of how a single dollar had once ensured that I had been promoted to seventh grade and how a single dollar now, from each of the four hundred people I planned to reach, would help a boy who'd never been more than a hundred miles from where he was born go to Washington and learn how the laws that affected all of us were made.

Almost everybody bought in. Some folks didn't answer my knocks, though I could tell they were home. But most listened to my pitch through a screen door or invited me inside while they fetched their purses or wallets from another room. I rapped on door after door, trekking up and down one street after another, until just before dark.

By the second Saturday, after knocking on nearly three hundred doors—some folks gave me more than a dollar—I made my goal and stopped. The next school day I handed the cash to my counselor—a pile of mostly ones and some fives—and told him it was for the trip. It was only then that he informed me that I'd gotten the scholarship. Since it couldn't be transferred to anyone else, we used my money to cover the cost for another student who couldn't afford it. People had handed me their money to help a needy kid go to Washington, and I insisted that's what it would be used for.

At seventeen, I was about to leave Texas for the first time.

———

FORTY YEARS AND NEARLY THREE million airline miles later, I boarded another flight bound for DC. I didn't need an air sickness bag this time. My ultimate destination was Congressional Country Club, founded in the 1920s and enjoyed ever since by presidents, senators, and those in their orbit. When I landed, the late-November morning was chilly, but the course remained playable.

Congressional marked the halfway point—the fifty-first course on my list—and it was the last northern, cold-weather course I'd play before heading south and west for the winter. I'd spent five months crisscrossing the country. There had been long days and short nights. There had been hurricanes and forest fires. There had been flight cancellations and unbearable traffic delays. I'd flown more than thirty thousand miles, driven more than ten thousand miles, and walked more than three hundred miles over fairways and roughs in twenty-six states. I still had a long slog ahead.

Six months into retirement, I was back in DC, where so much of my life had unfolded. A few years after that high school trip, it was where I was first paid to do something that required more than muscle and sweat. No one in my immediate family had ever been paid for anything but blue-collar work, and I was eager to prove that we could contribute beyond our well-proven ability to perform manual labor. Now that I'd returned, it was hard not to reminisce.

In the months between leaving the University of Houston and enrolling at Prairie View A&M, my brother Art helped me land a job as a machinist's helper at Drilco, a drill pipe–manufacturing company in Houston. Art had moved up the ranks from an entry-level position to foreman. His crew admired him: he was the rare manager who understood from personal experience the needs and challenges of even the least-ranking among them. And though he was a manager, he often stood up to management on their behalf. He had their backs. More than one of them told me they believed that they could accomplish anything when Art was in charge.

I, on the other hand, was at the bottom of Drilco's pecking order, paid to do a single, simple task: help a machinist set up a horizontal boring machine to cut a hole in the center of a twelve-foot-by-six-inch-diameter steel bar. I was grateful for the money; I was always grateful for any money. But it was the last manual labor I'd ever be paid to do.

Every night from 11:00 p.m. to 7:00 a.m., I performed that task over and over. It required attention, strength, and very, very little skill. It was repetitive, monotonous, and tedious. By 3:00 a.m., I fought to stay awake. By 5:00 a.m., the anticipation of the end of another night provided the surge of energy I needed to make it through the last two hours.

I continued working there when I started at Prairie View, but after a month of juggling graveyard-shift work, daytime classes, and evening studying, I was overwhelmed. One early morning, leaving the plant to rush off to school, I momentarily dozed off behind the wheel and drove my car into a shallow ditch. I wasn't hurt, but I gave my two-week notice the next day.

My experience at Drilco strengthened my resolve to pursue a career that would rely more on my mental abilities than my physical strength—one that would point toward a life I dreamed about. I knew I was cut out for a path that would lift me, like Art, to a place where I wanted to be. So I spent all my free time on campus at the career placement center researching the skills and traits I'd need to succeed as a white-collar professional. I was starting at zero; I didn't have a role model to follow. All I knew for sure was that there was a whole lot I didn't know.

That was when I discovered internships. A counselor told me about a program that alternated semesters on campus with semesters at a job related to my engineering studies. The concept seemed almost too good to be true: you trained in a job that would enhance your analytical, communication, and leadership skills before you even looked for a real job. I applied and landed an internship with the National Bureau of Standards in suburban Gaithersburg, Maryland, a government research facility that studies every aspect of measurement.

I arrived my first day in slacks, a dress shirt, and a tie—thanks to a career placement center tip—and was assigned my own office. Dressing in business attire and working out of an office are what most aspiring professionals do. But for me it was as if the world itself had just cracked open—as though I'd been given a secret code to success.

The job was heaven. Nerd heaven. I spent part of the day performing engineering calculations in my office and part of it conducting lab experiments on the flow dynamics of simulated urine (bromine) and simulated solids (small brown plastic tubes) that streamed through transparent pipes after we flushed them down a test toilet. We were researching how various toilets conserved water. The work was cutting edge: the bureau published an article about it in its in-house magazine, including a photo of me in a lab coat staring at the automated system we'd designed. Some of the other interns joked that I'd finally been potty trained. I didn't let on that in the span of a little more than a decade, I'd gone from an outhouse to the high-tech commodes of the future.

I felt incredibly fortunate. I mailed pictures of myself sitting in my office or working in the lab to my mother, and she showed them off at the nursing home where she worked. I knew how good they made her feel. It's also why I visited her at work whenever I went home from college, and later, when I worked at Exxon, making sure I arrived right before the end of her 7:00 a.m. to 3:00 p.m. shift so I could give her a lift home. At one time or another, most of my siblings did the same.

My mother would show us off and beam when coworkers and residents told her, "Thelma, you have such good children!" It was a source of pride and validation for her. Art was a foreman; Jen was married with children and thinking about going to college; Jerry was out on his own making a living; Ernest had joined the Job Corps. My three other siblings were home and in school.

There had been long years when so many relatives and neighbors had told my mother that her kids would "end up in the pen" because she was raising them all wrong, not giving them what they needed. Those verbal slaps reminded her of all the material things she didn't have and couldn't provide. But during our visits at Autumn Hills, when one of us wrapped an arm around her and smiled from ear to ear, she felt the full impact of all the unseen gifts she'd bestowed. It let her know that we were as proud of her as she was of us.

I RETURNED TO PRAIRIE VIEW after my internship more focused than ever. I had a better understanding of how to apply the theories and concepts in my textbooks to real-life technical problems. It was as though I were back in Mr. Calvin's sixth-grade math class, living in an imaginary world without limits. For once, I also owned something that many of my classmates did not: relevant work experience. I suddenly didn't feel as less than as before.

My second internship at the National Bureau of Standards was even more meaningful. I exchanged and challenged ideas rather than merely following orders. I worked with a group of physicists to research the effect of residual stresses on the strength of metals, coauthored an article published in a peer-reviewed journal, and had an epiphany on leadership. I was pouring the foundation of a better life, one layer at a time.

The epiphany came during my final performance evaluation. My supervisor noted that I had excellent leadership skills. I didn't understand. Nobody on our team had less of a leadership-level position than I did; I was way down at the bottom of the pecking order, after all. He explained that leadership wasn't a position but an ability to inspire others to work toward a common goal. He told me that my ideas and initiative inspired the team. The concept was earthshaking for me. In that instant, my idea of a leader went from someone who simply told others what to do to someone who motivated people to achieve shared goals.

From then on, I understood that the value I brought to a job would be determined by my capacity to contribute, not my title or job description. Ideas mattered more than position. Later on, that view irked some of those above me on the organizational chart at ExxonMobil, managers who expected deference based on their positions. Some didn't want me working for them, and that was fine by me—that was their right. Regardless of the consequences, I stuck to the principles validated for me during that second internship. They aligned with who I really was.

I could've made different choices during my career, and I likely would've advanced more quickly and farther up the ladder if I had. But making those choices would've meant giving up a piece of who I was to become someone others thought I should be. One principle never wavered: be true to yourself. There were many things I'd been ashamed of in my life, and there were times I tried to hide who I was. Once, as a child, I pretended to live in the house in front of our shack in La Marque when a music teacher came by to pick me up for school. I did that out of shame, and I never forgot the feeling. During my career, I never pretended to be someone I wasn't.

———

I SPENT TWELVE OF MY thirty-three years at ExxonMobil working within a chain of rectangular glass buildings connected by circular towers on a wooded campus just a few miles from the deep, thick rough bordering the manicured fairways of Congressional Country Club. That was where my dream of being a businessman who worked around the world was fully realized. During that stretch, I traveled to more than thirty countries, most of them numerous times. The world shrank while my mind expanded. Mr. Calvin's math problems were no longer my only outlet to a life beyond the borders of poverty and Texas.

During one of many trips to Paris, I spent a day with a truck driver while he delivered heating oil to homes outside the city, seeing firsthand just how important it was to those people's lives. On another visit, I spent a night in a penthouse suite at the Waldorf Astoria Versailles–Trianon Palace overlooking the gardens. Once while in Thailand, I visited the Grand Palace to inspect the tanks that stored the fuel we supplied for the king's vehicles. Afterward, I dined for the first time on sticky rice and the insides of a fish head. During a trip to Singapore, I bought pearls for Erika and Alexandra; Jordan's closet is filled with *fútbol* jerseys I picked up for him in Spain, the United Kingdom, the Netherlands, Argentina, Brazil.

Amid meetings and facility tours overseas, I also squeezed in some golf. I almost dunked an ace on a par three outside London—only days after recording my first ace on a course in Virginia. At the Olivos Golf Club outside Buenos Aires, I darted past groups of capybaras—grunting, three-foot-long water hogs—in search of my wayward tee shots.

I also trekked to towns desperate for fuel and energy and came face-to-face with poverty that was both familiar and deeper than my own childhood experiences. In a village in Colombia, raw sewage flowed through trenches that emptied into streams from which residents drew water for washing their clothes or bathing, as I had during summers on my grandparents' farm. Day laborers toted stones, dug holes, or worked in fields while women bent over tubs, cleaning, just like my mother, their kids playing all around them. When I caught a whiff of poverty's familiar scent around shanties built of cardboard and discarded crates—the same stink I'd once carried—I didn't flinch. Instead, I thought: "I've found my people."

I could've chosen not to go to those places. But I was proud to work for a company that could help give those destitute people the opportunity to better their lives. The correlation between quality of life and access to energy is clear. It's easy to demonize energy companies. I get it; when they make a mistake, the impact can be devastating. When I worked in Boston, a woman seated beside me on a commuter flight asked what I did for a living.

Her cool response when I told her: "I guess somebody has to do it."

"With all due respect," I replied, "I don't do it because somebody has to. I believe bringing energy to people around the world makes their lives better."

It's easy to take energy for granted. But I remember what it was like to grow up without it and the magic it could hold. I remember walking into the house we moved into after the Sawmill Quarters and turning the bathroom light on and off, on and off, on and off.

Darkness.

Then light.

———

CONGRESSIONAL FELT A THOUSAND MILES from anywhere, even though it was only about a dozen miles from the bustle of downtown DC. Set amid suburban Maryland's rolling countryside striped with horse farms and white fences, it's barely out of earshot of Washington's traffic-clogged Beltway.

I rolled in early and waited for my host inside the 140,000-square-foot, multitiered Spanish Revival clubhouse, the country's largest. You'd need almost a full day just to tour its three swimming pools, duckpin bowling alley, grand ballroom, and 10,000-square-foot fitness center. Its membership has included seven presidents, as well as Charlie Chaplin, Andrew Carnegie, and Vince Lombardi. It exudes power and prestige as much as golf.

Nancy Carlson joined me a few minutes later for a preround breakfast. A club member, Nancy had invited me to play the Blue Course at Congressional when she'd heard about my yearlong chase. We'd been longtime colleagues at ExxonMobil, and together we'd navigated many of the same cultural shifts that our presence, and the presence of others like us, had sparked.

Nancy was a trailblazer who had successfully scaled the corporate ladder in a male-dominated industry. She was proud of the barriers she'd broken. She'd started in the 1970s at a Mobil facility—before the merger with Exxon—as a night-shift foreman and learned the business from the ground up. The place wasn't always ready for her. There were no bathrooms for women at some facilities when she showed up because, well, the energy business was man's work. That thinking didn't change overnight. She worked with people who still believed that a woman should be home with her babies baking cookies. Any job a woman got, they felt, was one less job a man could have.

I observed more than once the objectification of women in the workplace. I'd hear men make remarks about what women managers were wearing and how they looked during presentations, when they should've been focused on what those women were saying. It was shocking how frequently that happened.

I watched another female colleague deal with harassment even more awkward and offensive. In meetings, there was a senior manager who always tried to sit next to her. At dinners, he'd do the same and flirt. I'd try to get there first and sit between them as a buffer. But on the road, she confided, there was always the potential for things to get worse. After meetings, she'd go back to her hotel room and get a call from one of her bosses, who'd say he was at the bar and did she want to join him. She knew what was going on.

Nancy was deeply involved in the company's affinity groups, helping women get a fair shake and advance. The overall sense of how women, African Americans, and other underrepresented employees were treated and perceived by some inside the company was the same. When a white man was promoted, it was generally seen as adding value to the company. When women or African Americans were promoted, it was often viewed as the company doing them a favor. We all just wanted to be valued for who we really were.

Nancy rose through all of it and helped advance the culture. Her presence was felt in every room she walked into. Her smarts, perspective, grace, and focus on details put everybody at ease. In every meeting of hers I attended, she commanded respect.

When Nancy invited me to play Congressional, she said I could also invite Malcolmn Pryor, who'd hosted me at Merion.

Then, during our breakfast, Nancy told me her brother couldn't join us for the round. I mentioned that Malcolmn had arranged for his cousin Powell, also an avid golfer, to drive him to Congressional, and before I could say anything else, she invited him to join us. Powell, like all chronic golfers, keeps his clubs and shoes in his trunk, so he was ready to go. And he later returned the favor by getting his college roommate, a member at Essex County Club, a stately Top 100 course in Manchester-by-the-Sea, Massachusetts, to host him and me near the end of my quest.

We all met up on the range. Greeting us there was our forecaddie, an older Black gentleman named Maurice. Maurice is something of a legend around the club. He started working there in his teens, and he told me he'd caddied for presidents dating back to Dwight D. Eisenhower. I'm not sure his math adds up, but that was Maurice's story, and he was sticking to it.

We then made our way to the first tee box, where the markers were shaped like the Capitol dome. I pulled my drive into the left rough, about twenty-five yards short of a bunker—and then off we all went: four Black men and a white woman, rolling across the Blue Course's manicured fairways as Maurice entertained us with his colorful, if sometimes dubious, stories.

Were we a small sign of golf's incremental progress?

We sure would've been a sight to those three Black men who decades earlier had been turned away at nearby East Potomac, only to jump onto the course a few hours later and proudly play all eighteen holes accompanied by US marshals and white hecklers.

None of us mentioned those men as we made our way around Congressional that crisp morning. I'm guessing that none of us even thought of them. But playing on the same grass where presidents, senators, industrialists, and celebrities had duck-hooked drives, topped approach shots, and left three-foot putts three inches short just like the rest of us—the golf gods don't discriminate—surely served as a kind of unspoken tribute to each one of those trailblazers at Potomac.

Even if none of us broke 80.

CHAPTER SIXTEEN

WHISPERING PINES

When our hearts turn to our ancestors, something changes inside us.
We feel part of something greater than ourselves.

—Russell M. Nelson

Henry David Thoreau famously went into the woods to live deliberately and learn what the simple life could teach him. As fall gave way to winter, I returned to the piney woods of East Texas where my family and I had once lived a spartan existence—not by choice, as Thoreau had done, but out of necessity.

Whispering Pines Golf Club, one of only two Top 100 golf courses in Texas (the other being Dallas National Golf Club), slips through the woods about twenty-five miles northeast of where I first learned resourcefulness, self-sufficiency, and an appreciation of the simple things in life, much like Thoreau. My golf odyssey had returned me to my American ancestral roots.

I couldn't help but think about my great-great-grandparents Tankie James and Tiny Profit and the impact that their resilience and determination had on my own early life, long after tobacco and cotton farms in East Texas were replaced by the two industries that dominated Huntsville when I was growing up: timber and incarceration.

Five state-run prisons operated in or around town. I passed by the most fearsome of them, fittingly nicknamed the "Walls Unit," during my daily bus ride to Scott E. Johnson Elementary. It rose over downtown like a medieval fortress, its fifteen-foot-high redbrick walls taking up four square blocks. Armed guards watched from tall towers. The message was clear: whoever went in wasn't coming out.

That message often rang true. The Walls Unit housed Old Sparky, a straight-back wooden electric chair used to execute death row inmates. We heard that the town's lights flickered when the switch was pulled, but since we didn't have electricity in the Quarters, the surges didn't affect us.

During Tiny and Tankie's time in the mid-1800s, tobacco, sustained by chattel slavery, was king. Tankie was considered plantation property; had the Emancipation Proclamation not been issued, she could have been sold, just like lumber unloaded in the Sawmill Quarters, to an enslaver at another plantation. Had that happened, she would have never met my great-great-grandfather or borne his son whose name I carry. I would have been something even less than ILLEGITIMATE. I would never have been born.

As children, my siblings and I were aware that the matriarch on my mother's side had been enslaved and that her resilience was at the roots of our ancestral tree. My mother's determination to endure and work to overcome all the challenges she faced can likely be traced back to Tiny and Tankie. And because Tiny and Tankie were determined to build a family together, I was able to return, more than a century later, to a place near where they'd met and play a game as whimsical as golf, enjoying a freedom they couldn't have possibly imagined.

———

MY SIBLINGS RECALL THAT DURING my earliest years I rarely wore a stitch of clothing. Now, leaving the native-stone clubhouse at Whispering Pines in a pair of black PGA Tour shorts and a turquoise Nike golf shirt, I couldn't help but feel pride in my roots and how far my family had come from this ancestral soil.

I knew I would need to channel all the strength I'd learned from the woods into my golf swing if I was going to dispense with Kevin and Richard, the two friends I'd dueled with months earlier. We were reuniting at Whispering Pines, with its wide but treacherous fairways, for our rematch. They'd had my number back at Valhalla, but I'd been playing exceptional golf lately, shooting in the mid-80s in the two rounds leading up to our rematch.

A week earlier, I had played at the storied Pinehurst No. 2 in North Carolina, with turtleback greens that threatened to turn perfect approach shots into nightmare recoveries, and I'd managed an 84. My caddie, Jeff "Ratman" Ferguson, preached finesse as he helped me navigate the many minefields. He'd carried Davis Love III's bag in the 1980s and told me he had been inducted into the Pinehurst Caddie Hall of Fame.

Ratman was born to loop. Literally. He entered the world in a hospital adjacent to the second tee at nearby Southern Pines Golf Club and joked that he'd likely leave the world through the same building, since it had been converted into an assisted living facility. Before the round, he wisely steered me away from the driving range and toward the short-game area to practice my chipping. During our round, landing precise shots on those humped greens saved me far more strokes on my scorecard than any ego-stroking drives.

I followed that round with another 84 the next day at Eagle Point Golf Club in Wilmington, a tricky Tom Fazio design off the Intracoastal Waterway.

I was ready to dominate. Kevin and Richard had other ideas. They didn't wait long to start in with their head games, relying on the same tactics that had worked during our Bout in the Bluegrass at Valhalla. Knowing how much importance I put on routine, they went all out to disrupt my habitual rhythm and cadence. From the moment I arrived at the course, they rushed me. Kevin had arranged the round through someone at his home club, which meant that I hadn't had to take Dylan Rowe (the intern I'd met at Valhalla) up on his offer to ask his dad, the club's head pro, to get us on the course. It also meant that I had no control over anything.

Kevin gave me our tee time and that was it. He didn't inform me until the last minute that we were going to play the club's par-three course before teeing off on the main layout. That led to chaos: we lost our original tee time when the starter couldn't find us. Then, a few holes later, we were abruptly rushed off the par-three track when a new time opened up on the main course, all of us forced to scatter like fire ants kicked from their mound.

I gathered myself on the first tee box but couldn't decide where to aim my drive on the short par four with a hard dogleg left. Thick pines and a gator-friendly Caney Creek flanked the left side, while the tee box pointed toward the trees to the right. I finally hit a 5-wood toward the trees, hoping that my ball would stop before it reached the edge of the fairway. It didn't. It flew beyond and settled in the dirt under low branches. I never recovered and made double bogey. All the resourcefulness I thought I'd stirred up on that ancestral soil with my memories counted for nothing on the golf course.

I had a few pars here and there the rest of the round, and I scored well on what are considered two of the three toughest finishing holes in Texas. But my day was mostly one disastrous shot after another. I drove my ball into the water on the twelfth trying to cut off too much of the river that ran between the tee and the fairway. And though I made the green on the par-three sixteenth, my ball ran off the back, never to be found. Maybe a gator got it.

The three of us always play our worst golf when we compete against one another. Kevin and Richard are too busy trying to get into my head, and I'm too busy trying to ignore them. But, as always, we made promises at the end of the round to do it all again.

I HEADED BACK TOWARD HOUSTON. The route was at once familiar and disorienting. I had spent the first eighteen years of my life at one stop or another along the 112-mile segment of what's now I-45 between Hunts-ville and Galveston. Most of the region's rural history has since been plowed under and paved over by Houston's relentless boom-bust-boom exurban push. Through my windshield, I watched a continuous-seeming succession of strip malls and car dealerships and chain motels.

As I was growing up, it was still small-town Texas that whooshed by me as I held on for dear life in the bed of Frank's pickup truck. The road-side was still thick with wild grasses and tall pines and cattle. Houston was already Houston, even then, with downtown traffic clogged like a pig in a python. But as we inched our way through and approached Texas City, just south, I could spot derricks bobbing for oil on the dwindling patches of undeveloped land.

On my way home from Whispering Pines, I didn't swing through Huntsville. The sawmill is long gone. The dirt road we lived on is over-grown and barely visible, and the shacks that lined it have all been leveled—or, just as likely, simply disintegrated. The last time I'd visited, I'd had to ask directions just to find the little opening that marks the top of the road. People live nearby on what's now called Boettcher's Mill Road—Black folks who spent parts of their lives in the Sawmill Quar-ters or had relatives who did. Most were wary of me, now grown and a stranger, until I mentioned some obscure memory I knew would bind us, such as the scent of Miss Truelove's tea cakes wafting through the morn-ing air. We'd all give anything for a chance at one more bite of one of Miss Truelove's sweet tea cakes.

But neither my siblings nor I live there anymore, physically or psy-chologically. Yet the past still lingers. During my last visit, I ran into a rel-ative and his longtime girlfriend. She'd heard all the stories and lived near all the ghosts, and she summed up her takeaway of that now-disappeared world.

"Scary and haunted," she said with a chilling remove.

Asked to elaborate, she shook her head. "Scary and haunted," she repeated.

When I think back on all the misery Frank caused in our lives, I have to give him this: he got us out of there. Leaving the Sawmill Quarters changed the trajectory of our lives, at least eventually.

CHAPTER SEVENTEEN

LOS ANGELES
COUNTRY CLUB

We all carry, inside us, people who came before us.

—Liam Callanan

P eople are resilient but life is tenuous.

During my third trip to play golf in California, the rain poured down in sheets. Hills stripped of their protective vegetation by wildfires got so soaked that they slid toward the Pacific. Montecito, the wealthy Southern California enclave sandwiched between the foothills of the Santa Ynez Mountains and the ocean, where I was scheduled to play at the Valley Club of Montecito, was hit especially hard. More than twenty people lost their lives. Some were washed out to sea.

Tragedies like that are a sobering reminder of life's fragility. I lost a close friend and work colleague early in my career with Exxon. An African American mechanical engineer who graduated from the University of Kansas, Ed and I cemented our friendship over long days solving challenges with operating equipment inside the Baytown refinery. He died of acute leukemia at age thirty-one. I sat with him at the hospital a few hours before his last breath.

I'd witnessed death before, like when Boogie had been shot just yards away from me in the projects. But he had been dead by the time I'd gotten to him. Before I sat beside Ed in the hospital, I'd never heard a death rattle, the gurgling sound made by a dying person too weak to cough.

In my early years at Exxon, work consumed me. I sat at my desk until late at night, designing equipment, solving equations, studying operating materials. I spent most weekends inside the refinery, donning a white hard hat and steel-toed boots to learn more from the workers who operated it.

My job was my life. I loved it.

Ed's passing was a wake-up call. I began to seek more balance. I started taking what I called "stop and smell the roses trips": drives across the country to soak in the sights and appreciate friends and strangers alike. I explored national parks, toured local museums, ate in roadside diners, nosed around mom-and-pop shops. I talked with folks everywhere along the way. I'm a people person—not just by choice but by nature.

Decades later, I was back at it, crisscrossing the country, but this time on a golf odyssey often impacted by existential events: the mudslides in Montecito; wildfires that raged within yards of Mayacama, a Napa Valley club where during a charity event pro athletes scrambled for their lives; an underground fire at the Atlanta airport that knocked out power hours before my flight and almost prevented me from even getting to Mayacama and the Olympic Club in San Francisco, another course I was scheduled to play that week.

The tragic events in Montecito disrupted my plans to play the Valley Club, but I rearranged my schedule during that trip and completed rounds at the Los Angeles Country Club and the Quarry at La Quinta in Palm Desert.

Six months before my round at LACC, while vacationing in Ireland, Erika and I were interrupted during dinner by a gray-haired man at the table next to ours. He'd overheard us talking about the first five courses I'd played and asked if the Los Angeles Country Club was on my list. When I acknowledged that it was, he said, "Well, they don't allow Blacks, Jews, or movie stars, but if you can promise me you aren't a movie star, I can probably get you on."

His comment caught me off guard until I realized he was joking about LACC's past discriminatory policy, one that had long been abandoned (except for the movie star exception). I appreciated his offer, but I already had a host. A former neighbor from our time in Charlottesville, Jim Haden, had asked his brother Pat, the former football star, to host me. I'd golfed regularly with Jim at Glenmore before I joined the group with the guys who seemed to long for the days when Blacks and Jews— but I assume not movie stars—were shut out of private clubs.

Jim was the CEO of the hospital where Alexandra was born. Even if we'd never played golf together, he might still have known about me from one of his hospital's delivery rooms.

JIM'S KNOWLEDGE WOULD LIKELY HAVE arisen from a fateful summer morning in 2004 when Erika awoke and declared that our second child would be born that day. I grabbed the bag she'd packed for this very occasion and we headed to the office of her ob-gyn.

Dr. Siva Thiagarajah, fondly known as Dr. T., immediately confirmed that Erika was in labor and sent us across the street to the hospital where she could relax in a tub of warm water until delivery.

Erika lay across the delivery room bed while a nurse filled the whirlpool bath. She asked the nurse for something to relieve her discomfort. To ensure that she wasn't administering medication too close to delivery, the nurse checked Erika's dilation and confirmed that we had plenty of time. She handed Erika a couple of pain pills and said she'd be right back.

Erika never made it to the tub. Moments after the nurse walked out, Erika exclaimed, "The baby's coming!"

That was when I said four of the most foolish words ever spoken by a man whose wife was in labor with a second child: "How do you know?"

In a voice I'd never heard before, from a deep place where no man dares go, Erika yelled, *"Get somebody now!"*

I sprinted to the nurse's station: "My wife said the baby is coming."

As the nurse and I rushed back into the room, we saw the baby's head crowning. The nurse mashed the call button and told me to wash up. Several other people dressed in scrubs and head coverings ran into the room. But before they could assist us, the nurse and I had rotated Alexandra to untangle her from the umbilical cord and then, together, pulled her from the womb.

One of the staffers who'd charged into the room took my shiny new daughter from my hands and placed her on a table next to Erika's bed, immediately suctioning fluids from her nose and mouth. The nurse I'd just assisted assured us that everything was fine. Amid all the chaos, I don't even remember who cut Alexandra's umbilical cord—me, the nurse, or one of the other people who came racing into the room.

The setting and circumstances were much different, but it seemed that another circle had suddenly been closed. My three oldest siblings and I were all delivered in a country cabin by a midwife. Now as an adult, in bright hospitals surrounded by the best medical staff and the latest technology money could provide, I'd helped deliver both of my own children.

———

JIM HADEN'S BROTHER PAT IS a well-known two-time national champion quarterback at the University of Southern California. He's also a Rhodes Scholar, NFL quarterback, TV color commentator, and former athletic director at his alma mater. Now he'd agreed to host me at LACC, set on a multibillion-dollar strip of real estate along Wilshire Boulevard, between Beverly Hills and Westwood. But despite its high-priced acreage, many of the fairways on LACC's championship North Course are generous enough to hold even my free-range drives.

Still, danger lurks: treacherous bunkers, dry creek beds (known locally as *barrancas*), and slopes that send drives that land on the wrong side of the fairway into deep, ball-clutching rough. Survive those, and there are still the bunker-patrolled greens, which are fast and firm, i.e., dangerous.

Every great golf course should have a short par four, and the sixth hole at LACC is one of my favorites. It measures 320 yards from the blue tees, with a hard dogleg-right fairway that widens in the landing zone. Golfers much stronger than I might try to drive the green by cutting off the dogleg, but if the ball flies to the right, trees and a *barranca* stand ready as par killers. A deep trap off the green's collar catches balls that are short, leaving a tough up-and-down to a shallow putting surface backed by yet another bunker with a steep slope behind it.

I took the safe route, hitting a 3-hybrid to the dogleg's spacious bend. The ball kicked toward my target, leaving just eighty yards to the pin. That was when I got greedy. Rather than staying conservative by going for the middle of the putting surface, I took on the back-left pin placement. The ball carried a couple yards too long and landed on the slope behind the green. It took a chip and two putts to get into the cup. I enjoyed the entire course, but the sixth hole sticks out. It presented so many challenging options; I could've played it eighteen times, eighteen different ways, and called it a round.

Throughout our round I was struck by Pat's unassuming manner. He didn't tell stories about his national championship seasons at USC or the All-Pro NFL season he'd had while simultaneously attending Oxford. I can't tell you what he thinks about any of his accomplishments. As we walked the fairways, he pointed to Lionel Richie's backyard and pool and, later, the wall that separated a fairway from the former Playboy Mansion. But our conversations centered mostly on his wife, Cindy, his kids, and his grandkids, including one grandson who's a terrific golfer.

As for me, who worried about fading into obscurity after a fulfilling career, Pat's humility was a heartening reminder that our lives are defined more by who we share them with than by what we achieve at the office.

On that day, he was more of a loving husband, proud father, and doting grandfather than a former football star.

Pat hosted me again several weeks later at Cypress Point Club in Northern California, where every hole challenged me in its own way. On a lot of courses, you hit a driver off every tee except on the par threes. A certain dullness creeps in. That wasn't a problem there. Between all the club choices off the tee on the par fours and fives and the never disappointing beauty of the ragged coastline that runs along holes thirteen through seventeen, there's neither time nor space for boredom at Cypress Point.

The sixteenth hole exemplifies the seaside course's seductiveness. Set on the Monterey Peninsula's westernmost point, the 220-yard hole is arguably the par three with the most dramatic risk-reward ratio in all of golf. It plays entirely over a deep-blue cove carved into the Pacific, with a mere five to seven yards between the cliff's edge and the front of the green. With the wind in our faces, everyone in our foursome but me avoided the cove by bailing out to the fairway to the left and short of the green. That line requires a carry of just 120 yards. From there, they could take their chances with a pitch-and-putt par.

But I hadn't flown five hundred miles an hour in a pressurized tube at thirty-five thousand feet from one coast to the other to bail out left on a golf course. I went right at the flag. For 185 of the 187 yards needed to clear the ocean, my ball looked splendid. Then came the last 2 yards. My ball caught the edge of the cliff, kicked back, and plummeted toward the beach.

After a penalty stroke, I teed up again and hit to the bailout area. A pitch-and-putt later, I penciled in a double bogey that could have been a par had I taken the safe route to begin with.

I CONCLUDED WHAT HAD BEEN my third trip to California on one of the lushest fairways I'd ever seen—smack in the middle of the desert.

I'd played my first desert course a few weeks earlier, the Estancia Club in Scottsdale, Arizona, and been blown away by how green and fertile it looked amid that arid landscape. The course superintendent, noting my disbelief, jokingly said that they watered the fairways with Evian.

If the Estancia Club irrigates with Evian, the Quarry at La Quinta, in the Coachella Valley near Palm Springs, must use Dom Pérignon. The fairways and putting surfaces were even greener and as immaculate and tight as artificial turf.

The course conditions of the Quarry rivaled those of Augusta National. Fairways wound like emerald ribbons among lakes, streams, boulders, waterfalls, mesquite, and cassias near the base of the Santa Rosa and San Jacinto ranges. Divots appeared to fill themselves, and the rough, cut slightly higher than the fairways, was in better condition than the fairways on some of the other courses I'd played.

The head pro had agreed to let me play the course after a single phone call, and he paired me with Justin, an assistant pro. Justin splits his year between Castle Pines in Colorado, where I'd met him during an earlier round, and the Quarry. He's originally from little Norfolk, Nebraska, the hometown of Johnny Carson, the late-night TV host who kept me up until midnight on school days when I was a teenager.

During those years, I didn't really understand my fondness for Carson. Looking back, however, it had a lot to do with my memories of summers spent with my grandparents. Three of my mother's sisters, who'd moved to California to escape the Jim Crow South in the late fifties and early sixties, when defense contractors were hiring everyone they could, even women of color, had chipped in to purchase a TV set for them in 1969.

The mahogany-stained console was about half the size of a dresser. It had a large round knob with numbers for the channels and smaller knobs for brightness, contrast, and horizontal hold, which prevented the picture from scrolling off the screen. The first summer they owned it, all of us kids sat on the floor, with my grandparents behind us on the sofa, and watched in awe as Neil Armstrong set foot on the moon.

My grandparents loved Flip Wilson's variety show and, on the rare Sunday nights we weren't in church, *The Ed Sullivan Show*. The television was usually turned off right after those shows ended; Jamama and Pa Pa told us that the TV needed to rest.

I recall one exception: the night Joe Frazier was a guest on *The Tonight Show*. I think it was after his first fight with Muhammad Ali. My grandparents admired Frazier but had mixed feelings about Ali after he changed his name from Cassius Clay, though I believe they would've appreciated the man he became if they'd lived to see it. That episode of *The Tonight Show* was the last TV show I remember watching with them. That fall, my grandmother, who hadn't shown any signs of illness, suffered a stroke and passed away at seventy.

As her body lay cold and still inside a half-open casket just below the pulpit in Mount Zion Baptist Church, her original church home before she and my grandfather had met, I sat in disbelief. I kept expecting her to wake up, step out of the casket, and walk right out of the church. She was the first person of significance in my life to die. The death of my father, whose name wasn't even on my birth certificate, had had zero effect on me. But at thirteen, I struggled to process my grief at my grandmother's sudden passing.

After they lowered her casket into the ground of the Mount Zion Cemetery, I not only said goodbye to my grandmother, I also said goodbye to my summers of endless exploration, tub baths with ticklish tadpoles, drinking water drawn from a well, and hopscotch across squares sketched in the dirt.

My grandfather passed nine years later, at eighty-nine. He was eulogized in the roadside church he had helped build, the Galilee Church of God in Christ, where we had spent all those endless Sundays, and then buried next to my grandmother at Mount Zion.

The quiet death of that man, who had been such a towering figure in my life and whose grandmother had been a slave, reminded me that life is tenuous, no matter how resilient we are.

With his death, the family legacy fell on my mother and her siblings.

CHAPTER EIGHTEEN

SEMINOLE

Forgiveness is the fragrance that the violet sheds
on the heel that has crushed it.

—Mark Twain

Despite the hurtful things my mother's siblings said to her about having kids out of wedlock and the awful ways they sometimes treated her, she never let it break her spirit. Although they weren't there for her as a teenager when one of their husbands raped her—an incident she never spoke of and that I learned about only after her death—as an adult she always summoned the inner strength to be there when they needed her. My mother didn't learn to read until late in life, but she possessed a remarkable memory. She recalled every detail of everything she ever saw and anything ever said to her. Even more remarkable was her ability to forgive. She never held a grudge or harbored resentment—a trait she passed down to all of us.

In the summer of 2018, as my mother's youngest and last surviving sibling lay bedridden in her small bungalow near Crenshaw, Los Angeles, my younger brother Jeron, who lived about forty miles south in Santa Ana, moved in and became her caretaker.

Jeron, who was born Earnest but changed his name as an adult, was the second of my four siblings fathered by Frank. He had a troubled childhood, dropping in and out of school and constantly getting into fights. But he turned his life around after attending a Job Corps program in Texas: he moved to California to drive eighteen-wheelers, got married, and raised two great kids.

He was divorced by the time our aunt Tanza's health began to fail, and he stayed at her place to help whenever he was off work. Despite her eighty-four-year-old body's breakdown, our aunt's mind remained strong. One day near the end of her life, as my brother returned her to bed after he had helped her to and from the bathroom, she looked up at him and asked, "Why are you here?"

"Because you need me, Auntie," he replied.

The answer didn't satisfy her. "But why are *you* here?" she repeated.

Jeron wasn't sure what she was getting at. Then she added the one thing that still weighed heavily on her mind: "After all the horrible things we said and did to your mother, why are you here taking care of me?"

Jeron finally understood. "You're my mother's baby sister," he said simply. "I'm just doing what she would have done."

My mother's jobs required few professional skills. She cleaned and cooked for other people. She mopped floors and washed bedpans. Yet she had a rare gift. She excelled at being authentic and true to herself and instilling those values in her children.

A LONG, EARLY WINTER BECAME my odyssey's nemesis. With freezing temperatures and snow blanketing much of the Northeast and Midwest, I focused on playing elite courses in the warmer, clearer South and West. I had played almost sixty courses in my first six months; I played just ten across the three months of winter.

After the California trip, I made a couple of February stops in Florida: Seminole Golf Club, the course many consider the best in the state;

Calusa Pines Golf Club, my personal favorite there; and the challenging but fun layout at TPC Sawgrass in Ponte Vedra Beach.

As Lin Rogers's jet, the same one that had whisked me to Augusta, touched down at Palm Beach International Airport, I was reminded right away of the six-year-old illegitimate colored boy that is always with me. I'd never seen so many private jets in one place, not even when I was with ExxonMobil, when I occasionally flew on the company plane. Gulfstreams, Bombardier Challengers, Cessna Citations, and the like were flanked by rows of Range Rovers and black Chevrolet Suburbans.

Although I had become accustomed to the trappings of privilege and wealth during my visits to so many esteemed clubs, I was shocked by how quickly I again felt out of place. I'd stepped into a world even more elevated than the elevated worlds I'd stepped into before, something I hadn't thought possible.

I didn't have too much time to spend in somber reflection, though. Lin's copilot threw our clubs into the back of a Suburban, and off we darted to Seminole. Attendants greeted our group, which again included Danny Yates, in the semicircular driveway in front of the terra-cotta Spanish-style clubhouse, its white window awnings gleaming in the bright sun. They told us that our lone responsibility at the club was to enjoy ourselves. They'd take care of everything else.

It reminded me of a weekend excursion I had taken about a year before retiring, to ExxonMobil's hunting ranch in South Texas. Our fleet of private jets was greeted by a procession of black SUVs that dropped us off at the lodge, where a staff of attendants lined the driveway to welcome us. I hadn't been hunting since I was a young boy, when I had done it for survival rather than sport. I have no muscle memory for golf after taking up the game so late in life, but my muscle memory for shooting birds remained intact. Armed with a shotgun rather than my childhood weapons—a slingshot or a rubber gun we crafted from a wooden stick, a clothespin, and rubber from a worn-out inner tube—I quickly reached the state's limit on kills. I was less proficient at shooting clays, which felt to me like pretend hunting.

The most fascinating moment came just before dawn on the second day while I hunted with soon-to-be CEO Darren Woods. Out in tall weeds along a narrow dirt road, I nailed a wild hog. It was almost too easy. I stood with my feet shoulder width apart, my right leg back a bit, my knees bent slightly in a relaxed, balanced stance—just as I'd do with my golf swing. With the butt of the shotgun's brown stock pressed against my right shoulder, I peered through the scope in the dim light and put the crosshairs an inch to the left of the hog's front quarter as it stood about four hundred feet away. Our guide said that that would ensure a quick kill. I took a light breath, then pulled the trigger. The two-hundred-plus-pound beast dropped instantly.

If we'd had black-barreled Remington shotguns with scopes when I was a boy, I probably wouldn't have been so lanky.

As much as I enjoyed that trip, I almost hadn't gone. I was worried about succumbing to the good old boy culture I'd spent my career avoiding. I thought that becoming part of it would signal that I approved of it. I talked it over with Erika, and she advised that I couldn't work to change the culture if I wasn't at the table. Throughout my career, I'd learned that it wasn't enough to fight for equality; I also had to combat the things that perpetuated inequality. As it turned out, my presence at the ranch, along with that of some female colleagues, wound up being a step in the right direction.

It wasn't a total success. Before I left for the ranch, Erika offered one piece of advice: don't get shot. I failed. While hunting dove, a colleague went beyond his designated shooting arc, and I soon felt the sting of hot buckshot raining down on my arms and chest. They had to be removed with tweezers.

I wasn't worried about buckshot on the first tee at Seminole, yet I remained unnerved. The fabled Bob Ford, who for years had split his time as head pro between Oakmont in the summer and Seminole in the winter, stood just off the tee box, eyeing our first drives.

Seminole caters to highly skilled golfers. Ringed by towering hedges and set between dune ridges along Juno Beach and US Highway 1, the wide-open Donald Ross design offers plenty of room off the tee. But if the bunkers or waste areas don't get you, the fast, firm, wavering greens likely will. The course is hard. It's even harder when the wind blows, which, as at Prairie Dunes in Kansas, it almost always does. But unlike those winds off the plains, which generally blow from the northwest, the Atlantic gale at Seminole seemed to come from every direction.

Unable to relax, I hooked my drive on the 370-yard par-four first. Fortunately, the tall palms along the left side had plenty of space between them. My ball rolled through the first of the fairway bunkers before settling in the rough, leaving me 215 yards to the pin.

My second shot flew between two more palms before curling toward the center of the fairway. Watching it soar, I felt good. That feeling didn't last: the ball landed short of the green, ran right through it, and came to rest just off the back. My putt from the tight fringe rolled for what seemed like an eternity before stopping ten feet below the hole. My next stroke pulled up five inches short. I tapped in for a disappointing bogey.

There are no easy holes at Seminole, just holes that are less difficult than others. I played sixteen of them without a single par. I wasn't even playing that poorly—the universal duffer's lament—I was just making one insufferable bogey after another. The shortish par-three seventeenth was emblematic. I stroked a beautiful tee shot on a hole separated by hedges from the beach and the aqua-blue Atlantic. The ball rode an ocean breeze down the left side and faded onto the green. Then it did what so many balls had done that day: it didn't hold. Instead, it rolled off and into one of the billion (or so it seemed) bunkers that encircled it. I blasted it out and back onto the green—where, again, it didn't hold and, again, rolled into another bunker on the opposite side.

It took me one swing to get within a few yards of the cup, then four more strokes to get to the bottom of it—my day in a nutshell.

Golf in a nutshell.

With one last chance to make a par, I lined up my drive on the closing par four just as I had when I had taken aim at that wild boar in South Texas. My knees were slightly bent, but this time my left foot was set about a foot behind my right, so I could hit a fade. I flipped my wrist at impact, drawing the ball slightly to the left rather than curving it to the right—a double cross. The ball sailed toward a waste area. My prospects for a round-ending par were grim.

For once I lucked out: the ball rested neatly atop the sand in the last of three bunkers. An easy but firm swing picked it cleanly and sent it on a direct line toward the pin. My shot landed in the center of the oblong green, then rolled to just eight feet below the cup.

I walked up the middle of the final fairway side by side with Danny Yates, dressed in his trademark beige sweater and khaki pants. It was the first time all day we both had putters in our hands as we strode together toward the green—my round's most memorable moment.

I missed the birdie putt. So did Danny. But an easy tap-in saved me from my first-ever round without a par.

———

MOST GOLF COURSES IN FLORIDA seem to me like the same song played by different orchestras—an ensemble of lagoons, palm trees, bunkers, and waste areas, all arranged on flat, sandy terrain.

Calusa Pines is the exception. Its long fairways rise and fall along a series of twists and turns through an array of vegetation—big pines, oaks, maples, and pampas bushes. If there were palm trees, I didn't notice them. The course does have four lagoons—it's Florida, after all—but water doesn't come into play on every hole. I was told that the sixteenth tee box might be the highest point in all of south Florida.

My host was JFK, John Francis Kennedy, a gray-bearded retired CFO from Boston known affectionately in golf circles as "The Prez" because his initials and home state match our thirty-fifth president's. He'd played nearly all the Top 100 courses; Augusta was his white whale. Now he was my ultimate blind date. I'd met him through a nearly uncountable number of introductions: a friend of a friend of a friend eventually led me to JFK. It was the longest, most random chain of connections I'd used to gain access to a single course.

———

Two weeks later, on my way to Las Vegas to attend a memorial service for a cousin's son with my siblings, I was hunting for a private club in the hills of Northern California.

Laid out eight miles south of the Golden Gate Bridge, near Lake Merced, the San Francisco Golf Club isn't an easy find. The barely marked entrance is off a narrow street that runs between a preschool and a Catholic church. It's further shrouded by the surrounding houses and apartments. I got the impression that it was hard to find by design.

A. W. Tillinghast's only original course in the West is as old school as his 1923 design suggests (no carts, no yardage markers, no cell phones), with wide, severely undulating fairways and large, comparatively level greens. My caddie, J.C., wore black from head to toe because, he explained, his initials matched those of the Man in Black himself, Johnny Cash. Virtually all the SFGC loopers are longtimers, and J.C. was no exception. He told me that my normal club distances were irrelevant in the Bay Area's cool, thick air. He said he'd hand me the club he thought I should use and that I should swing it without looking to see which club it was. I was skeptical. But after hitting the green in regulation on the first two holes, I was sold.

The most interesting hole is the 165-yard downhill par-three seventh tucked into the southeast corner of the property. It was built on the site of the last known legal duel in America. In 1859, one hundred years before my birth, David Broderick, an abolitionist US senator originally from New York, was mortally wounded on the site by David Terry, a pro-slavery former Kentuckian and recently resigned chief justice of the California Supreme Court. The two men had been close friends and political allies until they fell out over slavery. Broderick died three days after Terry shot him. Terry was killed three decades later by the bodyguard of a US Supreme Court justice he attacked on a train car. The percussion-lock, .58-caliber Belgian pistols used in the duel hang on the wall behind the clubhouse bar.

Reflecting on that bit of history, I thought our country could probably use more of what my mother had: the ability to forgive.

CHAPTER NINETEEN

RIVIERA

My hope is that we continue to nurture the places that we love,
but that we also look outside our immediate worlds.

—Annie Leibovitz

I have a simple palate that I come by honestly.

Until my senior year of high school, I'd never eaten in a sit-down restaurant where you order off a menu. That changed thanks to being on the student council. We invited imprisoned drug offenders to a school assembly in the hope that their shared pasts would deter classmates from drugs and crime. Afterward, another council member and I hosted the inmates and their guards for dinner.

We gathered around the table at a cozy Mexican restaurant along Highway 6, the main drag through Hitchcock. It was the closest I'd been to inmates since my childhood days, when almost every day I had walked past white-clad prison trustees sweeping the streets of downtown Huntsville. When it came time to order, I stared at a menu filled with unfamiliar Mexican dishes and finally just ordered a cheeseburger. One of the inmates immediately cut me a look. There was no mistaking its meaning: "Don't embarrass yourself by ordering a cheeseburger in a Mexican restaurant." I scanned the menu again and hurriedly ordered the closest-sounding thing to a cheeseburger I could find: beef burrito con queso.

Now, decades later, on a brisk Thursday evening in Evansville, Indiana, a river town on a horseshoe bend in the Ohio, I walked into a Golden Corral off Interstate 69. Spring was closing in, and I was looking forward to playing Victoria National Golf Club, just east, the next day. A young cashier with flowing dark hair slid my debit card through the reader to deduct $13.95 before I made my way to the all-you-can-eat food station. The choices seemed limitless: mashed potatoes or sweet potatoes, drumsticks or thighs, sweet corn or corn on the cob, string beans or black-eyed peas. I prefer choices like these over the menus of fancy dishes I have to consult Erika about.

Surveying the room with my plate piled high, I saw people as diverse as my food choices: Blacks, whites, Asians, Latinos, young families, elderly couples, mixed-race couples, singles—a melting pot in the middle of the country.

Sitting alone amid a symphony of voices, I filtered out conversations that, at their core, weren't much different from the ones I had listened to in the dining halls of the most privileged clubs I'd visited. People talked about family, work, their kids' education, doctors' appointments, health issues.

Although we have a long way to go in achieving equality in our country, the principle of *e pluribus unum* was evident inside that Golden Corral. As I wolfed down my fried chicken, sweet potatoes, and green beans, I couldn't help but feel a sense of hope for a more united and inclusive future—across the country and on exclusive golf courses alike.

TOM FAZIO DESIGNED VICTORIA NATIONAL Golf Club atop an abandoned strip mine. The picturesque routing passes between and around mounds of mining spoil and deep finger-lake lagoons. The course is demanding—higher handicappers sometimes grouse that it makes "a good golfer feel average"—but my early-spring round of 87 was less about my game than the between-swings conversations with my caddie as he un-wound the story of his circumstances and life.

Corey grew up around Philly but moved to Kentucky and got mar-ried. Now he was recently divorced and had taken a sabbatical from his banking career to focus on a start-up. He'd invented a device that prevents scam artists from using skimmers to steal information from debit and credit cards. It was his retirement ticket. He caddied to have a flexible schedule while developing his product and taking care of his daughter on weekends.

Corey projected both optimism and the weight of his life's burdens. He was trying to reinvent himself while dealing with day-to-day issues—making a living, coparenting—that remind you just how fast and relent-lessly life can come at you. In that way, golf provides a handy analogy: you keep adjusting, just as Corey had me do through eighteen holes on that tough, unyielding course; and you never really break the code, you just try to figure it out and learn from the process.

And lastly: if you break 90, you've done good.

That night, still stinging from my finishing-hole double bogey, I drove north toward Columbus in a massive rental SUV. My wipers brushed aside a misty rain the entire drive. I passed time on the phone with an old college classmate, reminiscing about how much my travel style had changed since the days when I had driven from Texas to Wash-ington, DC, for my internships.

Back then, I had loaded everything I owned—clothes, books, a small black-and-white TV—into the back seat and trunk of my 1978 burgundy Chevrolet Monte Carlo and hit the road. I'd drive twenty-four hours straight (the speed limit was 55 miles an hour) to avoid having to pay for a hotel, stopping only once, at a roadside rest area in the middle of the night, for an hours-long nap. I did splurge on one trip, spending the night at a motel where I found a room for less than ten bucks.

As we chatted about those not-so-good old days, an orange dash-board icon flashed for low tire pressure. I pulled over in the dark and the rain and instantly heard a hiss coming from the rear passenger-side tire. At that hour, in that weather, with eighteen-wheelers whooshing by, there was no way I was changing the tire on that unfamiliar monster of a vehicle. I called the rental's roadside assistance and waited for help.

A tow truck showed up an hour and a half later. It beeped and flashed its lights as it backed up to the front of my car. A chubby, gray-haired guy stepped out and pulled the lever to lower his flatbed. Realizing that he was about to put my car on the hook, I walked over to him and extended my hand. "Hi, I'm Jimmie," I said.

As we shook, I felt the same calluses and scars I'd felt while holding my grandfather's hands as I had helped him out of bed during the waning years of his life. Pa Pa's calluses and scars had been earned from a lifetime of hard work. I sensed that this man's were, too. Even in the pitch black, his eyes looked tired.

"I'm George," he said, his voice gruff and short.

I told him that I needed a tire changed, not a tow. He stopped dead and frowned. "They told me you needed a tow," he said.

He walked to the other side of his truck, mumbling to himself as he pulled a lug wrench from a metal toolbox. I tried to soften the moment. "Where you from, George?" I asked.

He ignored my question and pulled the spare from the back of my SUV. The tension was palpable. So I asked him, "Why does it matter whether it's a flat or a tow?"

"I just drove fifty miles," he answered flatly, not looking up, "for ten fucking dollars."

I was stunned. He'd come out on a miserable night to make what would add up to a couple dollars an hour.

"How much do you get for a tow?" I asked.

He looked more beleaguered by the minute. "Twenty," he finally responded.

With the rain falling on a chilly night, two contrasting Americas had collided along the side of Interstate 71: George, a white man in his midfifties who looked older than his years from a lifetime of working with his hands and his back, feeling gut punched by the thought of making only ten bucks for changing a tire; and me, a Black man traveling across the country while spending thousands of dollars to chase a dream most folks would consider whimsical at best.

I doubted that George would believe that I could relate to the way he was feeling.

After ten years at Exxon, I finally made it to 800 Bell Street—the gleaming, Oz-like headquarters in downtown Houston. Yet month after month passed without any advancement. I finally asked my boss, Chris, for a meeting and requested that he invite his boss, John, as well. (Yes, it is a company of many bosses.) Not many Black employees had advanced more than I had—at the time I was the only one in headquarters on the junior manager track, and only three other Black men had come and gone before me—and I wanted to give them a sense of what it was like for me, for *us*, to navigate multiple worlds. I wasn't asking outright for a promotion. I was asking for them to see something they might be blind to.

When we all sat down for the meeting, I allowed that I was concerned that I wasn't progressing as quickly as I thought I should. I told them that there were challenges I dealt with at Exxon that were separate from my abilities. I wanted to be sure it was not those challenges that were getting in my way.

They stared at me quizzically. I pulled out four magazines I'd brought into the room: *Life*, *Money*, *Ebony*, and *Black Enterprise*. I held up the issue of *Life*, which featured a beautiful white family on the cover, and asked John if he was familiar with the publication. He was; in fact, he subscribed to it. I then held up the copy of *Ebony*, whose cover featured a successful Black family. When I asked the same question, John said he thought he'd seen it on a grocery store rack but that he'd never bought or read it. I did the same thing with *Money* and *Black Enterprise*, with the same result.

"That's the challenge for me," I told them. "I'm from this world"—I held up the two Black-oriented magazines—"and then each day I walk through the doors of this building and into this world, the one depicted in *Money* and *Life*."

Lights flickered in their eyes.

"You get to live and work in just one of these worlds, while I have to navigate both," I went on. "And I want to make sure it's not the challenge of having to live in those two different worlds that's keeping me from advancing—that's keeping you from advancing me."

Slowly, they seemed to get my point. I was promoted a short time later. I probably would've been promoted anyway. What I took as my career stalling was merely the kind of temporary bottleneck that occurs all the time at a company as big and complex as ExxonMobil. Yet it was important to me to help them recognize that a homogeneous workplace designed long before, in a time of exclusion, needed to adapt to its changing workforce.

Was George dealing with challenges that his bosses couldn't comprehend? As I held a flashlight over his shoulder while he broke the lug nuts, I wondered what had led him to a life where his labor was worth less than what I had spent earlier that day to buy a peanut butter and jelly sandwich and a Powerade for my caddie at the turn.

The reason the social worker encouraged me to lower my expectations during my high school years was because the most successful Black men she knew were those who worked menial jobs at the refineries and chemical plants in nearby Texas City. Back then, however, even those men earned enough with their hands and backs to buy a house and educate their kids. I wondered if George could do the same in today's America and whether he believed in the American Dream as much as I did.

I told George that my tip would make his trip worthwhile. After he finished with the tire, I handed it to him—fifty bucks. His resentment blew out of him as rapidly as the air had evacuated my rental's back tire. In the dark, in the rain, amid the splashes and flashing headlights of the passing cars and trucks, he smiled and extended a hard, now-gritty hand.

We shook and went our separate ways—George to his America, where a single dollar still mattered, and me to mine, where I hoped I'd never forget that it's the Georges of the world who keep things moving.

In the end, it's not about which America we live in. It's about understanding and respecting both. It's about realizing that we are all in this together.

———

ALMOST ELEVEN MONTHS INTO MY quest, and a week and a half after my encounter with George, I finally played my twelfth and final course in California.

It didn't start well. David Roemer, who'd heard about my quest through a mutual friend, arranged a round at Riviera Country Club in the ritzy Pacific Palisades neighborhood on the west side of Los Angeles. He and I would be joined by one of David's work colleagues, Campbell, and our host, Michael, a friend of David's friend. David had played golf at Emory University in Atlanta and attended the University of St Andrews in Scotland as a graduate exchange student in a program that honored the memory of Bobby Jones, who'd also attended Emory and was beloved in St Andrews.

Unfortunately, Michael was expecting just two of us. He'd planned to play a match that day with another club member.

Ideally, every group on a golf course has the same number of players. This helps ensure a consistent pace of play throughout a round. Tee times are based on how long it should take four golfers to play a hole. Smaller or faster groups spend a lot of time waiting between shots, and groups larger than four can slow the pace of play for the entire course. Fortunately, we were allowed to play as a fivesome.

The first thing Michael asked me as we began our round was how old I was when I took up golf. When I told him I had started playing at forty-five, he shot back, "You can't be that good, then. It's going to be a long day." His remark, coupled with the fact that he and the other member were engaged in a high-stakes match, made it the most uncomfortable round of my quest. David, Campbell, and I stayed out of their way.

"Now on the tee, from Cherokee Town and Country Club, Jimmie James," the starter announced as I addressed my ball on the first tee box high above the fairway on the short, straightaway par five. With a strong wind at my back, I hammered a 265-yard drive down the fairway's right side, staying 35 yards short of the gravel cart path that cuts across it. I laid up to a comfortable 50 yards on my second shot and opened my round with a par on the course's second easiest hole.

With the wind blowing directly into us on the next hole, the toughest on the course, my drive flew 50 yards shorter than my first and landed in the right rough. I followed with one of the few double bogeys I carded all day, then rebounded with two straight pars.

My play on the 220-yard par-three fourth, with its expansive 40-yard bunker off the front of a 20-yard-deep green, made for one of my most satisfying moments of the round. Shooting into a two-club wind, I hit a driver off the tee on a par three for the first time in my life. I aimed for the right side of the green to avoid the massive front bunker. The ball landed pin high, just off the right edge, leaving forty feet for a birdie. I stroked the putt on a good line, but it ran out of gas five feet from the cup. I rammed the next putt home for my par.

I completed the front nine with a respectable 41.

Our host, a thirtysomething guy who played every day after having made his fortune creating two successful TV shows, was struggling, and was totally consumed by his match. He seemed to avoid David, Campbell, and me as much as we avoided him. David and I glanced at each other but said nothing about it.

Many golfers regard the tenth hole at Riviera as the greatest short par four in the world. It measures just 301 yards, but the strategically designed fairway and greenside bunkers create a dilemma: risk driving the green or lay up, which requires dropping the ball into a 50-yard area between two deep, raised-face bunkers. Meanwhile, the narrow green is protected by long traps to its left, to its right, and behind it.

It all makes for an interesting risk-reward proposition.

But even the most bedeviling golf dilemma in the world is less consequential than those I faced during my career. One of the most challenging occurred in 2010, following nineteen inches of torrential rain in Tennessee, south-central Kentucky, and northern Mississippi. The downpour caused the Cumberland River to crest well above its flood level and inflict significant damage in Nashville. A bulk fuel facility under my watch was situated on the Cumberland there, between Tennessee State University, an HBCU, and a golf course named for Ted Rhodes, the second Black man to compete in a U.S. Open. (Coincidentally, that 1948 tournament was played at the Riviera Country Club.)

During that catastrophic flood, river water rushed through the bulk fuel storage facility, causing one of the half-full gasoline tanks to float several feet above its concrete base. Two small pipes connected to the flanges near the tank's bottom were the only reason it didn't float away. To keep the tank in place and avoid a disastrous spill of hundreds of thousands of gallons of gasoline, we encircled it with stout half-inch-diameter steel cables anchored to bulldozers.

Then we had a challenging decision to make. One option was to pump water into the tank, allowing the lighter gasoline to float to the top. That way if the flange bolts were strained enough that the flanges separated, the water would leak out before the gasoline, giving us time to promptly retighten the flanges before any gasoline escaped. However, it was crucial to consider that putting water into the tank would increase its overall weight. That would increase the stress placed on the flange bolts and raise the potential risk of the tank bottom puncturing as it resettled onto its base once the floodwaters receded.

After engaging our emergency response experts and engineers, the manager responsible for the facility's operations and I decided to pump the water in. I told the manager that if our actions were successful, I'd give him the credit, but if they failed, I'd take the blame. Fortunately for everyone, the flanges held, and the tank ultimately settled back onto its base without leaking a drop of gasoline.

On the tenth hole at Riviera, my caddie and I decided to drive the green. It didn't work out as well as the decision to put water in the tank in Nashville. But thankfully, the only thing at stake on the course that day was my pride. I hit a low drive that caught the lip of one of those fairway bunkers, then kicked back into it. I took the blame. A bogey was the result. My caddie said that even the pros struggle with that hole and make more double bogeys than eagles.

The twelfth green features a tree off its left front commonly called the Bogart tree. Rumor has it that Humphrey Bogart sat beneath it during Los Angeles Opens there while sipping his favorite whiskey.

I saved par with a fifteen-foot putt on the long eighteenth hole, which plays uphill to a green just below the Spanish-style Riviera clubhouse. After we all shook hands, our host, Michael, asked about my score. I told him 83 and added, "Not bad for someone who didn't start playing until forty-five, huh?"

He winked and then wrote a check to his friend to settle the match he'd just lost.

It was way more than the tip I'd given George.

CHAPTER TWENTY

QUAKER RIDGE

When we give cheerfully and accept gratefully, everyone is blessed.

—Maya Angelou

Thirty-five days, twenty-nine courses.

That was the daunting task ahead of me. Feeling its full weight, I said goodbye to Erika and the kids and told them I wasn't sure when I'd be back.

The remaining courses were spread across nine states in virtually every corner of the country, with most in the Northeast and Midwest, where for months it had been too cold to play. Yet my biggest challenge wasn't geography—at that point, I'd hop on anything at any time to go anywhere. It was that I still hadn't secured hosts for five courses, with three commitments having fallen through at the last minute.

Things had started to feel especially dire when the guy scheduled to host me at Shinnecock Hills Golf Club on Long Island called to cancel a week before our tee time—his brother-in-law had passed away. He put his assistant on the line to reschedule, but the earliest opening she found was in August. I pushed her to find something sooner, but in my desperation, I think I pushed too hard; the guy got back on the phone to reiterate that August was the best he could do.

It was a major setback. I felt as though I were a field goal away from winning the Super Bowl—only to fumble inside the ten-yard line. Shinnecock, set to host the U.S. Open, had limited the number of guests each member could bring during the year leading up to it. The championship was now only a month away, and I worried that members had either reached their guest limit or already made commitments. I questioned my decision to save Shinnecock for the end of my year so I could play it under U.S. Open conditions. Now I could fail because of it.

I'd also let my self-imposed deadline become an obsession. My quest wasn't just about golf, and it certainly wasn't just about me; it was about determining whether America was still a country where the kind of grit, self-reliance, gratitude, and generosity that had helped me claw my way out of poverty and deal with barriers created by racism still mattered. In the grand scheme of things, completing my quest in August instead of June wouldn't have had any bearing on that determination. However, the boy my mother had raised and the man I had become didn't want to let down all those who had helped me so far. I wanted to do exactly what I told them I would do. The salesman in me also wanted to close the deal; closing validates your premise.

The challenges mounted as time ran down. I also needed hosts for the two other courses where my commitments hadn't panned out—Pine Valley Golf Club and Quaker Ridge Golf Club in New Jersey and New York, respectively—and invites for two courses in Idaho. The improbable was looking more and more impossible.

Still, I refused to give up. A few days later, I boarded a plane to LaGuardia to play Winged Foot Golf Club in Mamaroneck. As I walked through rows of cars in the rental garage on the other side of the Grand Central Parkway, an attendant named Nathan noticed the bulky black travel bag I was pulling behind me. He asked if I was a golfer. I mentioned my quest. He seemed unimpressed and told me that he held the course record at a golf club in Hawaii. After a brief pause, he added, "No one has ever shot higher than the 143 I scored there."

Didn't see that coming! We both laughed out loud. For a moment, he made me forget my crazy challenges. We can all use the pressure-relieving levity of a Nathan now and again.

————

LIN ROGERS, WHO'D HELPED KICK-START my journey at Augusta, had gotten a friend to arrange for me to play Winged Foot's two Top 100 courses with Mike Ballo, one of the club's assistant pros. The West Course, which has hosted major championships dating back to 1929, was undergoing a renovation in preparation for the U.S. Open a few years down the road. So Mike and I played its back nine, along with ten holes on the East Course. Fortunately for me, that unconventional routing included the West's eighteenth hole.

The eighteenth is probably most famous for denying Phil Mickelson his third consecutive major during the 2006 U.S. Open. From the tee box, needing just a par to win, Phil stared out at a right-to-left fairway that swept between the tall elms lining both sides. But his drive flew well left, bouncing off a white hospitality tent and into the rough.

Rather than pitching safely back into the fairway, Phil foolishly did what a duffer like me would do: tried to reach the green with a miracle shot around one of the elms. The ball struck the tree and kicked right back at him. His third shot buried itself in the left greenside bunker. Phil, one of the best short-game players on the planet, failed to get up and down from there. He carded a double bogey and lost by a stroke to Geoff Ogilvy, who'd birdied the final hole.

As for me, I hit a booming high drive down the right side. The ball landed in the fairway, then rolled into the first cut, stopping less than a yard from the hole's lone fairway bunker. It left me 160 yards to a middle-left pin. I striped a dart straight at the flag. The ball landed inches beyond the hole, then rolled out to twelve feet. My birdie putt narrowly missed the cup. Disappointed, I tapped in for a par.

My caddie, Dawnie, a Scottish lass with red hair, white shirt, khaki shorts, and shades, noticed my dejected look. "Phil Mickelson would have paid a million pounds for that par," she half joked in her Scottish accent.

As Dawnie cleaned my clubs after we completed the ten holes on the East Course, I mentioned that I planned to drive to the Hamptons to knock out four more courses. She and Mike suggested that I take the more scenic and less stressful route to Bridgeport, Connecticut, then ferry across the sound and drive the remaining twenty minutes to the Hamptons. Little did any of us know that their suggestion would put me onto a collision course with destiny.

Their route took me north rather than south and sent me immediately down Griffen Avenue, between Winged Foot and Quaker Ridge Golf Club, directly across the street. I hadn't driven far when I noticed a commotion on the side of the road. A couple of guys in golf attire were in a heated discussion with a taller fellow standing next to a blue pickup truck with a cracked windshield. One of the golfers had apparently hit a ball over the low stone wall between the course and the street and it had pinged the truck's glass.

Curiosity got the best of me. I parked on an intersecting street and watched until the tall fellow angrily got into his pickup to move it from the middle of the avenue.

At that moment, along that unexpected route, I reflected on all the serendipitous encounters that had gotten me onto courses. I also thought about all the doors I had knocked on in my youth to sell a product or an idea. I got out of my car, walked over to the guys, introduced myself, and told them I was sorry for whatever calamity had occurred but that every dark cloud had a silver lining and I wanted to be theirs. They just blinked back. I then explained that I was on a mission, with a rapidly approaching deadline, to play the country's most exclusive courses in a year. I pointed over the wall toward Quaker Ridge and said, "I have thirty-four days left to play twenty-seven courses, and I need to play that one this Saturday."

Throughout the year, I hadn't asked anyone directly for help other than the pros at my own clubs and two or three others. But as a former salesman, I knew that to close the deal I would have to ask for the sale. Standing on a street I'd never been on, still wearing the blue polo and khaki pants from my round at Winged Foot, I knew that if I was going to achieve something never done before, I had to take risks and do things most people wouldn't.

My pitch couldn't have been clearer. "I need one of you to host me on Saturday," I said to the group of strangers.

They continued to stand there, shocked and speechless, I think, by my boldness. Then one guy, dressed in a shirt with a Quaker Ridge logo, broke the stunned silence. "These guys can't help you, they aren't members," he said flatly. "But I'll tell you what: we need to deal with this cracked windshield right now, so give me your cell number and I'll call you this evening."

With that, I slid into my rental and drove off. I didn't know whether I'd hear from the guy or not, but I knew that when it comes to achieving aspirations in the face of adversity, it helps to believe in fate.

He called that evening as I sat in my Hamptons hotel room, introducing himself as Mario Guerra. I recognized his name from my research: he was the head pro at Quaker Ridge. Mario told me he appreciated the way I had approached him and the other guys on the street. At the time, I'd had no idea who I was talking to. Then he added, "I, too, believe in fate intervening in our lives as a force for good."

He asked about my background. I told him I had been born into poverty in Texas but overcame those beginnings to have a successful career in the energy industry. He told me that his family had come to America as political asylum refugees from Cuba.

As a boy, I'd played baseball with a stick and a doll's head on the dusty roads of the Sawmill Quarters. When Mario was a young boy in Cuba, he used a broomstick for a bat and a rock wrapped in tape as a ball. He played basketball on a dirt court with a hoop made from the metal ring of an old wine barrel that was attached to a corner of his house. We were kindred spirits whose lives intersected on destiny's path.

Mario told me that Quaker Ridge didn't allow unaccompanied play on Saturdays during peak season. I understood that the members wanted unfettered access to their club after a long winter. But he said he admired what I was trying to do and that he'd request an exception from the club's president and general manager.

It was granted the next day. On the Saturday I had originally been scheduled to play Shinnecock Hills, I'd now be teeing it up with Mario at Quaker Ridge. My improbable quest had become a little less impossible—thanks to someone I hadn't known twenty-four hours earlier.

———

During the three days between my rounds at Winged Foot and Quaker Ridge, I checked off the four courses I'd traveled to the Hamptons to play: Sebonack Golf Club, Friar's Head, National Golf Links of America, and Maidstone Club.

The experience at Friar's Head began with the most sensible scorecard I've ever seen. After declaring that all natural sandy areas would be treated as bunkers, it wisely stated, "With respect to all other matters, common sense shall be exercised." The fabled Coore/Crenshaw design is situated just inland from the sound on the North Fork of eastern Long Island. Its neatly maintained fairways are carved from dunes and punctuated by bunkers and waste areas crafted to look as though they've been there for millennia. It gives the course the rugged elegance that's one of Coore and Crenshaw's hallmarks.

That throwback charm is enhanced by a strong reliance on caddies. A caddie is required; you can't survive the course without one. There are no yardages on the scorecard or yard markers in the fairways. My young caddie, Jason, a college student, carried a yardage book that helped us determine how long holes played and distances for approach shots. Jason also toted a pole on his back and rake teeth on his belt so he could assemble them swiftly when he needed to tend the bunkers; there are no stray rakes on the course. Playing Friar's Head is a return to golf's true roots.

My experience was capped off by what I consider the most stunning view of any Top 100 course on Long Island. Beyond my caddie and me on the elevated fifteenth tee, the fairway wound through sloping, tree-covered dunes toward a green that appeared to drop straight into Long Island Sound. Even more stunning: the walk to the sixteenth tee along a narrow wooden boardwalk that hung off a sandy cliff, also falling toward the sound. The sweeping vistas had little effect on my up-and-down game: I rolled in a ten-footer to save par on the picturesque fifteenth but made double bogey on the sixteenth after hitting a drive into the lone fairway trap.

The next morning, I drove around the Great Peconic Bay to play at National Golf Links of America, a course made up of a string of template holes. It's bordered to the south by Sebonack Golf Club, which I'd played two days earlier, and to the east by Shinnecock Hills, which I still needed a host for.

When I'd played Old Macdonald at Oregon's Bandon Dunes, with its oversized, quirkily configured greens, I'd thought it was the silliest course I'd ever played. I couldn't comprehend why it was ranked among the country's best. That was before I played Yeamans Hall Club, a Seth Raynor design running through the low country of Charleston, South Carolina, bordered by salt marshes and peppered with trees dripping Spanish moss. I found those holes so intriguing that I researched their architect. That led me to C. B. Macdonald and template holes.

National Golf Links is the outcome of several journeys through the British Isles that the Chicago-raised Macdonald, the mustachioed son of a Scottish father and part-Mohawk mother, took in the early 1900s to study golf courses. He found roughly twenty different links-style holes that he thought both beginners and expert golfers could appreciate. Those holes became known as template holes, and he used them as models to design National.

The holes include the Redan, like the one I had been fascinated by at Somerset Hills, a par three with a right-to-left, severely sloping green protected by a bunker off its front left. It's modeled after the fifteenth hole at North Berwick Golf Club, east of Edinburgh, Scotland. Then there's the Punchbowl, which at National is next to the course's iconic windmill, with a concave green reminiscent of the ninth hole at Royal Liverpool Golf Club in England. And there's the Road Hole, named for the infamous seventeenth hole on the Old Course at St Andrews. It's a hole that plays along a road and has some obstacle or hazard—in the case of St Andrews, the Old Course Hotel—that golfers must hit over to get to the fairway. At National, that hindrance is the crest of a hill and several bunkers.

Every hole at National forced me to strategize shots from tee to green, just as I'd done in business when mulling over market conditions, equipment reliability, and logistics for product delivery. Everything had to be in sync. Standing on the tee at National's short, drivable second hole, I had to decide whether to lay up onto the sloping diagonal fairway or drive the green and flirt with the tall fescue and massive bunker. I opted to lay up. But blessed with great luck at the worst time, I managed to hit the best 3-wood of my life. The ball sailed 260 yards, speeding along the fairway before finding a home in the right rough. My pitch from sixty yards landed thirty-five feet from the pin—a great (and welcome) save. Yet the challenge wasn't over. On an enormous green that both sloped and undulated, I three-putted for bogey.

It was bliss for a business strategist, engineer, and dedicated duffer like me.

"JIMMIE, WHY DO YOU THINK so many people have been so helpful during your quest?"

Sergio Galvis, the Colombian attorney who'd just hosted me at the

Maidstone Club in East Hampton, asked his question as we sat at a window table inside the East Hampton Grill, looking out at the boutique-lined Main Street.

We were there with our other playing partner, Geoff Whalen, whom I'd met a year earlier on the Ocean Course at Kiawah. Geoff was an executive at AMC, a cable TV network and studio headquartered in New York. When Geoff had asked during our round what I did for a living, I'd told him I was about to retire and embark on a journey to play the country's most exclusive courses. He'd brightened instantly and said he had a college friend who was married to a member at Maidstone, one of the more prestigious spots on my list. He hadn't guaranteed anything but had promised to ask his friend's husband if he'd host the two of us.

Now here we were.

Before I answered Sergio's question, Geoff piped in, "Because what he's doing is an amazing thing and people want to be a part of it." Sergio agreed but said he thought there was something deeper at play. In short: Sergio said that helping a stranger was as much a gift to him as it was to me. He thought the others who'd chipped in probably felt similarly.

I hadn't thought about it that way, but it made sense. Allowing people to do something for you that makes them feel good about who they are and what they've achieved is a gift that lasts.

———

AFTER PLAYING FOUR COURSES IN three days in the Hamptons, I drove back to Westchester County so Mario could be my silver lining.

Dark clouds hovered over us that Saturday, but luckily only a light rain fell as we made our way around the old-school Tillinghast design burrowed so snugly inside a quiet Scarsdale neighborhood that there isn't even room for a practice range.

Mario and I jokingly referred to each other as brothers from different mothers. During our round, I grew to appreciate the remarkable journey that had shaped his life. His grandfather's property was seized after Fidel Castro rose to power, and his father and uncle were eventually sent to work camps for their opposition to communism. Their persecution led his family to seek political asylum in the United States, leaving what little remained of their lives behind on the island. The US government offered his family free housing and food stamps in Chicago, but they chose to fly instead to Atlanta, where relatives had agreed to take them in.

As a boy, Mario dreamed of becoming a basketball player. That dream was dashed when he stopped growing at five feet, five inches, rendering meaningless all the shots he had made on that wire rim back in Cuba. Having played baseball with a broomstick and a rock made him a better-than-average high school player but not quite good enough to earn a college scholarship. He took out student loans to attend Valdosta State University in South Georgia.

During his sophomore year, while working as a residential assistant in a dorm, he met a couple of avid student golfers. Like me, Mario had grown up thinking that golf was something played by "them," not "us." But the students' enthusiasm piqued his interest. After playing hours of Tiger Woods's video golf game, he emptied his bank account to buy a sixty-dollar set of clubs from Walmart and borrowed money from his big sister for a bag. On the sixteenth hole of his first round ever, he hit a shot so pure that he neither heard a sound nor felt the slightest vibration of the club—the ultimate golf shot. It changed his life. He later confessed that if golf had been against his religion, his addiction to the game would surely have labeled him as a sinner.

Fate intervened a couple years after he graduated. During a round at a local course, he was randomly paired with the director of a Florida tournament on one of the PGA developmental tours. The guy offered Mario a volunteer job as a "runner," basically fetching whatever anybody needed fetched, but Mario completed that task so efficiently that he was reassigned to drive TV broadcaster Michael Breed around in a cart. By the end of the first day, Breed was so impressed by Mario's tenacity that he offered him a job at Sunningdale Country Club in New York, where Breed was head pro. Mario flew up the ranks there until he left to become assistant pro, then head pro, at Quaker Ridge.

By the end of our round, it was clear that the life journey that had put Mario on Griffen Avenue the day we met was as challenging and fateful as my own. I left Quaker Ridge with a friend for life.

———

ON SUNDAY, I RESTED. YES, it was only golf, "a good walk spoiled," as Twain mocked it, but hiking thirty-five to forty miles across seven courses in five days had still been a mental and physical grind.

I felt rejuvenated the next day, however, when I got to the Fishers Island ferry terminal in New London, Connecticut. I met up there with Bill "Billy from Philly" Allen, one of my Black Jacket buddies, and Tim Greene, the guy who'd invited me to join him and his son to get the first tee time at Bethpage. Those rounds felt as if they'd happened a lifetime before, but when my host at the Fishers Island Club had said I could bring friends for my unaccompanied round, I'd thought of those guys right away—Billy to thank him for his help getting me on at Prairie Dunes and Merion and Tim for welcoming me, a total stranger, in the Bethpage parking lot. We boarded the 7:00 a.m. ferry together for a forty-five-minute ride to a tiny island at the eastern entrance of Long Island Sound.

The pedigree of the 1926 design is maybe second to none: a collaboration between Seth Raynor, a C. B. Macdonald disciple, and Frederick Law Olmsted, Jr., a son of the renowned landscape architect credited with designing New York's Central Park and the grounds surrounding the US Capitol in Washington. Routed along the eastern end of the little two-mile-wide, eight-mile-long slip of land, the water-ringed course was shrouded in fog as we hit our inaugural tee shots. The opening hole is an unremarkable par four with a wide, hazard-free fairway until a small pond pops up beside the front of the green. It seemed pretty ho-hum, and at that point, I didn't understand what all the fuss was about. I felt the same way on the second hole, a standard Redan not nearly as captivating as Redans I'd played at Somerset Hills and National Golf Links.

All of that changed on the fourth hole, which plays along the sound and culminates with a Punchbowl green. By the par-three fifth, the fog had burned off, providing us with a clear view of the elevated, bifurcated Biarritz green, as well as a stunning panorama of the sound. That was when Billy turned to me and exclaimed, "Now I see why this is a top-ten course." The holes got even better after that; sky, land, and water often blended into one, creating a simple but singular landscape that brought the three of us together in a kind of communal awe.

Playing layouts like the one at National Golf Links had been fun, but the camaraderie among Billy, Tim, and me at Fishers Island, which we navigated without a caddie, made me regret having played so many courses as a single just to meet my self-imposed deadline.

Golf is a solitary sport best played with as many people as possible.

THE NEXT DAY, WHILE DRIVING to the Country Club in Brookline, Massachusetts, I passed the Park School, which Jordan and Alexandra had attended when we lived in Cambridge while Erika taught at Harvard Business School. The kids had been six and four. Precious memories from our time in the area flashed through my mind.

One Friday evening after I'd returned from a business trip, Erika told me that Jordan's first-grade adviser was concerned about the amount of time he spent alone during recess. Jordan was passionate about Boston's transit system, an outgrowth of the annual trips he and I took on Amtrak. His classmates' fascination with buses, trains, and trolleys waned after about five minutes, but while they moved on to other things, Jordan remained by himself to study more bus and rail schedules.

I explained to Jordan that although his classmates were fascinated by his knowledge of the transit system, he also needed to show an interest in them and their hobbies. He said he understood. So I asked him to spend the next week engaging his classmates on their pastimes. It was my version of giving him a bag of books like the one a coworker had once given me to broaden my own nerdy focus.

That Sunday evening, while putting him to bed, I asked Jordan if he had remembered the advice I'd given him. "Yes, Dad," he said. "I made a chart." He then showed me a chart he'd created with names of his classmates listed down one column and the days of the week listed across the top. He had placed check marks that identified which classmate's pastime he would show an interest in on each day: baseball, Batman, bugs. I smiled: no paternity test was needed to prove that he was my son.

Another cherished memory occurred during a weekend when Erika was away. I took both kids to a McDonald's a few blocks from our house. Jordan ordered chicken nuggets, and I got a cheeseburger for Alexandra. The look on her face when she bit into the sesame seed bun, beef patty, and cheese was priceless. "Mmm," she purred. "Can I have one for dinner, too?" No paternity test needed for that one, either.

As I turned into the Country Club entrance and drove over the road that cuts across the fifteenth fairway, my thoughts turned to the yellow clubhouse up ahead. Established in 1882, the Country Club is one of the oldest clubs in the United States and a charter member of what evolved into the United States Golf Association.

The club is also renowned, *still*, for the 1913 U.S. Open, when Francis Ouimet, a young American amateur and Country Club caddie, defeated the top British players at the time to capture the championship. The story is chronicled in Mark Frost's book *The Greatest Game Ever Played: Harry Vardon, Francis Ouimet, and the Birth of Modern Golf*. How I got to play the course, more than a century later, turned out to be a pretty great story, too.

My original host had canceled a couple weeks before our tee time because of a work conflict. In stepped Don and Caroline Young, a couple I'd been briefly introduced to by my host only a month earlier while finally playing at the Valley Club of Montecito in Southern California. After hearing about my Country Club host's cancellation, Don and Caroline, who were also members there, instantly rearranged their family vacation so Don could host me on the day I had originally been scheduled to play. It was one more inexplicably generous act by strangers that helped my increasingly long-shot goal remain in sight.

Another unlikely scenario led to my getting on at Shinnecock, which was fast becoming my white whale. While talking with members in the locker room at Old Sandwich Golf Club on Cape Cod, I ended up meeting the club's president, Andy Neher. When he learned about my odyssey, he asked if I was having trouble getting on at any remaining clubs. I told him that Shinnecock worried me the most, then brought up the "break glass in case of emergency" option I was reluctant to use. I explained that I'd been introduced by email to Jimmy Dunne, an almost universally known member of Shinnecock and other Top 100 clubs, as a potential host at Chicago Golf Club. Shinnecock members who no longer had guest privileges had told me that Jimmy was probably one of the few guys who could still take guests to Shinnecock ahead of the U.S. Open.

"You trying to play all one hundred courses, or just ninety-nine?" Andy asked.

I told him all one hundred, of course. Andy pulled out his phone. He knew Jimmy. "I'll call him right now."

I begged him not to call at that moment, promising that I'd get the person who'd introduced me to Jimmy to call him later. The truth is, I was finally afraid of "no." I wasn't ready to deal with the consequences.

I wrapped up my long, productive trip through Massachusetts with rounds at the Kittansett Club, Essex County Club, and Boston Golf Club. Twelve exhausting days after telling my wife and kids I didn't know when I'd see them again, I headed home.

Sixteen courses remained. With three weeks left to play them.

CHAPTER TWENTY-ONE

SHINNECOCK HILLS

Aerodynamically, the bumble bee shouldn't be able to fly, but the bumble bee doesn't know it so it goes on flying anyway.

—Mary Kay Ash

One winter night when I was five, sitting barefoot and bare-chested in worn coveralls at a table cobbled together out of more discarded wood from the sawmill up the hill, I made a promise to myself: I would graduate from high school.

At the time, I didn't know anybody who had done it. Even as a young child, I understood that following the same path as everyone else would lead me to the same place as they were in. If I wanted a different life from what I was experiencing in the Sawmill Quarters, I would have to do something different. Graduating from high school would be a start.

I sat a while longer in our shack's small, dimly lit front room, my toes freezing and my arms shivering in the weak heat thrown off by our makeshift wood-burning heater. I watched the smoke from a kerosene lamp curl toward the ceiling already darkened by years of soot.

It was the only light I had.

BEN HOGAN FAMOUSLY REFERRED TO the long par-four first hole at Oak Hill Country Club in Rochester, New York, with its narrow, slightly left-to-right fairway, as the toughest opening hole in major championship golf.

I birdied it.

But arranging rounds on a couple of the last courses during my quest had been much more challenging than that tap-in birdie. It's often said that the last mile of any journey is the hardest. I was finding that to be true.

It had certainly been the case during my pursuit of a high school diploma. It wasn't schoolwork or poverty that had made my last year of high school difficult; the biggest hurdle was overcoming my own fears. Growing up, I was sometimes accused of thinking I was special, and although at times I behaved in ways that distinguished me from others—bringing books home from school to study; not joining others to swipe stuff from the local supermarket—I knew deep down that that didn't make me better than anybody else. Having been labeled illegitimate at birth, I already felt as though I was less than everyone else. As my high school graduation got closer, I expected something to happen to prevent me from receiving a high school diploma, just as it must have happened to others. I didn't know what it would be, but I knew that something had prevented people more capable than I was from graduating.

As I ticked off the remaining courses on my list to accomplish a feat no one had attempted before, that same fear haunted me. I worried that weather, an injury, a last-minute cancellation, a flight delay, or any one of numerous other unforeseen pitfalls would keep me from achieving my goal.

I was down to sixteen courses, and I still needed hosts for Pine Valley, Shinnecock Hills, and two Idaho courses. Erika asked if I'd still play the other twelve even if I didn't get invites to those four. With the same resolve I'd had in high school, I told her I was going to play as many of the Top 100 courses as I could prior to my June 11 deadline. Though I had lined up hosts for twelve of them, I'd come to understand that nothing was certain until I was bending over on the first hole pushing a tee into the ground.

My fears were calmed a bit when people I'd met earlier along the way fulfilled their promises. Peter Korbakes, the cheery, enthusiastic fellow who'd raced down the fairway on the final hole at Milwaukee Country Club to offer an invitation to Olympia Fields Country Club, followed up and welcomed me to the sprawling course just south of Chicago. David Roemer, who'd secured a host for me at Riviera Country Club a month earlier, arranged for a friend to host me at Garden City Golf Club outside New York, known as much for its strict jacket requirement everywhere outside the locker room as for its classic Raynor design. Kevin Reeves, who had hosted me at the Golf Club near Columbus, Ohio, got a friend of a friend to host me at Camargo Club, a wide-open Raynor-designed course—the greens average a quarter acre—situated in a bedroom community north of Cincinnati.

At Butler National Golf Club, a men-only club in Chicago that plays deceptively longer and harder than it appears, I was granted membership for the day after my head pro from Cherokee requested playing privileges. Those privileges wouldn't have been granted for a woman. Though no club that I'm aware of still openly discriminates against Blacks or Jews, there are several that still ban women. Nancy Carlson, my longtime colleague and host at Congressional, would be out of luck at Butler. I only hope that one day soon, clubs decide it's as wrong to discriminate against women as it is to discriminate against others based on immutable characteristics.

My head pro wasn't the only club pro to help me in the final weeks. Relationships I'd established with other pros at previously played courses paved the way for a door-opening phone call with Peter McDonald, the head PGA professional at Shoreacres, a Seth Raynor course routed skillfully along ravines that abut the shore of Lake Michigan, north of Chicago.

My yearlong odyssey had been inadvertently ignited by Erika's request to her advisory board to help get me an invite to Augusta National. It had spun into a world of networking and encounters with golf royalty, self-made success stories, inheritors of family legacies and wealth, hardworking fathers and sons, immigrants, sympathetic caddies, and random strangers—all seemingly interconnected.

It's indeed a small world once you are in a particular world.

After playing Diamond Creek in North Carolina, then making the eight-hour drive to play Aronimink Golf Club, Donald Ross's self-proclaimed "masterpiece," outside Philadelphia, I had just nine courses left—and success or failure now rested on whether I could get onto Shinnecock Hills and Pine Valley. I'd locked in the two Idaho courses after an out-of-the-blue call from someone who'd heard about my mission and got a friend to host me.

It was time to break the glass.

I jetted off to join my friend Jeff "J.J." Johnson, the Flint Hills National president who had gotten me onto several courses, at Chicago Golf Club before playing my final Chicago-area track, Rich Harvest Farms, another billionaire's vanity layout that had begun as a six-hole backyard playground.

Over dinner after our round together, I asked J.J., who'd introduced me to Jimmy Dunne via email back in the fall, to reach out to him to see if he'd host me at Shinnecock.

He called over dessert.

I heard J.J.'s end of the conversation. He reminded Dunne who I was, then told him that my whole year now hinged on whether I got on Shinnecock. Was there anything Jimmy could do?

Me and the three others at our table stared at J.J., so quiet you could hear a pin drop. My heart pounded. I knew that the answer, one way or the other, wouldn't take long. Jimmy is a man of few words. In all the emails we'd exchanged, he'd rarely responded with more than four words; when he had, it had felt as though he'd written a novel.

J.J. smiled. "He can do it."

I put my face in my hands and breathed the biggest sigh of relief in the history of sighs of relief.

———

THE NEXT DAY, AS I pulled my rental into the parking lot of a Marriott in Naperville, Illinois, west of Chicago, I got a call from a stranger. Unbeknownst to me, a guy who had hosted me in Ohio had pleaded with his friend and Pine Valley member Jim White III to get me on at his club. Timing was tight: there was only one day when I could play Pine Valley and still complete the remaining courses by June 11.

Jim and I quickly realized that the one day that worked for me wouldn't work for him. We talked a few more minutes to avoid ending the call awkwardly. But as I sat in the car holding the cell phone to my ear, Jim decided to do something he never did: ask another Pine Valley member to host a stranger. Jim understood as well as anyone else that a reputation built over a lifetime could evaporate in an instant if you stuck a fellow member with a jerk for eighteen holes. But although he didn't know me, he knew a few others who did. Thankfully, they'd said nice things.

As I stared through my windshield with Jim on the other end of the line, it appeared the concerns I'd had at the start of my quest about being sabotaged because of my race had been unfounded. Instead, what mattered most, at least there, in that half-empty parking lot at my most desperate time of need, was whether or not I was a jerk.

I guess after playing almost all the country's most exclusive clubs, I hadn't embarrassed anyone.

Yet.

An hour later, Jim had arranged for another Pine Valley member to host me.

The dominoes had begun to drop.

By the time I left Chicago for Rochester, I had tee times for all seven remaining courses on the calendar. All I had to worry about now was weather, injuries, last-minute cancellations, and flight delays.

———

DURING THE TEN DAYS BEFORE I pressed that first tee into the ground at Oak Hill in Rochester, I had been to Ohio, North Carolina, Pennsylvania, New Jersey, Illinois, and New York twice. My birdie on Hogan's "toughest opening hole in major championship golf" on the ninety-fourth course on my list was surely the golf gods' gift for my iron-man efforts. I can't think of a better reason. My host seemed to acknowledge as much when, after our round, he handed me a commemorative golf tag engraved with my name, the date, and the words "Top 100."

After that: a seven-hour drive from Rochester to Southampton for my round at Shinnecock with Jimmy Dunne.

———

JIMMY DUNNE IS A DIMINUTIVE giant. He was in his early sixties when we played, and he was built like an aging wrestler, with specks of red peeking out here and there from a full head of graying hair. We arrived at Shinnecock's clubhouse, the country's oldest, within minutes of each other. Jimmy had flown into New York late the night before, having interrupted his college reunion at Notre Dame to be my host. He introduced me to the club staff and signed me in before we headed to the practice range together. We hit practice balls out into Shinnecock's rolling expanse, spreading over the unincorporated acreage nestled between Peconic Bay and the Atlantic.

No oddsmaker would've laid money on my being there, let alone being there with Jimmy. In fact, no oddsmaker would've laid money on either of us being alive.

Jimmy's survival story is one of the many legends, both tragic and heroic, born of 9/11. He was a hard-charging senior managing partner of Sandler O'Neill + Partners, a top national investment banking company once headquartered on the 104th floor of the World Trade Center's South Tower. He was also an avid golfer with a single-digit handicap and membership in numerous clubs, Augusta National among them.

Those details merged on September 11, 2001. Back then, Jimmy played so often and so well that he decided to try to qualify for the U.S. Mid-Amateur Championship, the leading tournament for amateur golfers twenty-five and older. His original plan was to qualify on a course in Connecticut on September 10. But Chris Quackenbush, Sandler O'Neill's head of investment banking and Jimmy's oldest and best friend, heard his plan and told Jimmy he'd have a better chance if he played at the Bedford Golf & Tennis Club, forty miles north of New York City. He thought that that course, challenging but straightforward if you keep the ball in the fairway, better suited Jimmy's game.

"Go to Bedford on the eleventh—you'll break par," Chris assured him.

Jimmy got an application for Bedford, filled it out, and handed it to his assistant, Debbie Paris. She sent it right in.

You can guess where this is headed. A cofounder of the firm and Jimmy's mentor, Herman Sandler, told Jimmy not to check in that day and to concentrate on playing his best. Jimmy showed up at Bedford early that crisp, clear Tuesday morning and, after a frost delay, got off to a strong start. He was one under par through four holes, feeling great about his chances, when a tournament official approached him with news of the tragedy unfolding in lower Manhattan.

Eighty-three of Sandler O'Neill's 171 employees were working on the 104th floor that morning. Sixty-six of them died—including Chris Quackenbush, Herman Sandler, and Debbie Paris. Golf saved Jimmy from the same fate.

Jimmy led the rebuilding of the decimated company. Every aspect had to be restored: financial records, phone records, computers. Meanwhile, he made sure that salaries and bonuses were paid, medical insurance was taken care of, and a college scholarship fund was established for the children of the employees who had died. In the following weeks, he spoke at no fewer than twenty funerals.

As we walked the narrow, fescue-framed fairways of Shinnecock less than two weeks before the U.S. Open, I didn't tell Jimmy what a miracle I thought it was that we were playing together or what a miracle it was that either of us was alive. I didn't share with him that my own brush with death, banal compared to 9/11, had been my impetus to wind up with a life that had brought me beside him on turf as exclusive and hallowed as Shinny's windswept layout.

Almost five decades earlier, on a warm Friday evening, when I was nine years old, I had found myself in one of poverty's traps. During my early childhood in the Sawmill Quarters, friends' lives were permanently altered when they ate the lye we used to make soap or drank the kerosene that filled our lamps. I avoided those ever-present dangers. Yet a couple of years after leaving the Quarters, I draped a red beach towel across my shoulders and tied it around my neck. I was Superman, running through the house with my hands stretched out toward the sky. As my sister Jen and brother Jerry sat on a sofa watching TV, I pretended to fly above imaginary clouds before finally landing in a storage room at the back of our house.

Catching my breath, I spotted an old refrigerator; they were common in our neighborhood. The abandoned appliance's size and heft reminded me of a scene from a comic book I'd read where a villain had stuffed Superman inside a locked safe and dropped it to the bottom of the ocean. Mimicking that episode, I crawled inside the fridge and yanked the door shut.

After a few glorious minutes of fantasizing in the dark about escaping to exact revenge and save the world, I pressed my hands against the inside of the door to open it. The door didn't budge. I pushed again. Nothing. It started to get hot, and I had trouble breathing. I couldn't see a thing and could hardly move in that tiny space. I was scared to death—literally scared I was about to die. Dripping with sweat and tears, I yelled out, "Somebody please help me!"

Nothing.

I pressed my body against the back of the fridge and pushed my skinny arms and legs against the door with every ounce of strength I had. It remained resolutely shut. I don't remember how many more times I tried, but I eventually bowed my head between my knees and gave up. I accepted that my life was ending. I started to pray, finding peace in my sanctified grandparents' teaching that children who die before they turn twelve always go to Heaven. Dazed, gasping, unable to see even my own hand in front of my face, I suddenly thought I heard a voice. I stilled myself and listened; the voice wasn't coming from outside the refrigerator door but from inside my head.

"Don't give up, Jimmie," it said. *"Never give up!"*

I took a deep breath and pushed one last time with what little strength I had left. The door flew open. Air and light poured over me. I stumbled out. When the numbness finally left my legs, I raced back into the house, where Jen and Jerry still sat on the sofa, as indifferent to me and my plight as strangers. Tears filled my eyes. I pummeled them with my fists. "Why did you want me to die?" I screamed. "Why didn't you come save me?" They had no idea what I was talking about.

But I was alive, and so were my dreams. From that day forward, everywhere I went, anywhere in the world, I carried with me the belief that the only superheroes we can rely on are the ones we carry inside ourselves. I vowed I'd never give up again.

Now there I was, along with Jimmy Dunne and his longtime Shinnecock caddie, Lenny Bummolo. Lenny, athletically built with calves like those chiseled into the legs of Michelangelo's David, had made loops around Shinnecock for more than thirty years. His skills were obvious to me from the moment he sensed my nervousness and, with a firm handshake and friendly glance, worked on putting me at ease. Everything went off without a hitch.

Standing on the tee box at Shinnecock's par-three eleventh hole under an overcast sky punctuated by shards of blue, Jimmy and Lenny shared the story of Jimmy's hole in one in 2010, the day he had set the course record. It was a June afternoon with blue skies that seemed to stretch into infinity. The flag fluttered in a light breeze as Jimmy hit an 8-iron straight at the pin. Then there was a *thwack*.

"We all heard the ball hit the flagpole," Lenny recalled.

"I thought it probably kicked off the green," Jimmy said.

"I told him, 'No,'" Lenny said, "'you got a one.'"

Jimmy's baritone voice cracked slightly when he told me what had happened next. They couldn't see the ball when they walked to the green, and Jimmy still believed that it had rolled off. But he reluctantly followed Lenny to the flag.

"We looked in the cup," Jimmy said, "and there the ball was, with the 'Q' staring straight up at the sky, illuminated like it was on fire by a single beam of light."

Jimmy marks his balls with a "Q" to honor his late best friend, Chris Quackenbush. I swallowed hard as goose pimples blanketed my arms.

Lenny added a coda: "The course record he went on to break that day had been held by Jimmy's friend Mike Williams, whose son was one of the Sandler O'Neill employees who perished that tragic day."

Finished with his story, Jimmy striped another 8-iron off the eleventh tee. It looked eerily reminiscent of the one he'd hit eight years earlier: straight at the flag, slight breeze behind us. "You might have another one, boss," Lenny only half-joked while the ball was still in the air.

It stopped four inches from the cup. Not a hole in one but a tap-in birdie.

After our round, over lunch in a corner of the clubhouse restaurant that overlooked the eighteenth green, I felt compelled to tell Jimmy that even with all that he had accomplished, I believed that his greatest contributions lay ahead.

He didn't shrug. He didn't ponder. He didn't object. He just smiled. "I hope you're right."

I hoped the same for me.

———

THE DAY AFTER MY ROUND with Jimmy at Shinnecock Hills, I rolled up to the gate at Pine Valley. When I asked the security guard for advice on playing a course many golfers consider the greatest skills test in the country, he said wryly, "Just have fun."

Wise words on any course.

I met my host on the practice range with his two other guests. All three of them sent balls out long and straight with seeming ease. I always wish it could seem that easy for me.

I'd played ninety-five of the country's best courses, but I still felt first-tee jitters on the ninety-sixth as I looked at a layout with no safe harbor for errant shots. My caddie, Owen, a young Jamaican sporting a neatly trimmed beard, sensed my anxiety as I faced the narrow fairway cutting through thick pines. "Relax, my brother," he reassured me in a smooth, singsong accent. "You got more room out there than you think."

I exhaled and sent my ball down the middle; it leaked slightly to the right before it dropped in the fairway. Owen winked.

My next drive on the short par-four second didn't fare so well, slamming into the face of one of the many bunkers that dotted the left-hand rough. It was plugged beneath prickly weeds that overlapped the edges. I couldn't have imagined a worse result on a drive just slightly off the fairway.

Welcome to Pine Valley.

Straddling the trap, I took a steep backswing, then hit down hard. Owen and I breathed a sigh of relief as the ball shot out of the bunker and back into the fairway. My approach plopped three feet from the cup.

I looked around, hoping that one of my partners would call out, "Pick it up." No one did. With the steadiness of a jackhammer, I pushed my putt for par to the right.

Welcome to Pine Valley. Again.

My fifty-foot birdie putt on the 185-yard par-three third took forever to get to the cup, yet just a fraction of a second to speed four feet past. I dropped the comeback putt in for one of the few pars I'd make on that grind-it-out course, where even my slightest misses, off the fairway or the green, were severely punished.

On most courses, the par threes rate as some of the easiest holes. At Pine Valley, ten holes play easier than the 220-yard par-three fifth, which requires a carry over water, rough, and sand to reach a green shoehorned between more traps and backed by tight trees. I swung and prayed. It didn't help. My ball shot into a bunker's gnarly weeds well short of the green.

We used the butt of a club, like the snout of one of my childhood hogs rooting for scraps, to unearth the ball. I then summoned all the strength I had to advance it a mere ten yards. My confidence was shattered. Ahead of me: more sand and pricklier rough than my game could handle. I proceeded to hit one shanked, topped, pushed, toed, skied, hooked, and sliced shot after another. Or so it seemed.

Pine Valley was almost as challenging as West Virginia's Pikewood National, the only track where my score had topped 100. But without spectacular views to distract me, I finished this course in ten fewer strokes.

CHAPTER TWENTY-TWO

THE OCEAN COURSE
AT KIAWAH

Be with someone who inspires you and makes you be the
best version of yourself.

—Roy T. Bennett

I'd planned to play my final round on Kiawah Island's Ocean Course. But fate intervened. Renovations had kept Wade Hampton Golf Club in North Carolina closed during most of the previous twelve months, and the course reopened only about a week before my deadline. The golf director at my Atlanta club found a member there to host me—on June 11, my D-Day. So I played the Ocean Course, my ninety-ninth, the day before.

I flew into Charleston, South Carolina, after spending an afternoon speeding across Idaho's Lake Coeur d'Alene in a white Cobalt 302 sport boat, music blaring, between rounds at the Golf Club at Black Rock and Gozzer Ranch Golf & Lake Club. I'd left Idaho on the cusp of accomplishing something no one else had ever done. Short of the sky falling, it was hard to see anything stopping me now.

I first visited Kiawah with my young family in the summer of 2006. Jordan was four and Alexandra two. Pristine beaches stretched along the Atlantic, cordgrass coating the salt marshes in yellow and green. Wildlife lurked everywhere: sea turtles and dolphins swam in the estuaries, while bicycle and hiking trails slipped through the natural habitat of deer, cougars, and all species of loud, shrill birds. My kids loved it.

Yet the space between their childhood experiences and mine wasn't lost on me. Whereas my childhood summers had been spent in torn coveralls romping through prairies and piney woods bounded by barbed-wire fences, my kids wore boutique beachwear as they ran up and down the raked sand of a gated luxury resort.

At the time, golf was my new passion, and the Ocean Course was the first top-flight layout I played. I can't remember my score from that first round, but I do remember my caddie, Patrick, whom everybody called Puddles: on his first day as a looper at the Ocean Course, his cart had hit a bump and he had flown face-first into a puddle.

I requested Puddles for the ninety-ninth round of my quest.

I jumped on the shuttle cart to the first tee with Kenny Warren, a former work colleague and longtime friend who'd flown in for that penultimate round, and a couple whom an assistant pro paired with us at the last minute: Dominic "The Domino" Chu, markets reporter for CNBC, and his wife, Meghan.

By now I'd tackled Pete Dye's beachside masterpiece on the island's eastern end countless times. With more holes bordering the Atlantic than any other course in the country, it can sometimes seem like one long, menacing sand dune, especially when there's a stiff wind off the choppy sea, which there almost always is. But Dye designed it with strategic lines that allow you to avoid most of the trouble—if you choose them, that is. Some prefer to take on the course's more treacherous routes.

The course opens with one of its easiest holes, a 365-yard par four that plays relatively straight, with sandy waste areas on either side from tee to green. I opted for one of Dye's generous lines and unleashed a drive that soared over mounds on the fairway's left side before fading back into the middle. It left me a no-sweat 143-yard approach to a back pin on a spacious green.

"With that wind, hit your one-thirty club and let the ball run back to the flag," Puddles advised.

I hit my pitching wedge on the money. The ball dropped below the cup, then chased past the pin before settling just off the back of the green.

The smart play from that extremely tight lie was to putt rather than chip. Puddles pointed out my line, but the fast, firm putting surface spooked me, and I tapped the ball too tenderly. It stopped dead a foot and a half from the cup. An opening birdie would've been great, but my jump-starting par was still sweet.

By the time I got there, a par on the 406-yard, right-to-left-bending ninth hole would have given me my lowest front-nine score there ever. Precisely a day short of my deadline, maybe I had finally worn down the golf gods. But following a strong drive, I flubbed an easy approach, then two-putted from fifteen feet.

Golfers hope. The golf gods laugh.

———

ERIKA MET US ON THE back nine. The original plan from a year earlier was for her to walk the final nine holes of my quest beside me. Wade Hampton's closure had spoiled that plan, but it still seemed fitting for her to accompany me on what is essentially my home course. Like every other significant milestone since our lives became one, we were in this together.

The first time my friends met Erika, they instantly recognized her impact on my life. When she was with me, I transformed into a kinder, gentler version of myself. Far into adulthood, I'd projected unwavering strength, a facade meticulously crafted to mask the unshakable feeling of inadequacy I still carried from my formative years.

Erika tempered that. When I was with her, I didn't hide my frailties from myself or others. I felt safe enough to reveal my deepest fears and flaws. Through her, I discovered a profound truth: that love flourishes in the delicate garden of vulnerability.

Erika's strengths—thoughtfulness, empathy, toughness—come from her own struggles. She grew up in Sherman, Texas, which at the time was legally integrated but functionally segregated. She lived just far enough on the white side of the tracks to find herself caught between two worlds and never fully embraced by either the Black or white communities. Black kids ran through her high school hallways yelling, "Erika Hayes is an Uncle Tom!" because she dared have friendships with white kids. Meanwhile, the parents of those white kids scolded them for having a Black friend.

Her parents, who had met in college while studying music, divorced when she was six. Her father, a music teacher and composer, moved to Michigan. Erika and her mother, an opera singer and later an educator, relocated to St. Louis. That was where Erika's mom met her second husband, Marshall Rosenberg, a renowned Jewish psychologist who eventually worked around the world as a peace advocate.

Trapped between two worlds, Erika poured herself into school. Whereas I found solace and purpose wandering the woods of East Texas and the refinery-lined streets of Texas City, she found both her peace and her drive in achieving academic excellence. She didn't settle for just good grades. She wanted to be the best in her class.

There were challenges. During a middle school honors social studies class, where she was the sole Black student, her teacher illustrated his concept of affirmative action by noting, "Take Erika, for instance. She'll get any job she wants because of affirmative action." As her classmates stared at her, she wanted to shrink under her desk, not because of what her teacher had said—she was too young to fully understand the impact of his words—but from the sheer embarrassment of being called out.

It wasn't until high school that her social studies teacher's words began to take an insidious toll on her. When Erika scored higher on a ninth-grade biology test than a student everyone considered to be the class science whiz, the teacher accused her of cheating. When she started applying to colleges, she contacted Harvard and withdrew her application; rejecting Harvard before Harvard had a chance to reject her. Four years later, she withdrew her Harvard graduate school application for the same reason. Her self-doubt resurfaced again when the University of Michigan waitlisted her for its PhD program. She left her first job as a professor at Tulane University prematurely because she didn't believe she was capable of earning tenure.

Deep down, that social studies teacher's words about affirmative action had left her wondering whether any success she achieved would ever be attributed to her capabilities or hard work. His words were a devious attempt to give her a check mark of illegitimacy.

He failed.

Those words ignited an unquenchable fire in her. She never missed a high school honor roll. She excelled as a psychology major at Pomona College, and when she was eventually accepted into Michigan's organizational behavior PhD program, she made it her mission to graduate faster than anyone else in her cohort. She did. She completed her master's and PhD requirements, including the defense of her dissertation, in three and a half years.

For almost three decades, I've watched Erika earn everything she's achieved. I looked on as she did the research for her dissertation; designed curricula for classes she taught at Tulane, the University of Virginia, and Harvard; built a leadership team while leading Emory's business school. In her first full-time administrative role at Virginia's Darden School of Business, she redesigned the executive education group while sitting up in bed with rollers in her hair. At each step in her career, she's poured herself into every detail, weighed every decision—while raising two great kids.

That social studies teacher couldn't have been more wrong, though he's not alone in his thinking. Erika was never handed anything during college or her career. She took advantage of every opportunity she had with brilliance, relentlessness, and hair-curlers-be-damned hard work.

And now she strode down the fairways on the back nine of the Ocean Course at Kiawah, supporting a dream she had helped ignite.

She and Meghan Chu hit it off immediately. As they strolled down the twelfth fairway toward Meghan's ball, Meghan explained her approach to golf: "I just have two criteria for whether I've hit a good shot or not."

"What's that?" Erika asked.

Meghan responded, "If I can find the ball and it's closer to the hole than it was before I hit it, it's a good shot."

Erika laughed. "Now, that's the kind of approach to golf I could learn to enjoy," she said.

It seemed like forever since I'd kissed her asleep the night before my round at Augusta National.

CHAPTER TWENTY-THREE

WADE HAMPTON

So many of our dreams at first seem impossible, then they seem improbable,
and then, when we summon the will, they soon become inevitable.

—Christopher Reeve

The improbable had become the inevitable.

After I dropped Erika off at the airport in Charleston, I pointed my rental car toward Cashiers, North Carolina, three hundred miles northwest. I was headed to my hundredth course on the 365th day of my quest. The forecast called for no rain. This was really going to happen.

Driving from South Carolina's low country into North Carolina's Blue Ridge Mountains, I suddenly felt the weight of everything I'd experienced during the past twelve months. I swallowed a few times to fight back the tears. I usually stop in the small towns I drive through when traveling across our vast and diverse country, talking with locals in the mom-and-pop stores along the way. I often get a real sense of a place from the people I meet and chat with.

But driving through the Carolinas on the final leg of my odyssey, I was overwhelmed thinking back on the many kindnesses shown to me throughout my life, both as I had fought to overcome poverty and racism and again as I had crisscrossed America, seeking access to its most privileged and exclusive golf venues.

Faces flickered through my mind's eye: Joe, the double amputee World War II veteran who had given me my first shoeshine box and taught me about our invisible history; Mrs. Thompson, the fourth-grade teacher who had spent her Saturdays guiding me through advanced math modules, teaching me that I was as capable as anyone else; Nestor Moreno, the Cuban immigrant who had taken me under his wing and mentored me during my early days at Exxon, continuing what Joe and Mrs. Thompson had begun.

There were also more recent allies: the couple from Boston who had changed their vacation plans to host me at the Country Club at Brookline, even though they'd only just met me; the head pro at Quaker Ridge, whom I had met by accident along the street outside his club; Lin Rogers, who had kick-started it all with an invite to Augusta; Jeff Johnson, whose vast network had made gaining access to remote courses a lot easier; John Sokol, who had joked with me in the short-game practice area at Merion and then, before he even knew my name, offered to help me get onto four other courses; and, of course, Jimmy Dunne, who had flown to Southampton from his reunion at Notre Dame to host me at Shinnecock when it looked as though I'd fall short of my goal by a single course and then flown back to rejoin his classmates once we'd finished.

None of those people had to do what they did. Yet each of them affected, even permanently changed, my life. I believe that we're all connected, essential to one another's success, and that great achievements are rarely, if ever, the result of just one person's efforts. In the end, our successes and failures are determined not only by how we deal with the challenges we face but also by the help and support others provide and the breaks we get along the way.

As I drove from the marshes to the mountains on that bright Monday morning, all the shops and shacks, church steeples and town halls, billboards and fruit stands I passed by faded into the background. It was nature, yet again, that most caught my attention: the sunlight reflecting off lakes, the morning mist filtering through steep forests, the circling hawks, the spooked, retreating deer. That beauty and tranquillity have always made me sentimental for the most pleasant surroundings of my childhood: the tall pines, the fields of wildflowers, the mockingbird's morning songs. The tadpoles wriggling in the bathwater I'd lugged from my grandparents' farm pond.

WADE HAMPTON GOLF CLUB IS smack in the middle of the Blue Ridge Mountains, where generations-old mountain culture mingles with the vacation homes of newcomers. Opened in 1987 on land that once belonged to a slave-owning Confederate general, it's tucked in a corner of the state that borders South Carolina, Tennessee, and Georgia. A section of the Appalachian Trail is not much more than a handful of long par fives away.

It's a glorious spot. At an elevation of almost 3,500 feet, with views of peaks reaching even higher into the high clouds, the course slips through the surrounding mountains so intentionally that virtually every shot sails into a postcard-worthy vista. Designer Tom Fazio has thirteen courses in *Golf Digest*'s Top 100 (2017–2018), but Wade Hampton is widely considered his masterpiece. The scheming bunkers, the false-front greens, the deceptively angled tee boxes and fairways are all pure Fazio—not to mention the routing, which weaves through an undulating valley like its own version of the Appalachian Trail. Yet amid all that beauty, he does what he can to mess with your head.

Although it's not Fazio's most difficult course to play—it probably ranks somewhere in the middle of the pack—it might be his most difficult to get onto. The club has only about three hundred members, which include, by one count, at least four billionaires. Though most members come from the Southeast, others are drawn from around the country by the course's reputation as golf's premiere mountain layout. They often stay throughout the clear, temperate summer months in homes set around and above the eighteen holes; on-site home ownership is a membership requirement, along with the reported $140,000 initiation fee.

Yet the club exudes—in fact, insists on—a lack of pretension. My host recalled a half-dozen members once engaging in a lively discussion during a club tournament rain delay about who has the better meat department: Costco or Sam's Club. With the exception of its breathtaking views, the overriding feel of the place is one of refined understatement.

The pro at Cherokee, my club in Atlanta, had connected me with Steve Hindman, a past president at Cherokee and member of Wade Hampton. I'd never met Steve, a tall, slim, silvering former tech company turnaround guy in his early seventies, but he welcomed me enthusiastically and without hesitation. We were joined by Terry, a neighbor of Steve who was anxious to hear about my quest, and Kelly, whom I'd bonded with after he'd gotten a childhood friend to host us both at Oak Hill Country Club in Rochester, New York. The foursome that day was emblematic of my quest: 75 percent of the people I played with that year were total strangers before I showed up.

Fazio's genius was on full display from the first tee. Looking out at a perfectly framed mountain snapshot, you might think you're in for a pretty conventional downhill par five with a slight dogleg right; it reminded me of the eleventh hole on the South Course at Cherokee. But Fazio had other ideas: the tee box angles to the left while the fairway bends to the right, with three bunkers of various shapes and sizes that throw your depth perception off. The design subtly causes you to swing down one line in your mind while your body swings along another.

But before I could let any of that get to me, my young caddie, sporting shades and a black boonie hat, grabbed the driver from my bag and handed it to me. "Lead us off, Jimmie," Steve commanded.

No matter how long you've played golf, that first drive—especially on a new course with new playing partners—is always a bit of an audition. Despite Fazio messing with my head by trying to get me to cross my lines, I passed that one: with a confident swing, I sent the ball sailing down the middle of the fairway. It felt great to land that one in the short grass.

The ensuing par felt even better. Yet my final round wasn't going to be about the score. I'd achieved all the goals I had set for my quest except one: an ace on a Top 100 course.

A hole in one is golf's no-hitter. We all hope for it, but no sane golfer stands on a tee box expecting to get one. No matter how good you are, an ace still requires a lot of luck. I'd made two during the thirteen years I had played golf. Tiger Woods has just three across his decades-long career. Nevertheless, I'd set the goal, and after close calls on several of the previous ninety-nine courses, I still hadn't bagged one.

My first opportunity at Wade Hampton was the 182-yard third hole, a stunner from the tee box, with water cascading down rocks behind the green into a small pond on its left edge. The cup was cut this afternoon on the front-right portion of the green. Steve offered his advice: "Land the ball to the right of the pin, and it should roll down to the hole."

My ball sailed right—*way* right. That left me with just three more chances.

As we played the next couple of holes, my partners questioned me about my year. Terry wanted to know my favorite course. I got that question a lot, and although I had my answer honed like a well-rehearsed elevator speech, it felt especially appropriate on this final day. "It's hard to name just one," I began, because in fact it was. "Instead, I have five, each for a different reason."

I went through my list: Augusta National for the experience of playing on such mythic grounds; Pine Valley, because of its unrelenting difficulty; Merion, for its traditions; Cypress Point, for its unparalleled vistas along the rocky Pacific coast and how each of the eighteen holes can be played multiple ways off the tee; and Fishers Island off the Atlantic, with its string of template holes crisscrossing the island's tip amid a background of cottages and lighthouses.

We stepped up to the sixth hole. At just 142 yards, it was probably my best chance for an ace. The pin was placed just beyond a rocky creek, off the front of the green.

The ball sprang off my pitching wedge and headed straight for the flag. But it landed on the bank of the creek, a few feet from the green, and rolled down into the fast-flowing stream. Fazio had lured another sucker.

"I think you're trying too hard," Kelly allowed.

He was right, of course. But I wasn't going to give up on going for it all now. Two more par threes still lay ahead.

By the par-three eleventh hole, all the miles I'd driven, flown, and walked and all the golf swings I'd taken in between were finally exacting their toll. In the past two frantic weeks alone, I'd played eleven courses in nine states. My muscles were tired and resisting the commands of my unfocused brain. I'd figured the shorter sixth hole was my best chance for an ace, but according to the golf raters, the 151-yard eleventh was the easiest on the course.

I took dead aim, swung, and heard a sound I rarely hear: the click of a pure ball strike—almost an absence of sound. I looked up to see the ball flying on an undeviating line toward the pin. It finally plopped down just short of the cup, then raced past it before coming to rest four feet beyond the flag. Kelly, Steve, and Terry all let out a moan.

"Oh, man, that was a close one!" Steve said.

None of my fellow golfers that day had ever recorded an ace. They didn't say it, but I'm sure they all thought it was just plain silly for me to have set that as one of my goals.

The holes between eleven and seventeen were a blur. My new friends peppered me with more questions about my quest. "Which course was the hardest to get on?" Milwaukee Country Club. It has a small local membership, which had made it difficult to meet a member or anybody who knew one. "What round was the most fun?" The one I'd played just a couple days earlier at the Golf Club at Black Rock in Idaho. I'd played in a fivesome that included two firefighters and a cop. My host, a commercial real estate developer, had blasted rock music from a Bluetooth speaker during the round to liven the mood.

Their interest was strangely satisfying, despite how tired I was and how many times I'd been asked many of the same questions. I can't remember a time in my life when I wasn't either setting goals or working to achieve them. I also can't remember many times when I wasn't ridiculed for the goals I set. Not many of the people I grew up with believed me when I said I would graduate from high school. When I told a social worker I wanted to be a globe-trotting businessman, she told me I should lower my aim. The only person who initially truly believed I could play America's hundred greatest golf courses in a single year was . . . my wife.

I've been fortunate to achieve many of the challenging goals I set in life. But I've missed a few, too. And I've learned from both the success and the failures over the years that setting a goal, and mustering up the determination and persistence that go into trying to accomplish it, usually matter more than the goal itself. I had to remind myself of that on number seventeen, the final par three on the course. It's the second hardest one at Wade Hampton, which I proved after my ball hit the tree blocking the pin on the left side of the green, then dropped into the creek. *Again.* I took a drop, pitched back over the creek, then two-putted for my third double bogey on the course's par threes.

So much for an ace.

When I fail to reach a goal, I spend very little time lamenting it. I learn from it, then move forward in pursuit of new goals, all the wiser for the lessons learned. The lesson I took away from trying so hard to get an ace that day at Wade Hampton was that I should've picked my battles and not shot for the pin on every par three just because I wanted that ace. The three doubles on my scorecard would remain a handy reminder.

————

As WE WALKED THROUGH THE trees separating the seventeenth green from the eighteenth tee box, something went out of me. Time stood still.

It felt weird—really weird—as though I were there but I wasn't. It was as if I were an observer of my own story rather than an active participant.

Only once before had I ever experienced a similar phenomenon. It had happened at my mother's funeral as my seven siblings and I sat in the front row under a green canopy at her gravesite in a churchyard cemetery. While they lowered her casket into a two-and-a-half-by-eight-foot hole dug in the hard Texas clay, the voice in my head that always protected me said, "One day you will be doing this for your mother."

My mind wouldn't accept that I was doing it that day. My subconscious refused to grasp what was unfolding before my eyes.

My mother died in her sleep on April 23, 1998, a month and a day after my thirty-ninth birthday. Her youngest grandchild had bedded down beside her and was asleep in her arms when her heart made its final beat. Her death was unexpected: she was only sixty-six and had not been sick. Years earlier, she'd had what we thought was a mild heart attack, which had kept her in the hospital for a couple days. She'd smoked since she was thirteen, and a doctor had said she wouldn't last many more years if she kept it up. The day the hospital released her, she placed a pack of cigarettes on her nightstand, where it remained, untouched, for the next year. When the year was up, she grabbed the pack, threw it away, and never smoked again. That was the quiet strength of my mother.

I was at work in a colleague's office when I got the word she died. I collapsed in shock. Later that evening, while packing alone for the drive from my home in Baton Rouge, Louisiana, to Sweeny, Texas, where she'd lived for more than a decade, my chest tightened. It was as if the refrigerator I had once been trapped in was pressing down atop it. My heartbeat raced; I had trouble breathing. I thought I was having a heart attack and called 911. Within minutes, flashing red lights filled my driveway. EMTs listened to my heartbeat, took my blood pressure and temperature.

"Any traumatic events in your life recently?" one of them asked.

"My mother just died."

I had never experienced stress like that before. The EMTs assured me that I would be fine and advised me to try to get a good night's sleep before heading out the next morning. I sat weeping in the dark for most of the night in a chair that had been my mother's favorite whenever she visited: a brown recliner in the keeping room, just off the kitchen.

The next morning, I drove to southeast Texas, near the coast. I passed signs for the small towns whose high schools I'd once competed against in football and track: Angleton, West Columbia, and finally Sweeny, an oil refinery town dotted with company-built housing for workers, much like the Sawmill Quarters.

I spent most of the next few days sitting in a rocking chair on the front porch of the funeral home, keeping watch over my mother's body, which lay at rest inside the building behind me. I was calmed by the lush green field filled with leafy oaks across the street. Nature has always been the music of my heart, even when it's broken.

The church service was packed; latecomers were forced to listen from the front steps just outside the open front door. Our mother had been retired for a year and lived in a wood-framed two-bedroom house that I'd bought her a few years earlier.

Besides her kids and grandkids, my mother's life in Sweeny revolved around the church. She had always been spiritual, if not particularly religious. A church community for her wasn't about rules and restrictions—it was about having a personal relationship with God, about feeling his presence in a meaningful and purposeful way.

The seeds of that had been planted early. In her youth, she'd rebelled against the rules of her own father's church—don't wear makeup, don't wear pants, don't play cards, don't smoke or drink (she never drank)—yet she always believed in God and prayer and the power of being a faithful servant.

Her closest friends in Sweeny were the church's minister and his wife, and their intimacy came through gloriously that morning in the preacher's eulogy. Those of us who had known her best felt that he understood her soul. He talked of her kindness, compassion, and empathy and the care with which she ministered to others. If someone in the church was feeling sad and low, Thelma James could sense it and would be there to comfort them. She was truly a member of the congregation in every way, not merely another attendee.

But she was, of course, complicated. The preacher noted her individuality, the way her personality had refused to be put into any easily identifiable box. You couldn't say that she conformed to a template of any particular kind of person. She had a sense of herself and the world around her that was uniquely her own. When she needed to be on, she was. At times she might come across as mild or meek or reserved—or damaged and depressed, just trying to hold up under the accumulated burdens of her life—but somehow, pulling from some inner depth that only she knew how to reach, she'd always find something to give to others, precisely when they needed it. She had so many of her own hurts and demons to tend to, yet she was always there for others when they needed her.

My mother spent her entire life taking it as it came, one day at a time, playing from the rough. Her pregnancies spanned twenty-three years, from when she was sixteen or seventeen until she was almost forty.

I don't know if any parent ever regrets having their children. My seven brothers and sisters and I were not the product of some plan; we were the product of no planning at all. There's no doubt that we made her life harder when we were young; but we made her life easier when we got older. We bought her a house so she would never again suffer the indignity of having her possessions ripped from her residence and dumped onto the street by the local sheriff or constable before a padlock was put on the door without care or concern for where she and her kids would go.

Despite those challenges, by her own example, she taught us to take responsibility for our actions and our well-being. And people weren't always kind about her parenting style. One of her sisters would often chastise her, "Thelma, those kids gonna break your heart one day, they're gonna end up in the pen." My mother's flat, imperturbable response:

"You look after yours, and I'll look after mine." And look after us she did. And here we all were, leading healthy productive lives. She did good.

Her greatest gift: she taught us kids to love and depend on ourselves and one another. At her request, every one of us helped one of the others at some point. As kids, we taught the next youngest to read or to add and subtract. Later on, we helped one another financially whenever we were able to. She made sure of that. She taught us, through her own kindness and generosity, to believe that most people have a good and kind heart. I saw that that was true during my golf quest. She never held a grudge, and she forgave everyone who ever wronged her. And she never tolerated any of us speaking ill of one another.

Bunched shoulder to shoulder inside that cozy, packed church in Sweeny, I understood for the first time the importance of having siblings when a parent dies. It brought me great comfort to be with others who had known my mother their whole lives and could relate to the pain we all were experiencing, without any explanation. In her quiet way, my mother had prepared us all for the day she would no longer be with us.

Like me, I'm sure my siblings hold an enduring image of my mother at Thanksgivings and Christmases, sitting in that brown recliner. She'd settle in and smile, looking proud as she watched her children and grandchildren singing and dancing in a *Soul Train*–like line between the cabinets in my kitchen, or all of us with our arms around one another, swaying from side to side, as we crooned "Amazing Grace"—some of us on key and some of us, me especially, not.

One Thanksgiving, as we sat around the table and took turns announcing what each of us was grateful for that year, Momma looked around at all of us and said, "I'm thankful for all forty-four-eleven-hundred children and grandchildren that I have in my life." That made-up number was how she expressed the level of joy we brought her.

We left the church in South Texas amid hugs and tears, and our family drove in a procession of cars back to Huntsville, an hour and a half north. Once we got into town, the procession veered west, out into the country, until it rolled to a stop at the end of the dusty clay driveway of the Mount Zion Baptist Church.

My grandfather and grandmother are both buried there. So are aunts, uncles, cousins. My father, Austin Riles, and his father, Ous Riles, are also buried there, in one of the first rows to the left. Their headstones are the closest I can remember ever being to them.

One could say that the history of Zion, the Black settlement where we were all born, is etched in the slabs that sprout from those weedy, sparsely shaded couple of acres ringed by a chain-link fence. Rows and rows of them bear familiar family names—Archie, Crawford, Slaughter—some plain and weathered to the point that they're barely visible, others ornate and still relatively fresh. Husbands, wives, and in some cases their children are buried in the same plot. All of them have their simple histories chiseled in the stone.

Under a clear sky and bright white afternoon sun, my brothers and sisters and I huddled together beneath the green canopy, where we were joined by neighbors and friends from the life my mother had had there. Thelma "None" James was finally lowered for eternity into that unforgiving Texas hardpan. Other than the modest headstone that would later be placed above her, you won't find any other notices, statues, or monuments to my mother anywhere.

We are her monuments. We are her accomplishments. Not just our physical being but the way we live our lives, which is a direct result of the way she lived hers.

———

I FELT MY MOTHER'S PRESENCE after hitting a poor shot off the eighteenth tee. Steve had suggested I aim right because of the creek running along the left side of the fairway; I guess he wasn't worried about the bunkers on the right. He stood off to the right of the tee box and watched intently as I took the club back for my final drive. So many thoughts raced through my head as I brought the clubface back down that I lost my balance and plowed the club into the ground three inches behind the ball. The drive traveled less than 130 yards before landing in the rough just short of the fairway.

I felt everyone around me sag.

"You don't want to end it with that drive," Steve said. "Take another one."

I teed up another ball and delivered a blow that sent it sailing down the fairway's right side, leaving me with a perfect approach. Yet as my caddie and I went to retrieve my first ball, nestled deep in the rough, I could hear my mother again, just as I'd heard her admonishing me about those matches when I rolled out of Augusta. Her words this time: "This isn't how you want to finish something this special."

Before I bent down to pick it up, I looked at my caddie and said, "I can't play that second ball. I should play this one." I took responsibility for my poor tee shot. Now I had to find a way to make par from the rough on a green still 345 yards away.

Fortunately, the final hole at Wade Hampton is a par five, and my decision to play my original drive released all the tension in my muscles. I made my best swing of the round: the ball sprang off the face of what was normally my 190-yard club and flew 220 yards down the middle of the fairway, leaving me just 120 yards short of the pin.

Those extra 30 yards put me in a great position to shoot for the flag and end my quest with a birdie.

It just goes to show that when you own your mistakes and do what is right, you can overcome them. I'll never know if I would have shot an eagle, or a birdie, or a double bogey had I chosen to play the second drive, sitting so sweetly in the fairway, 225 yards from the green. As I walked by it with my caddie, I merely picked it up and put it into my pocket. I followed my mother's example: I did what I thought was right.

I approached my original ball with a clear conscience. Rather than attack the flag behind a bunker, just past a pond off the front left of the green, I did what I've done so often in life: gave myself a little extra margin for error. My last swing of that long journey sent the ball sailing toward the middle of the green. It dropped fifteen feet to the right of the cup.

I paused on my way to the green while Steve, Terry, and Kelly hit their approach shots. In what had to be a sign of approval from the golf gods, all four of our balls had landed within a few feet of one another to form a perfect square. Kelly and I took the final steps of my journey together.

With all of us standing on the green, it was as if we were playing the final hole of a major championship with the winner already determined. Steve, Kelly, and Terry putted out to clear the deck for me to sink the final put on my 1,800th hole of the year. They huddled around me to help with the read as I bent over and studied the line. They all wanted my journey to end with a birdie from the rough.

Finally I stood over the ball, pulled the putter back slowly while holding the rest of my body dead still, then pushed the ball toward the cup. I rose on my toes as it broke slightly left and appeared destined to drop. But just as it approached the hole, it stopped breaking. The ball rolled instead along the edge of the cup and then just past it.

I went limp. But only for a moment. I walked to the other side of the cup and, without hesitation, tapped in the one-footer—I wasn't taking a gimme for my final stroke. I closed out the year with a par.

From the rough.

———

THE GUYS CONGRATULATED ME AS we moved from the course to the clubhouse for a celebratory drink. Steve introduced me to a couple other members and told them we'd just made history. The membership board later asked Steve to invite me to join the club. I would've been Wade Hampton's first Black member—for no other reason, Steve told me, than that no other Black golfers had ever applied. I declined; Erika and I already had a vacation home in a golf resort.

I rolled out of Wade Hampton and drove back to Steve's house, where his wife, Suzi, joined us for what turned out to be one of the most meaningful discussions of my quest. While we unwound on a screened-in back porch, with its stunning late-afternoon view of Whiteside Mountain—Tom Fazio would definitely have approved—I told Steve and Suzi that the past year had been about more than just playing golf. I told them I had wanted to see if I could meet enough people who'd assist me in gaining access to some of America's most exclusive golf clubs—places where men like me had once been forbidden. I told them I wanted to test my own belief in the American Dream. In the end, I'd gotten onto 75 percent of the courses through people I met during the year. I was a stranger. A Black stranger. Yet folks unselfishly invited me into their clubs, their homes, and their lives. And most of those people were white.

It wasn't a referendum on race. Racism, whether outright hatred or the soft bigotry of low expectations, still creates barriers to success for African Americans.

Steve takes pride in the fact that his liberal friends consider him a conservative and that his conservative friends consider him a liberal. He's an issue-by-issue guy, and on this issue, Steve and I quickly discovered that we held different opinions about what it would take to improve equality in America.

Steve sees the dismantling of the barriers created by racism as something whites must do. I commended him on his understanding of our challenges but told him that his view inadvertently suggests that Black people, who have been fighting against centuries of slavery, Jim Crow laws, and overt discrimination in critical areas such as education, housing, employment, and medical care, have neither agency nor responsibility. I emphasized that our advancement won't depend solely on what whites do but also on what we do and on what our society—Black and white—does together. We don't necessarily have to eradicate racism for Blacks to succeed; we just need to render it impotent.

The sun dropped lower over the mountain as our conversation went on; the Blue Ridge turned bluer. Suzi dipped in and out with food and drinks.

I talk a lot about growing up in poverty, I continued, but I'll never say I was underprivileged. Privilege is not just about wealth. It comes in many forms. Mine came in the form of a mother who loved every one of her eight children equally but made each of us feel as though we were her favorite.

There are numerous things about all of us that we did not choose. I didn't choose to be Black, to be born in poverty, to be born in America. But I did choose to appreciate life and the opportunities that come with it. Regardless of the circumstances, I am glad that the mother who loved me, and the father I never knew, created me. No struggle, no hardship, no circumstance will ever rob me of that gratitude. I choose not to be angry.

That's not looking at the world through rose-colored glasses. I recoil at the injustices in the world. I'm not some Pollyanna who doesn't see racism. I've lived it. It's unfair. It's disgusting. It's immoral. But it can be overcome.

That doesn't mean that those who don't overcome it are flawed or weak. I understand why some give up. They get tired of working against it, and once they get tired it becomes so much easier to quit. Fatigue is the enemy of achievement. Chief Joseph, a great Native American warrior who never gave up on the hope that one day his people would achieve freedom and equality, said upon his surrender, "I am tired. . . . My heart is sick and sad. From where the sun now stands, I will fight no more forever!"

Whether as a child in tattered clothing being ridiculed at school, a high school athlete falling behind in a four-hundred-meter race, a starving college student struggling to pay tuition, or an engineer being hazed, I often felt like "fighting no more forever." But rather than quitting or turning bitter, I chose, like my mother, to embrace hope and optimism and to fight on. I'd chosen that, I concluded to Steve, because in America, where I was born playing from the deepest, least forgiving rough, I could.

Steve listened intently. Then he sat back. He said he saw my overcoming the multitude of challenges I had faced as an exception. I saw it as an example, because of all the people I know who look like me and are smarter and more talented than I am. They are capable of achieving much more than I have.

As our discussion stretched into the evening, Steve and I were struck by the civility of our exchange. Though we were both passionate about our positions, we listened and respected each other's views. In a world on the verge of losing both decorum and civility, our discussion never devolved into name-calling or dismissiveness. We found common ground— common ground that now stretched beyond golf. Despite its wretched history and current flaws, I found an America that remains a place where we can rise above humble beginnings—where we can still succeed even playing from the deepest rough.

It was now pitch black outside. The air was cooling and dead quiet except for the cicadas and bullfrogs just beyond us. Steve and Suzi were disappointed that I was leaving, but after 365 days of this, I was anxious to get home.

During the two-hour drive back to Atlanta under a star-filled sky, I reflected again on the journey. After 90,756 miles through 33 states, 8,797 strokes, 82 nights spent in hotels, and more money spent than I care to talk about, I was finished.

Done.

I'd gotten help from people of different races, genders, religions, and classes. I had the privilege of playing golf at clubs in every region of the country. Everywhere I went, I had felt welcomed, respected, and admired for the audacity of my quest and my passion for the game. I had felt *seen*. I had spent time with club members, security guards, locker room and parking lot attendants, caddies, and waitstaff, as well as people in the communities I visited, whether at a gas station, a restaurant, on an airplane, train, or bus, or inside bars and hotel lobbies.

At the clubs, I had found that a common passion for golf was enough to bridge many differences. But more than the bond of golf, I had found a common desire to love, laugh, cry, and hope for a better life for the ones we hold dear.

I reject the notion that we are only as strong as our weakest link. That holds true for a chain but not for a society. When we work together, we can leverage our strengths and overcome our weaknesses.

Early in my yearlong odyssey, I played in the shadows of our country's great monuments, including the one where Dr. King gave his enduring "I Have a Dream" speech. As I traveled through the years from a life of poverty to a life of comfort, I tried to leave bread crumbs along the way. I wanted others to see where I'd been. I am no longer invisible, nor is my life defined by being colored and illegitimate. Where I started is so much less important than where the opportunities I've been afforded have taken me. That, for me, is the American Dream.

Just as I had done the night I returned from Augusta National, I turned onto my street, its incline and length eerily similar to my childhood street in the Sawmill Quarters. Except, rather than shacks, the dead-end cul-de-sac is lined with multimillion-dollar mansions. Instead of small dirt yards, the homes are separated from the street by manicured lawns with neatly trimmed hedges and bushes and colorful flowers. Kids don't play baseball with a stick and a doll's head on dirt but rather lacrosse and soccer on freshly mown grass and paved asphalt.

I pulled into my garage around 1:00 a.m., dropped the keys onto a kitchen counter, and headed upstairs. In our bedroom lay the one person I could have never done all of it without. I kissed her—deeply, tenderly, gratefully—then whispered as she smiled:

"We did it."

LIST OF COURSES

In order played, with ranking:

ACKNOWLEDGMENTS

I n a life that has benefited from countless acts of kindness, it's a delight-ful challenge to acknowledge everyone who has shaped my journey. To all those who have left an indelible mark on my life, my golf quest, and the creation of this book, my heartfelt gratitude knows no bounds. Without your kindness and generosity there would be no story to tell.

To my seven beloved siblings, Art, Jen, Jerry, Bobbi, Jeron, Rose, and Alfred, thanks for allowing me to expose the most intimate moments, challenges, and joys of our family's remarkable journey.

I extend my warmest thanks to Don Snyder for his invaluable insights into the fundamentals of writing and storytelling. To Drew Jubera, whose countless hours of discussions, guidance, and revisions lent depth and context to my work, I am truly indebted. As I am to Farrell Evans for his insightful thoughts on my golf experiences and his fact-checking.

A special nod to my initial editor, LaShara Bunting, for her unwavering belief in this project. And to my ultimate editor, Ian Straus, your thoughtful edits have ensured that every page ignites the reader's curiosity.

Finally, to my agent, David Granger, thanks for your steady hand and wise counsel throughout this project.

ABOUT THE AUTHOR

Born in 1959 to a single mother of eight in Jim Crow–era Texas, **Jimmie James** emerged from humble beginnings, growing up in a shack without electricity or plumbing. He was the first in his family not only to graduate from high school but also to pursue and earn a college degree. He graduated from Prairie View A&M University at the top of his engineering class. In his thirty-three-year career with Exxon, James rose from an entry-level engineer to a globe-trotting executive, overseeing businesses across the world. Now retired, he splits his time between Atlanta, Philadelphia, and Kiawah Island, and enjoys golf, travel, photography, and chess. He and his wife, Erika, have two young adult children, Jordan and Alexandra.